North Coast Diaries
Strathy at the Time of the Great War

North Coast Diaries

Strathy at the Time of the Great War

Frank Bardgett

BIRLINN

First published in 2006 by
Birlinn Limited
West Newington House
10 Newington Road
Edinburgh
EH9 1QS

www.birlinn.co.uk

The Publisher acknowledges subsidy from the Scottish Church Society
towards the publication of this book.

ISBN 10: 1 84158 488 6
ISBN 13: 978 1 84158 488 1

British Library Cataloguing-in-Publication Data
A catalogue record for this book is available from the British Library

Typeset by Iolaire Typesetting, Newtonmore
Printed and bound by Antony Rowe Ltd, Chippenham

In memory of my father,
Stanley Bardgett
Born 1916 during the Great War
Died 2006 after a full and generous life

Contents

List of Illustrations

Maps

Pages from the diaries

Photographs

Maps were drawn by Mrs Alison Bardgett
Photographs were taken by the author

Acknowledgements

The diaries on which this book is based were most kindly made available by Peter Chester and I am delighted to be able to acknowledge his encouragement.

While the resources of numerous national archives have been used, special thanks are due to the archivists and librarians of the Highland Council and particularly to the staff of the Brora Library, who went out of their way to enable visits to be as productive as possible. Thanks, too, are due to Kathryn Mackay, Robert and Diane Mackay, Anne Cameron, Helen Miller and other friends for assistance and encouragement; and, as always, to Alison Bardgett for her contribution to this research and her continuing support and understanding.

The response of the Scottish Church Society to a paper entitled 'His Ministerial Office', read at their May 2004 meeting, was helpful at a time when I was pulling together the main themes from which this book has developed. Financial support towards publication from the Scottish Church Society is gratefully acknowledged.

The diaries on which this book is based, together with transcripts of their contents, are now deposited with the North Highland Archive of the Highland Council.

Frank Bardgett,
Tigh an Iasgair,
Street of Kincardine,
Boat of Garten

Abbreviations

£ s. d.   Currency is expressed in pounds, shillings and pence. There were 12 pence (d.) in a shilling (s.) and 20 shillings in the pound (£1).

CSVR   'Valuations Rolls for the County of Sutherland', published annually from 1855 by direction of the Sutherland County Council.

Fasti   *Fasti Ecclesiae Scoticanae* ed. Hew Scott and others, Edinburgh 1915–2000.

GROS   General Register Office for Scotland. The Census of 1901 and Registers of Births, Marriages and Deaths held by GROS have been consulted via the official website as maintained in 2005 at: www.scotlandspeople.gov.uk

HCA   Highland Council Archives, a service of the Highland Council, based in the Public Library, Inverness.

JG   The *John O' Groat Journal*, a weekly newspaper published in Wick. A full sequence of the paper is held at the North Highland Archives.

NAS   National Archives of Scotland

NE   *The Northern Ensign*, a weekly newspaper published in Wick. A full sequence of the paper is held at the North Highland Archives.

NHA   North Highland Archives, a service of the Highland Council based in the Public Library, Wick.

NLS   National Library of Scotland

NT   *The Northern Times*, a weekly newspaper published in Golspie. Microfiche copies of the complete sequence of the paper are available at the Public Library, Brora.

Scotsman   *The Scotsman*, a daily newspaper published in Edinburgh. A full searchable sequence of the paper since 1817 is available on *The Scotsman* archive website [2005].

Year Book   *The Book of the Church of Scotland (Year Book)* published for the Committee on Christian Life and Work, Edinburgh 1886 and thereafter annually.

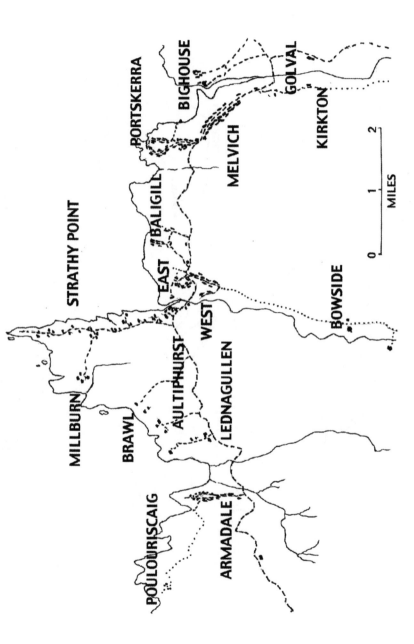

Map 1. The District of Strathy

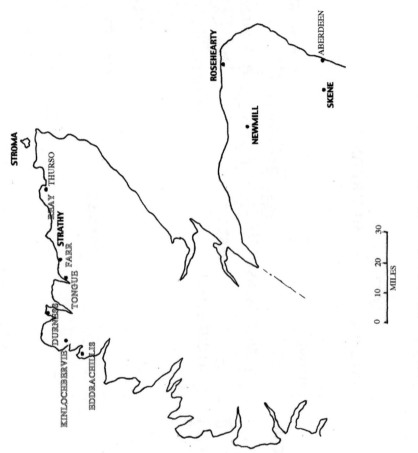

Map 2. Places and Parishes from Alex Youngson's career

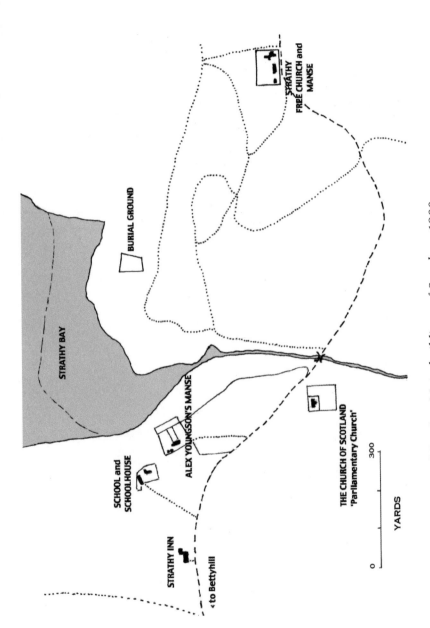

Map 3. *Main buildings of Strathy c.1900*

1

Introduction

This is a book about the parish of Strathy on the north coast of Scotland as viewed through the diaries kept for the years 1911, 1912, 1915 and 1919 by Rev. Alexander Youngson MA, minister of the established Church of Scotland at Strathy, 1909 to 1930. From the outset, it must be admitted that Mr Youngson's ministry attained no national significance in the Scotland of his day. He must have been virtually unknown beyond the northern counties of Scotland. He held no post of national importance under the General Assembly. Why, then, write and read about him almost a hundred years on?

Mr Youngson's ministry may be said to have been ordinary, but it took place in circumstances of lasting interest. The Highland Clearances are remembered for the eviction of the Gaelic-speaking populations of the Highland straths to make way for sheep; it was to such coastal districts as Strathy that the people came, those who remained in the Highlands. The time we are considering was separated by only a century from the final clearance of Strathnaver, which by 1883–4 had created an economy of extremes: on the one hand, the absentee landlords of impressive wealth and status and on the other, the mass of tenants paying rents of under £2 a year.[1] The history of Strathy is thus, in part, a history of what came after the Clearances. It helps answer the question: what sort of society did the dispossessed create? By Mr Youngson's time, most families in the area were described as crofters, holding secure and heritable tenancies under the 1886 Crofters Holdings Act. Still, the oldest in the community that he knew had actually been born during the period of clearance and settlement, and life remained hard; tensions and inequalities remained and landed estates still dominated a society in the process of emerging from feudalism. One of the interests of the Youngson diaries is the evidence they suggest of a growing grass-roots democracy, existing alongside the deference given to class, wealth and status. Further, between 1911 and 1919 lay the great gulf of World War.

In this north coast community, the Church of Scotland had an equivocal place. As the established Church in Scotland it was legally secure and not dependent on popular appeal. Its finances rested on state support: civil law ensured that the landed classes paid most ministerial stipends. Until 1874, the landlords (or 'heritors') of most parishes had nominated their chosen minister for appointment in a system of patronage. Part of the regular procedure for couples intending to be married was to have public notice of their wedding made in the parish church, even if they themselves belonged to another denomination. The assemblies (or 'courts') of the Church held a privileged status, largely independent within the British legal system; the monarch sent a personal representative to attend the General Assembly. Yet the population of the northern Highlands had largely abandoned the Church of Scotland in and after the Disruption of 1843 in favour of the Free Church of Scotland, a denomination born from rejection of patronage and of state control. This is not the place to recite the nineteenth-century divisions and reunions of the Scottish presbyterian churches. Suffice it to say that, by 1909, Strathy was home to four presbyterian congregations. Besides Alex Youngson's established Church of Scotland there was also the Free Church of Scotland (congregation from 1845; manse built *c*.1862; church completed *c*.1881); the Free Presbyterian Church (congregation after 1892, church 1909–12) and the United Free Church of Scotland (congregation from 1900, Strathy UF church and manse *c*.1911). In this situation, what was the role of the parish ministers and their minority congregations, so often neglected by historians seduced by the glamour, sacrifice and energy of the Disruption? What sort of ministry was attempted? What place in society did the Established Church fulfil? In Mr Youngson's own day and denomination, his contemporaries considered his ministry successful. Though few attended his church, he was well known and respected as a minister across the far north.

Much of the appeal of this ministry is, in fact, its ordinariness. Not many ministers attain to appointment as conveners of national committees or Moderators of the General Assembly and few, even of these, can be said to affect the course of church or Scottish life. The Church of Scotland has been likened to an ocean-going super-tanker: once set on a course, hard to turn from its direction and difficult to stop. As Tolstoy suggested in *War and Peace*, history is not driven by the leaders, the Napoleons of the age, but by 'the action of innumerable infinitesimally small forces'. Thus the mass and the energy of the Church lie not so much in its radicals or its Moderators as in the aggregation of its 'ordinary' congregations and ministers, those who undertake its daily and routine mission and who, together, set its direction. The pattern of ministry conducted by Alex Youngson in Strathy can be shown to be similar to other ministries in more than half the presbyteries of the Church of Scotland in the years immediately before its 1929 union with the United Free Church. In good faith, he followed a pattern that I describe as institutionally arrogant, a pattern that, because it was ordinary and unquestioned, still has implications for the church.

The ordinary, however, can be difficult to study and to understand: such ephemeral paperwork and documentation as it generates is often lost, destroyed within weeks and months. Chance governs much of what is preserved, and our opportunity to remember Alex Youngson's ministry is in part due to the chance that has brought down to us four – only four – of his pocket diaries. These four surviving diaries offer an almost random selection of Mr Youngson's time in Strathy. Fortunately, other sources also survive – kirk session and presbytery minutes, the local weekly newspapers, documents in Scottish national and local archives – these expand helpfully on the brief entries of the diaries. Through the lens of these diaries, then, a picture of an almost vanished world can be recovered: a picture of the people, institutions and daily life of crofting townships on the north coast of Sutherland around the time of the Great War.

Still advertised in 2006 as 'undiscovered', the north coast of Britain was visited before the First World War only by those whose business took them there, or by those with considerable resources both of time and money, usually bent on shooting deer or grouse, or fishing for salmon and trout. Roads to and in the north were poor, and the motor car was still a luxury. The railway reached to Caithness, but Forsinard, a full sixteen miles inland, was the nearest station to the Sutherland coast. Indeed, until 1921 no Moderator of the General Assembly of the Church of Scotland had been known to visit the Presbytery of Tongue during his term of office: 'its vast area of about half a million acres, and its remoteness from all railway communication, have always proved a formidable obstacle to such recognition on the part of the Church', *The Scotsman* reported [27 August 1921]. Yet issues within the story of this supposedly remote part of the United Kingdom continue to resonate.

A final comment by way of introduction. My interest in this history was begun during those years when I was minister in Strathy. But what people say to a minister, they do not normally expect to find in print, years later. Beyond examination of the Youngson diaries, this story is therefore told from public sources that anyone may see. It is interpreted with the help of my knowledge of the area and my experience of the community, certainly, but what follows is essentially history, not my personal reminiscences, and it does not depend on oral sources. Alex Youngson's diaries also recorded events, and not his opinions; at least, not explicitly.

2

The Youngson Diaries

The Diaries

A diary is one of the essential tools of the modern world. Look at the shelves of a stationer's or a bookshop at any time from September onwards – they fill with new diaries for the forthcoming year, published in endless variations: displaying a week or a fortnight or a month at a time, sometimes with pictures, with information on national holidays, or travel, or – the permutations go on. A diary manages time, resolves conflicting priorities, offers structure to life, embodies memories. Hence diaries fascinate, offering privileged insight into a personal world.

Alex Youngson's diaries were pocket-books, on the whole maintained in pencil though with some sections in ink. His entries recorded in outline the main occurrence of the day, whether this was an appointment, a township or person visited, or activity in the glebe. These diaries were thus kept as a record, written after the event – though in a few cases it appears that such appointments as meetings of the Presbytery were entered in advance. As diaries of record (albeit brief), the books show Mr Youngson's priorities – the matters he chose to commit to paper. So they reflect his mind as well as his tasks, and cover family and financial matters as well as his ministerial duties. Space was also given, almost every Sunday as a matter of routine, and on other significant days, to noting the weather. The north coast of Scotland can be bleak and windswept; winter blizzards not uncommon. As travel was largely on foot, the prevailing weather played a significant part in determining whether an ageing minister might venture from his manse, and also in encouraging or deterring attendance at Sunday worship. As one who farmed his glebe, Mr Youngson was also like his parishioners in looking for good weather to assist seed planting, lambing and at harvest-time: all these activities, too, find their place in his diaries.

The diaries for 1911 and 1912, both 4″ × 6″ in size, were published by Hodder & Stoughton (London), and were entitled: *The Minister's Pocket Diary and Clerical Vade Mecum*. Designed with appropriate advertising for clergymen working within the United Kingdom, these two books contain – beyond the pages for entries through the year – much other useful space. Besides those pages headed 'General Memoranda', Alex Youngson made use of the sections headed 'Cash Account', 'Visitation', 'Class Roll' and 'Addresses of Friends'. 'Baptisms' and 'Marriages' attracted some brief notes. He did not use the pages headed 'Poor Fund', 'Sick List', 'Private Communions', 'Letters received', 'Addresses delivered', 'Books read' and 'Books lent', 'Business for next Church or Parish meeting' and 'Committees'. Strathy was not such a large or busy charge that its minister needed assistance in remembering these matters and, besides, the congregation as such had no poor fund, and private communion was not practised by the Scottish Church in the Highlands of Mr Youngson's day.

In 1915, Alex Youngson used *Oliver & Boyd's Pocket Diary* published in Edinburgh by the firm of that name. A distinctively Scottish diary for general professional use, and also 4″ × 6″ in size, it contained lists of 'Fairs, cattle-markets etc in Scotland', dates of local Scottish holidays, and a complete list of Members of both the House of Commons and the House of Lords. Lacking the church-specific pages of the Hodder & Stoughton publication, the 1915 diary featured, besides general memoranda pages, a double-page spread per month 'Cash Book'. Mr Youngson used this 'Cash Book' on a daily basis carefully to record cash received and paid. A similar feature was also used in his 1919 diary. Published by Thomas de la Rue (London) as *The Onoto Diary*, besides the daily pages, the cash-book and space for general notes, the 1919 diary contained British, foreign and colonial postal, parcel and telegraph rates, currency conversion and other such general information. At 3″ × 4.5″, the 1919 diary is the smallest of the four to have survived, and contains the inscription 'With love from Violet'.

Alex Youngson completed most entries in all four diaries in pencil. His was a time when writing in ink meant using a pen and inkwell, or perhaps a fountain pen; but fountain pens were prone to leak and to stain the jacket in which they were carried. We can imagine that entries in ink were made in his study, with inkwell and blotting paper to hand, whereas for use in the community outside the house, a pencil would be carried with the pocket diary. The 'Class Roll' and 'Visitation' sections, however, together with some of the additional notes, were completed in ink in the diaries for 1911 and 1912. Thus the first names of the Class Rolls for the Sabbath School were entered in ink (in 1911, names 1 to 20 inclusive). We can imagine the minister entering the formal roll at the first session of the Sabbath School for the year. Thereafter, names were entered in pencil as new scholars (in 1911, names 21 to 33) arrived. The diary then served as an attendance register for the Sabbath School: in its printed form, these pages were laid out in columns, so that ticks or zeros in each scholar's row could be entered for each weekly session. In addition, another section of the diaries completed in ink was that relating to his support for local fishermen. The diaries for 1911, 1912 and 1915 all contain lists (in ink) of 'Boats and Crews – Strathy Point': the 'Lady', the 'Morning Star', 'Royal George', 'Busy Bee' and 'Vine'. Each had a crew of six. The Committee for the pier for Strathy Point, from which these boats sailed, is named in ink. In 1911 so too is a list of subscribers and donations under the heading 'Help for Portskerra Slip[way]'. As we shall see, Alex Youngson's priorities included education (in a broad sense) and using his administrative gifts for the benefit of the community.

The 'Visitation' sections of the diaries for 1911 and 1912 were carefully completed in ink; and space was found in the 1915 diary for the same content. The minister can thus be pictured, in his study, at the beginning of each year, carefully entering in the new diary the names of all the inhabitants of the townships within walking (and hence visiting) distance of the manse: Strathy West (23 households and one empty house), Strathy East (23 households), Strathy Point (39 households), Brawl (8 households), Aultiphurst (8 households), Baligill (15 households), Millburn (3 households) and Bowside (2 households).[1] These lists were compiled in walking order and are broadly comparable to those given in the official 1901 British Census. They include the entire communities, house by house, and with no indication of denomination or religious affiliation. This is clearly the diary of a parish minister: someone who would seek to be acquainted (at the least) with all his neighbours and not simply with those who belonged to his congregation. In addition, some names were given under the headings Melvich & Portskerra (9 households) and Bighouse (5 households): these names, however, were a very small selection from much larger communities, not at that time technically within the parish of Strathy. Curiously, headings were made for the townships in the west of the parish – Fleuchary, Ledna-gullen and Armadale – but no names were entered in the spaces carefully left between the headings.

To follow the minister around the parish, we need – like him – to be aware of both the geography and the history of the Strathy district of Sutherland.

The Parish

Where is Strathy and what are the borders of the parish?[2] The answer given to this seemingly easy question has varied over time. Church and state institutions have produced different answers, pushed by changing technology and economic imperatives. Nevertheless, for centuries these lands have been occupied by families of the Clan Mackay.

The name Mackay has been predominant in the north and west Highlands for many generations. In the Reay Papers (available to the public in the National Archives of Scotland[3]) the 1415 charter can still be seen by which Donald, Lord of the Isles, transferred Strathnaver and Strath Halladale to Angus Mackay and his son Neil. The chief of the Clan Mackay took the title of Lord Reay in the early seventeenth century. A clan with a strong military tradition, the Mackays mustered for the Hanoverian cause in 1745. In consequence, the Presbytery of Tongue (created on the then Lord Reay's advice after 1724 and comprising ministers from kirks built at his expense) sent a flowery address to the Duke of Cumberland in 1746, congratulating him as 'the Deliverer of the Oppressed' thanks to his notable victory at Culloden. Mackay of Strathy was a subordinate house of Reay, a younger brother of the first Lord, who was granted these lands for himself and his heirs. The laird's house for the former Strathy Estate was on the east bank of the Strathy River near its estuary, at the apex of a triangle of cultivated land stretching back along both sides of the river. In 1760, a visiting bishop of the Irish Church described the scene in a way that the modern traveller from Bettyhill can still appreciate: the green cultivated slopes still stand out attrac-tively against the peat of the hill behind: 'We came to a most charming vale between the bogs called Strathy Bay. It belongs to Captain Mackay, now in the Sutherland Regiment . . . Here is a good house and offices . . . This is a fine country situated between the foil of black bogs that hang over it.'

Similarly the seat of the Mackays of Bighouse lay at the mouth of the next river to the east, the Halladale. Unlike the Strathy laird's house, Bighouse Lodge still stands. These Mackay estates of Strathy and Bighouse were divided by the watershed between the Strathy and the Halladale, and for several centuries before 1800 belonged to separate parishes: Strathy was part of the parish of Farr (with its church at Bettyhill) while Bighouse and Strath Halladale were part of the parish of Reay (with its church in the Caithness settlement of the same name). Strath Halladale was thus in the anomalous position in being part of the County of Sutherland, but looking to a parish the bulk of which lay in the County of Caithness.

As a parish in its own right, separate from that of Farr, Strathy was thus not a historic pre-Reformation parish, but a product of the notorious Highland Clearances. In order to improve their estates, Highland landlords in the decades before and after 1800 created sheep farms covering vast acres of northern Scotland: the wool from sheep offered substantially greater income than the rents of the previous smallholding tenants. Captain John Mackay of Strathy, like Major Hugh Mackay of Bighouse, had followed the military tradition of their clan. His regiment, the Sutherland Highlanders, had served gallantly in the Revolutionary and Napoleonic Wars – but meanwhile his north-coast estate had been sold.

John Mackay of Strathy sold the Strathy Estate in 1790 to a lawyer, William Honeyman. Honeyman took the title 'Lord Armadale of Strathy' when appointed a judge of Edinburgh's Court of Session. He first began the process of 'improvement': the destruction of the old economic order and way of life, and its replacement by the new. An absentee landlord, Honeyman was concerned for the income to be generated from his lands in the north. By 1809, the laird's house at Strathy was reduced to a 'ruinous state' according to John Henderson's description of his tour of Sutherland.[4]

Strathy Estate was bounded on the west by Kirtomy; to the east it included Baligill but not Melvich nor Portskerra. Honeyman divided the estate into three: Strathy Mains (the lands at the estuary of the river, behind the laird's house); the old subtenanted settlements stretching for five miles up the Strathy river and occupied by ten families; and his new creation, Armadale Sheep Farm. In *A General View of the Agriculture of the County of Sutherland* (published 1812) John Henderson described Armadale as he knew it in 1809. Honeyman had given Armadale on lease to sheep-farmers from Northumberland. The lease was in the hands of one of these, Gabriel Reid, in 1794. Cheviot sheep had been introduced: a hardy breed, vastly more productive and profitable than the native flocks. To make way for greatly increased numbers of sheep, the original subtenants of the lands were removed – cleared – from their lands. Fourteen families were relocated, being granted holdings including some land already in cultivation and on the crofts of the present community of Armadale north of the main road. 'He has increased them (his tenants) and encouraged them to improve and be industrious seamen' wrote Henderson. Those who preferred not to accept the new, smaller, amounts of ground offered were able to sell their cattle and hence obtain capital with which to emigrate. By 1812, Armadale Farm was one 'of the most extensive in the North of Scotland' with a stock of some two thousand and more Cheviots. The pattern in Armadale was to be repeated throughout Sutherland.

Thanks to the added value that the Armadale sheep farm had brought to the estate, Strathy was sold to the Marquis of Stafford in 1813 for £25,000. Armadale's two to three thousand Cheviots now joined the 15,000 already grazing on the Sutherland estates in 1811. Elizabeth Gordon, Countess of Sutherland from 1811, held sway over the single largest tract of land then owned by any British family; as the Reay estates shrank, those of Sutherland increased until almost the entire county was owned by her and the man she was to marry – the Marquis of Stafford, subsequently the first Duke of Sutherland. The policies of the Staffords and their agents, policies also directed at 'improving' their estates and increasing their revenues, are forever linked with the Clearances. First William Honeyman and then the Staffords, in large measure, created Strathy as we now know the district.

'Improvement' continued apace. Maps made for the Sutherland Estates in this period still exist, deposited at the National Library of Scotland.[5] The intention was to extend the Armadale land devoted to sheep east across the hill into the basin of the River Strathy. All subtenants were to be cleared from settlements south of the line of the main road and relocated in 'allotments' to be created largely north of the road and along the coast. A map dated 1815 shows this particularly clearly. Originally endorsed 'Brae Strathy ground possessed by small tenants', these words are deleted and 'Armadale Sheep Farm' written in; while across the road is written 'Settlers here'. The ancient dwellings at Brae Rathy, Dalangwell, Bowside, Auchrugan and Daltine were to be abandoned. In their place, new 'allotment' communities were to be created at Portskerra, Baligill, on Strathy Point, at Brawl, Aultiphurst and beside the existing Armadale fisher-town.[6]

It is clear both from the maps that survive and from walking round the crofting settlements as they exist today that the patches of land north of the road allotted for each family were very small. This was a deliberate policy of the estates. Patrick Sellar, the Stafford's main agent in the parish of Farr, explained why in 1815:

> Lord and Lady Stafford were pleased humanely to order a new arrangement of this County. That the interior should be possessed by Cheviot Shepherds and the people brought down to the coast and placed there in lots under the size of three arable acres, sufficient for the maintenance of an industrious family, but pinched enough to cause them turn their attention to fishing. I presume to say that the proprietors humanely ordered this arrangement, because, it was surely a most benevolent action, to put these barbarous hordes into a position where they could better associate together.[7]

The crofting settlements of Strathy East and Strathy West are good examples of the crofting allotments in this area. Together, they occupy the arable lands once associated with the Strathy laird's house. The field divisions still to be seen largely correspond with an estate map of 1855.[8] Marked on the map are the assessments of total and arable acreage. No. 2 allotment, for example, had just over ten acres in total, of which three were reckoned arable. The original numbers 5 and 6 seem to have been combined; they were at first calculated to be barely a single arable acre each. For these 'pinched' holdings, rents of £2 and more were expected yearly.

These communities were not simply for those cleared from the hinterlands of Armadale and Strathy. Over ninety families were cleared from the Sutherland lands in the parish of Farr in 1809, from Strathnaver – cleared, notoriously, by fire if they delayed. Many of these were resettled on the barren lands of Strathy Point. The years 1811 and 1812 saw another round of evictions. In 1818, the then tenant of Armadale, William Innes of Sandside, agreed to surrender his coastal lands to assist resettlement from Strathnaver. In exchange, the thirty-eight families of the Strathy glen were cleared and their land added to the sheep farm according to the map made three years earlier. By 1847, a further map shows the Armadale Farm extending from Kirtomy in the west to near Baligill in the east; and from the road southward to Loch Strathy.[9]

By 1850, then, the ancient Mackay lands of Strathy had been almost totally transformed. The old settlements had gone; new allotments were created. The old family of Mackay of Strathy had gone – their house crumbled into ruin. In their place the North-umbrian Reid and his successors managed affairs under the absent Staffords' all-powerful manager, James Loch, a Scot from the south. Whereas the clearance of Armadale had been efficient, that of Strathnaver had been ferocious. The tenants found themselves driven out, unable to take the vital roof timbers needed to make new homes; unable to drive their cattle, to harvest the crops still in the ground or even, horrifically, to keep alive their old folk. In place of a self-sufficient society based on the rearing of cattle and their native sheep, those who now found themselves resettled were expected to cultivate ('improve') pre-viously barren peat moor; to survive on what potato crops they could grow, and to take to fishing off a coast devoid of protected harbours and exposed to the full blast of the ocean. Strathy Point had been uninhabited before 1800. The dangers of its situation were undiminished by 1902:

> Strathy Point lies 3 miles out into the north Atlantic Ocean, situated on the north coast of Sutherland, and is thus exposed on three sides to the full force of the Atlantic billows, their boats which are sometimes broken by the storm, or swept away by the waves can be drawn up only a few yards into a small narrow creek, hemmed in on three sides by perpendicular rock some 200 or 300 feet high, and this creek, naturally formed by the wear and tear of time, cannot be approached during a violent storm and thus their boats are at the mercy of the storm. Not infrequently do they lose their fishing gear, such as lobster creels, which must be

left in the sea all night as when a storm arises during the night they cannot launch their boats as the entrance into the creek is so dangerous by sunken rocks, or detached pieces from the adjacent perpendicular cliffs which shed occasionally on the surface.[10]

'Improvement' continued. The Marquis of Stafford bought Bighouse and the lands of Strath Halladale from Major C. C. Mackay in 1830 and, clearing the inhabitants from the head and the foot of the Halladale, by 1847 had created sheep farms at Bighouse (including Golval and Kirkton) and at Forsinard.[11] Some of the profits were spent on new roads and bridges and on the provision of inns: locally, the Strathy Inn and the hotels at Melvich and Forsinard. More went to sustain the lifestyle of the super-rich of their time, the aristocratic families of England, then building such palaces as Yorkshire's Castle Howard. The Staffords were, however, in their way, serious about creating new communities. A community needed a church. The Marquis therefore took the opportunity of finance available from the government in London to have Strathy created as, in effect, a new parish – with a new church, and a manse for the new minister.

After the Napoleonic Wars, Parliament in London voted the huge sum of £1,500,000 to build new churches for the Church of England as a victory thanksgiving to God. Belatedly, and only as a result of much lobbying, £50,000 was granted to Scotland by an Act of 1824 to build thirty churches and manses in the Highlands. No more than £1,500 was to be spent on any one site, while the most expensive church in England cost £76,677. The purpose of the Parliamentary legislation was to provide additional places of worship for huge Highland parishes, which – like the parish of Farr – covered hundreds of square miles. The architect appointed under the scheme was Thomas Telford, by then the most celebrated British architect and engineer of the age. Both the fabric and the ministers' stipends of long-established parish churches were the legal responsibility of the heritors of their parishes; 'Parliamentary churches', however, were funded by the British Parliament, which paid the initial cost of the buildings and endowed the stipends. Beyond granting the land needed for church, manse and glebe, no further liability fell to the heritors – a fact convenient to them, but of mixed blessing to the church. It was agreed that Strathy should receive a church under this scheme, the Staffords providing the sites from the Sutherland estate. Telford's church at Strathy was completed by 14 March 1828; a minister, Rev. Angus MacIntosh McGillivray, moved into the manse (built on the site of what was possibly the former Strathy laird's garden) and was inducted by the Presbytery of Tongue to his new charge on 25 September of the same year. At first the minister at Strathy was auxiliary to the parish minister for Farr, at Bettyhill. As part of its own programme for church extension, however, the Church of Scotland decided to give the Parliamentary churches their own parishes and Strathy was separated from Farr and erected *quoad sacra* (for spiritual purposes) under an Act of General Assembly of 1833.

The boundaries of the new parish were agreed in 1834 by the Presbytery of Tongue on the advice of the ministers of Farr and Strathy, and of the factor to Her Grace, the Duchess Countess of Sutherland. In brief, the line ran from Armadale Head to Drumbasbie, placing the settlement of Armadale in Strathy parish, and 'from then along the march of the old Strathy Estate, until it meets Kildonan'.[12] Underlying this division, whose recorded details mainly concern the new line between Farr and Strathy, was the fact that Strathy would inherit the existing eastern boundary between Farr and the Parish of Reay – which was also the eastern boundary of the Presbytery of Tongue itself. The Laird of Bighouse was historically a heritor of the parish of Reay: seating in the Bighouse Loft or gallery was reserved for him in the Kirk of Reay (built 1739). In its original form, therefore, Strathy did not include the lands of Bighouse – the fishing settlement of Portskerra, the crofting lands of Melvich or the fifteen miles and more of Strath Halladale – these remained within the parish of Reay.

By Alex Youngson's induction in 1909, however, the picture had been further adjusted by the civil authorities and (separately) by the church, both of which retained the traditional word, 'parish', to describe the area within which their different local institutions had jurisdiction. Though the Church of Scotland had separated Strathy from Farr, for local government and civil purposes the parish of Farr continued undivided. After the British state took over from the church the tasks of caring for the poor and of public education, the old boundaries of the parish of Farr remained the basis of the elected School Board, and of the elected Parish Council that administered poor relief. Further reforms, however, created in 1890 a new electoral ward based on Strathy that also included Portskerra, Melvich, Bighouse and Halladale as far south as Forsinard. By the 1901 Census, this 'greater-Strathy' area officially comprised the Registration District of Strathy for the purposes of civil registration of births and deaths. For electoral purposes, the same lands were named the East Ward of the Civil Parish of Farr. The Parish Council of Farr and the School Board of Farr meanwhile after 1890 exercised authority over a 'greater-Farr': the old undivided Farr together with the new areas taken from Reay. The annexation to Farr/Strathy for civil purposes of Strath Halladale and the lands at its mouth hence aligned local government institutions to the formal county boundary between Sutherland and Caithness.

The different presbyterian churches active in Strathy came to different decisions as to the bounds that they served. The Free Church fell in line with the new civic boundaries, maintaining a minister, church and manse at Strathy and a church in Halladale; and designated their parish, 'Strathy'. The United Free Church designated its parish, 'Strathy and Halladale', and maintained a minister, church and manse in Strathy together with a mission hall in Melvich and a missionary and mission (with a separate Deacons' Court)[13] for Halladale. The slowly changing established or parish Church of Scotland, with its minister, manse and church at Strathy, for formal purposes considered Strath Halladale and the lands of the Bighouse Estate to be part of the parish of Reay until 1930 and Mr Youngson appears to have visited in Halladale only rarely.[14] Nevertheless the minister of Strathy recorded in his diaries details of visiting, funerals and baptisms in Portskerra and Melvich, townships only three miles or so from his manse. The Free Presbyterian Church alone of the four Strathy congregations did not attempt to maintain a local minister.

The settlements of Strathy Bay with their neighbours of Armadale, Lednagullen and Baligill (and others yet smaller), and with Portskerra and Melvich, thus comprised the townships where those who looked to the ministry of the Parish Church of Strathy were concentrated 1909–30. Legally, the condition of the people of the townships had greatly improved since the period of clearance and settlement. As a response to the Crofters' War, an extended period of unrest often involving the illegal seizure of land, a Royal Commission of 1883 had taken evidence of the

causes that had brought the Highlands and Islands to the edge of
starvation. In 1886 the Crofters Holdings Act gave crofters
security of tenure, a heritable interest in their land and legally
controlled rents. For the first time, the powers of the estates over
their tenants were legally limited and it became possible actually
to improve the yield from the land without being penalised by
increased rents.[15] Yet the Act could do nothing to alter the
geography of the north coast, swept in winter with salt-laden
winds, too often rocky, barren moorland that even mechanised
agriculture can make little of. What was still needed was access to
the better arable fields of the hinterland, and to hill pasture,[16] but
meanwhile the lands of the old Strathy Estate had been sold,
1899–1900, by the 4th Duke of Sutherland to William Ewing
Gilmour Esq., who during the 1890s was reinvesting into land
funds derived from Clydeside industry.

The last decades of the nineteenth century saw a general decline
in the profitability of sheep farms, with land across the Highlands
being purchased or redeveloped for its sporting potential.[17] With
his primary Sutherland home at Rosehall near Lairg, Mr Gilmour
and his guests used the lodge at Bowside as a base for fishing and
shooting when visiting Strathy, though the hinterland of the
community was never formally constituted as a deer forest. At
the time of Alex Youngson's induction, 'Mr Gilmour' (as he
appears in the diaries) was thus proprietor of the lands around
Strathy Bay and the crofts there paid their rents to him. Apart
from the lodge at Bowside, itself somewhat remote from the
coastal settlements, the buildings most prominent around the bay
before 1914 were the four presbyterian churches and their three
manses, Strathy Public School, and the Strathy Inn (held by a
tenant of the estate). Thanks to loans from wealthy friends of the
community, a building was purchased as a public hall and library
in 1912. It was almost clear of debt by 1919: 'Strathy is very
fortunate in having a suitable and accommodating building (as a
hall) where the young people of the district can assemble together
for their social and intellectual interest.'[18]

To the west, Armadale was of sufficient size to have its own
community life, and besides the Armadale Public School there
was a house there provided for the area's doctor while serving as
Medical Officer of Health for the Parish Council. Both Armadale
and Strathy enjoyed local telegraph or post offices by 1909.[19] It is
worth adding that the current lighthouse at Strathy Point did not

exist in Mr Youngson's time; it was the last to be built by the Northern Lighthouse Board, becoming operational in 1958.

Meanwhile the 34,000 acres of the Bighouse Estate were still in the hands of the Duke of Sutherland in 1909. The profitability of sheep having declined, two sections of land around Forsinard had been redeveloped as a deer forest. Lying to the west of the mouth of the Halladale, Melvich was primarily a crofting settlement, while Portskerra (like Strathy Point) was a crofting/fishing township with its own harbour – of sorts. Between them lay the Melvich Hotel, tenanted from the estate and enjoying sixty-three acres of its own land: both this and the hotel at Forsinard had fishing rights on the Halladale for their guests. The Melvich Hotel rented further fishing on the Strathy lochs from Mr Gilmour and also offered its guests the facility of a billiard room in a corrugated iron extension. (By 1930, the hotel was advertising in Edinburgh's daily paper, *The Scotsman*: 'Situated in Fine Sporting Country . . . Trout Fishing in numerous Lochs, also Sea Trout Fishing, Free to Guests. Deep Sea Fishing . . . Pigeon Shooting by arrangement. Sea Bathing. Garage. Electric Light . . . Visitors met by Hotel Car if required'.[20]) There was a public school in Melvich and a telegraph office in the schoolmaster's house. A drill hall was opened in 1912, in which social events were also held. The bay was visually dominated, however, by the properties of Bighouse on the east bank of the Halladale. Just south of Melvich lay the tenanted sheep farm of Kirkton. Portskerra and Melvich as Alex Youngson knew them were helpfully described by an agent of the Board of Agriculture for Scotland in 1920:

The crofting townships of Melvich and Portskerra straggle along the hillside westward for about two and half miles from the most northerly point of Kirkton Farm and undoubtedly form one of the most congested areas in the County of Sutherland. According to the Valuation Roll, Melvich, which lies nearest Kirkton, contains 31 houses and crofts, 3 houses with gardens attached, 1 house (only), 1 piece of land, and Hotel with land and grazing, while Portskerra, which is a continuation of the last named, contains 53 houses and crofts, 4 houses with gardens attached and 2 houses (only). The crofts vary slightly in extent, but the average size is somewhere about 2 acres and the land, without exception, is of very poor quality. In addition to the individual crofts, there is an extent of common pasture which works out approximately at

27 acres per croft. It adjoins the townships and marches on one side with the hill pasture of Kirkton. Part of the common is fairly good heather pasture, but the greater part (possibly about two-thirds of the whole area) is of very inferior quality. While there are not a few modern and substantially built houses, the buildings generally are of very poor description, being small, drystone or clay built and roofed with straw thatch. The population of the combined townships, estimated at close to 500, are dependent for a livelihood on the produce of their crofts eked out by rather precarious returns from the sea. Owing to the lack of harbourage, sea fishing is at all times difficult and very often impossible. A movement is at present on foot to construct a harbour alongside the existing breakwater and that, if carried out, should tend to the development of the local fishing industry and so, to some extent, mitigate the existing conditions of living there.[21]

A generalised description of a typical crofting home at this time was provided in a report of the Sanitary Inspector for Sutherland, published in the press in 1912:

His [i.e., the typical crofter's] home, built perhaps 50 or 60 years ago of dry stone, in many cases of stone and clay, had originally a thatched roof, but recently was improved by a wood and iron or felt roof. The walls naturally were damp, not infrequently from foundation to wall head. They were lined with several layers of paper, hanging more or less loosely from the walls. A box bed with a wooden press at the foot divided the 'but' from the 'ben'. This box bed was also covered with layers of paper, and nearly closed in with a curtain in front. The windows of nearly all the houses were small, and in 50 per cent were 'fixed' and could not be opened. In not a few cases, every crevice was stuffed up so as to exclude draughts and fresh air. The attics in 95 per cent of this class of house formed a perfect triangle, with the couplings and sarking covered over with the never failing wall paper. It could easily be imagined how difficult a matter it was to disinfect such a place with anything like efficiency.[22]

In fact, the Inspector was over-optimistic about the extent of progress in the Strathy area. A survey conducted for the Inland Revenue around 1912 showed only eight homes with roofs of corrugated iron with twenty-five more slated in the settlements around Strathy Bay; but those slated included the inn, two manses, the schoolhouse and the estate's properties at Bowside. All remaining homes were thatched.[23] Poor land, small crofts, homes in which illness might flourish, dangerous fishing, precarious finances, a background of dispossession still within living memory; these features were common across the townships that lay between Drumholistan and Drumbasbie, clustering along the north coast around the mouths of the Halladale and the Strathy.

The Minister

It is more than time to make a better acquaintance with our diarist and his family. Alexander Youngson was born in 1841 in the coastal village of Rosehearty in the parish of Pitsligo, Aberdeenshire. His father was described both as a baker and as holding the office of Inspector of Poor for the parish.[24] Alex gained the degree of MA from the University of Aberdeen in 1861 and the next year began work as a schoolmaster in the parish of Skene, where he was also appointed Registrar for Births, Marriages and Deaths. The school was a parish school, under the management and control of the kirk session of the Established Church for the parish. As schoolmaster, besides essential numeracy and literacy, Mr Youngson was expected to teach his pupils Bible stories, the Shorter Catechism and the tunes for singing the Scottish metrical psalms. In 1870, and while he was employed at Skene, his marriage to a girl from his home village, Elizabeth Catherine Young, the daughter of a retired ship's captain, was celebrated at her home, Craighaugh House, Rosehearty. The home Mrs Youngson was leaving was (in its context) substantial, and confidently set back up and above the terraced cottages of the fisher-town. Bridegroom and bride were both aged twenty-nine.[25] Four of their five children who survived infancy were born during Alex Youngson's time as schoolmaster at Skene.[26]

In 1872, however, by Act of Parliament, the network of schools controlled by the Church of Scotland was taken over by the British State. The teachers formerly appointed by the Parish Minister and Session were now appointed by an elected School Board. Finance came in part from a local tax or *rate,* and from the central Scotch Education Department on the basis of payment by results. The local School Board's grant was determined by the number of pupils registered and by their attainments, discipline, etc. as assessed by an Inspector. From its income the Board was then free to set wage levels for its teachers. Whereas teachers in the church's schools had held their posts with much the same level as security as ministers, effectively for life, now their contracts were at the pleasure of the School Board. Depending on the ethos of the local area and the composition of the board, the religious culture of public schools could be much reduced, and the government-inspected syllabus was now secular.[27]

Perhaps these changes in the character of teaching as a profession were instrumental in Alex Youngson's change of career, or more likely he had always seen a period as a schoolmaster as a step towards the ordained ministry. After obtaining an MA, candidates for the ministry of the Church of Scotland were required (from 1866) to attend a Divinity Hall for either three full sessions or two full and three partial sessions, not to degree standard but to the satisfaction of their Presbytery. Employment as a schoolmaster was a regular route for obtaining an income and sustaining a family while satisfying the church's requirements.[28] While he was still a schoolmaster, Alex Youngson was nominated to be the first minister of a new parish church, that of Newmill, by Keith. Newmill had previously been a mission within the parish of Keith and had become a parish in its own right on 18 June 1877. Above the main-door gable-end of the church, aligned to overlook the cottages of the wide main street of the village, the date on the bell-tower reads '1870'. Under the congregation's constitution, the Trustees had the right to nominate the first minister of the charge. Alex Youngson must somehow have impressed the Trustees of Newmill: Alexander Duff, Viscount Macduff MP; James G. Brown, distiller; Alexander Thurburn, solicitor. Having preached to the approval of the congregation he then passed the trial Greek and Hebrew discourses, sermons and lectures set by the Presbytery of Strathbogie, was licensed as a minister on 2 August 1877 and was ordained and inducted to Newmill on 4 September.[29] The Youngsons moved into the impressive manse behind the church.

This was a period of renewal for the Established Church. Following the catastrophe of the Disruption of 1843, when more than a third of the ministers and membership seceded to create the Free Church, the Church of Scotland had gained greater independence from the British state. While the boundaries of historic parishes still had both religious and civil aspects, the

Church could now more easily create new parishes for its own ecclesiastical purposes, *quoad sacra,* and hence adjust its structures to a changing population and an industrialising nation. One of the goals of the Church was to acquire sufficient capital sums to *endow* (fund through the annual payments of interest from invested capital) the stipends of ministers of these new parishes. Its ideal was to offer a Christian ministry across the nation at minimum cost to the congregations, so that the poorest need not be compelled to pay for their own minister. While called by the congregation, a Parish Church minister was not dependent on the congregation for his income, and his calling was understood to be to the population of the parish and not simply to those who came to worship. Between 1846 and 1899, 405 new parishes like Newmill were thus created and endowed by the work of the General Assembly's Committee on the Endowment of Chapels, providing places of worship for some 1,482,000 people.

Complementing the work of the Committee on Endowment was the Home Mission Committee, which offered support to newly created congregations before they could be endowed and also to Mission Stations: congregations in islands, remote areas or mining communities that were judged for some reason not to merit parish status. The mission statement of the established Church of Scotland, increasingly vigorously followed, was to bring Christian worship and church life 'within reach of those who, owing to distance from church, or other circumstances, would otherwise be practically without adequate opportunity of sharing in them' and also of 'pressing upon them the offers of the Gospel, not only by public services in church but by personal visitation in their own homes'.[30] Alex Youngson's career as a minister, first at the new *quoad sacra* parish of Newmill, then as missionary minister at the Mission Church on the island of Stroma, and finally in the *quoad sacra* Parliamentary parish of Strathy, suggests that he sought to put these missionary ideals into practice.

There was, however, a three-year gap between Alex Youngson demitting office as minister of Newmill in June 1896 (aged fifty-five) and his appointment to Stroma in 1899 (aged fifty-eight). Records still extant in the National Archives of Scotland show that between 1890 and 1897 he was bankrupt, his assets seque-strated for the benefit of his creditors.[31] It seems that Mr Young-son's difficulties were associated with his connection with the sea:

after the Town and Country Bank, Aberdeen, his largest single debt was due to Guthrie, Macdonald, Hood & Co., ship brokers and owners. They claimed £354 0s. 6d. owing towards the voyages of the ships *Auldgirth*, *Keir* and *Durrisdeer*, commencing April 1893 and ending October 1895. That sum alone represented more than a year's income. Mr Youngson's assets by 1890 included 1/64th shares in the *Durrisdeer*, the *Ecclefechan*, the *Dunveggan* and the *Auldgirth*, and elements of his bank loans were secured by mortgage against these ships. It may be remembered that Mrs Youngson was the daughter of a ship's captain. Perhaps through his marriage her husband had obtained unsound assets or become entangled in business he did not fully understand? Both Mr and Mrs Youngson came from the same fishing village of Rosehearty, however, and it could have been their joint interest in the sea that had brought the couple together.

The financial failure was a serious one. Omitting shillings and pence, Mr Youngson's total assets in 1890 came to £913, wholly inadequate against secured liabilities amounted to £536 and an unsecured debt of no less than £2,586. He owed money to many in Keith itself, as well as to creditors in Glasgow and Edinburgh, and to a London bank. As costs escalated above income and increasing loans could not be repaid, much of the daily business of the Newmill manse had come to be run on credit. Debts were owed to a whole range of small firms: a bookseller, cabinetmaker & upholsterer, an umbrella maker, plumber, printer, coal & wood merchant, ironmonger, coachbuilder, baker & confectioner, chemist, jeweller, dressmaker, bootmaker, draper. School fees, presumably for Katie, aged twelve in 1890 – perhaps also for Alice (aged fifteen) – were owing to the College for Daughters of Ministers of the Gospel, located in Edinburgh. All of these debts were more or less written off by the bankruptcy. Once his household furniture and other personal goods had been sold, and his life insurance policies cashed in, Mr Youngson's creditors were paid one first and final dividend from his sequestrated assets, at the rate of 1s 6d per pound: a bare 7.5 per cent. Thus 92.5 per cent of his unsecured debts were left unpaid when he was released from bankruptcy on 9 June 1897. Ministers of the Established Church held a position in society and lived in manses of stone and slate, often large and impressive. They did not, however, own their manses and Alex Youngson's private means had been insufficient to meet the crisis that befell him and his family.

His financial affairs, of course, could not fail to have an impact on his ministry at Newmill. In December 1895, the Session Clerk wrote to the Presbytery of Strathbogie with documents to sustain a complaint by the elders against their minister, and to demonstrate the deteriorating financial circumstances of the congregation. The Presbytery met in public in Newmill Church to look into the case and heard the 'managers, elders and certain members of the congregation testify to the loss of confidence of the congregation in Mr Youngson as their minister'. Inevitably, a committee was appointed to discover the facts and, faced with its report, he resigned the charge on 1 June 1896, 'for the good of the church and parish of Newmill, the good of the Church of Scotland and to terminate the unhappy division which had arisen in the congregation'. Clearly, though some section of the congregation may have remained loyal, the elders had decided that a minister who could not pay his bills could not remain. It was later discovered that Alex Youngson had omitted to sign the minutes of his Kirk Session between 24 February 1895 and 31 May 1896: 1895 may well have seen stormy meetings between the elders and the minister. The members of Presbytery appear not to have been unsympathetic to the Youngsons: as he departed, he was commended to the Baird Trust for financial support and his son Alex was awarded the Scott Bursary for a course at the University of Aberdeen.[32]

Mr Youngson's move to Stroma in 1899 had thus an element of necessity about it if he was to be able to continue a vocation as a minister. Thanks to the abolition of patronage in 1874, Church of Scotland ministers were called by the election of a congregation and hence required recommendations and reputation. The financial failure at Newmill must have blighted his opportunities. The post of missionary minister was of less status and income than that of a parish minister.

Stroma, a small island in the Pentland Firth off the north coast of Caithness, fell within the parish of Canisbay, and besides the mission church had a public school of its own. The households raised crops on its arable land and also fished. Some fifty small boats were based on Stroma, and the population also provided crews for eleven larger herring boats. Before 1894, however, there was no harbour or pier on the island: the boats used a beach and a creek or geo, and on each return to shore had to be dragged above the high-water mark. Coal, fuel and goods from across the

Pentland Firth came the same way, as did (on occasion) the doctor. So in 1892 the population persuaded the County Council of Caithness to build a pier, subscribing £200 of their own against a total cost of £800. In 1901 the campaign began again. The inhabitants of Stroma petitioned a government agency, the Congested Districts Board, for a grant, claiming that the 1894 pier was 'utterly inadequate to the requirements of the district'. A total of ninety-eight inhabitants subscribed the petition, and at the very head of the list was the name 'Alexander Youngson – minister, Stroma'.[33] Clearly by 1901 the people of Stroma were content that their missionary minister's name should be prominently associated with this business, essential to the prosperity and well-being of their island. We may think that his failure at Newmill had been left in the past.

Once it had been agreed that Alex Youngson was to leave Stroma for Strathy, the congregation of the island made a leaving presentation to him and his family during an evening event held in the island's church. To their departing minister was presented a purse of sovereigns and a gold-mounted fountain pen, while Mrs Youngson received a 'handsome gold bracelet' and Miss Katie, 'a very beautiful travelling clock', all suitably inscribed. It was clear from what was then said that Alex Youngson came to Strathy well recommended by his former congregation on Stroma:

> As Mr Youngson is about to depart from our midst it is incumbent upon us to present to him before he leaves some small token of the respect and esteem in which he is held by all. He has laboured faithfully and successfully among us for over nine years, and during that time he has endeared himself to every one by his uniform kindness, sympathy and promptitude in coming to the help of all in their time of trial . . . all of us must recognise the debt of gratitude we owe to him.[34]

It may be that the pen with which Alex Youngson wrote the visiting lists in his diaries was that presented to him in 1909 by the people of Stroma.

On 21 July 1909, the Presbytery of Tongue formally inducted Rev. Alexander Youngson to the parish of Strathy. With no representation from the west coast parishes of Eddrachillis and Kinlochbervie, three ministers comprised this meeting of the Presbytery. The minister of Durness preached from Mark

3:35; the minister of Farr was Moderator and chaired the meeting, and the minister of Tongue (Rev. David Lundie), was Clerk:

> Mr Lundie did then in the name of the Lord Jesus Christ, the Great Head of the Church, and by authority of the Presbytery, solemnly admit Mr Alexander Youngson to be Minister of the Church and Parish of Strathy and to all the rights, privileges and emoluments pertaining to that office, and the Brethren present gave him the right hand of fellowship and he and the congregation received suitable exhortations from Mr Lundie.[35]

At an earlier meeting the Presbytery had approved a call from the congregation to Mr Youngson. Unfortunately no indication is given in the minutes of the size of the call, though we are told elsewhere that it was unanimous.[36] At the time Strathy (like other Church of Scotland congregations of the north coast) lacked sufficient elders of its own to form a Kirk Session. An elder appointed by the Presbytery from elsewhere acted as Session Clerk; the local point of contact for those wishing to vote in the call was the headmaster of Strathy School, Mr John M. Gunn.

In 1909, the year of his induction to Strathy, Alex Youngson was aged sixty-eight. His appointment to the charge was for life – Parish Ministers were entitled to remain in their charges until death (or unless their Presbytery removed them for some serious fault). He came to the manse with his wife; Mrs Youngson and a further four members of his family were entered in the communion roll of the congregation.[37] The fifth, his second daughter, Emilie, in 1898 and when aged twenty-five, had married John Begg, a 'gentlemen of independent means'.[38] Joining the congregation with their parents were their eldest, Helen (Nellie), Alice and Katie, the youngest, with the only son, Alexander William. Alex Jnr, however, then aged thirty-three, had maintained the family's maritime interests and was normally away at sea: he had obtained his certificate as a ship's Engineer (2nd class) in 1904, upgraded to 1st class in 1906. As the people of Stroma's presentation was, among the family, to Katie alone, neither Nellie nor Alice can have been normally resident on Stroma. Katie, however, married Thomas M. Martin and was removed from the communion roll in 1914; Nellie's connection with her parents' household continued to be limited to occasional visits. It therefore fell to Alice to become permanently resident at the manse at

Strathy as she took Katie's place assisting her parents. The manse was to remain Miss Alice Youngson's home for the rest of her life, as it was to be for both her parents. Stone-built and slated, it had four rooms downstairs, with a scullery and pantry, and four rooms upstairs with a bathroom supplied with cold water. A steading, stables and shed completed the complex of buildings.[39]

The family was not, of course, well off. Mr Youngson's life's savings, his two life insurance policies, had been cashed for the benefit of his creditors. On appointment to Stroma at the age of fifty-eight he had had to begin again. The stipends for missionary ministers and ministers of *quoad sacra* parishes, however, were among the lowest in the church. *The Church of Scotland Year Book* for 1912 shows the stipend for the Stroma Mission as £93 with a manse and that of Strathy as £120 a year with a manse. By contrast, the minister of the parish of Farr had a stipend of £223 in 1912; in the Presbytery of Caithness, the minister of Wick had a stipend of £358 with a manse. Moreover in 1909 the Church of Scotland had no pension scheme for its ministers. This was to come following the General Assembly of 1911, when a pension of £100 p.a. at age seventy was suggested as the suitable benefit for a compulsory contribution scheme. As a minister admitted to a charge before the creation of the fund and over the age of fifty, Alex Youngson was ineligible to join this pension scheme when it was created. The year 1911 was also the date of the beginning of statutory National Insurance. The detailed diary entries of pennies spent and received gain added significance: it is likely he was unable to afford to retire.

Alex Youngson came to Strathy in straitened circumstances. The former parish schoolmaster and registrar from Skene with connections with the business of the sea still retained an interest in parish administration, education and seafarers. At Stroma he had gained the confidence of a small and close community. Despite the humiliation of financial failure, he had found strength to begin again and now at an age when some contemplated retirement he was once again a parish minister. Mrs Youngson (at sixty-eight, the same age as himself) and his daughter Alice (then aged thirty-four), with a resident maid as a domestic servant, made up his household.

3

The People of the Parish

A Snapshot – the 1901 Census

Who were the people of the parish of Strathy? How many of them were there? What did they do? For this information we turn first to the latest UK Census from which personal information is available: that of 1901.[1] For this census, the enumerators listed each household in the district, showing for each person their relationship with the head of the household, their occupation and place of work, married status, age, district of birth and language: whether Gaelic, or Gaelic and English. These details can be compared with the lists of households given in Mr Youngson's diaries of 1911, 1912 and 1915 to gain a picture of the people of the parish to which he came as minister in 1909. The following table shows the total number of people and households, settlement by settlement (but excluding empty houses), according to the five census enumeration districts for the east ward of Farr, 1901. In the Church of Scotland parish of Strathy (excluding Portskerra, Melvich and Strath Halladale) lived some 680 men, women and children.

	Settlement		Hlds	Popl	Cf
1	Aultiphurst		5	18	
	Ardvinglas		3	18	
	Fleuchary		1	5	
	Lednagullen		13	49	
	Mains of Armadale		2	7	
	Armadale		34	130	
	Drumbasbie		1	1	
		Total	**59**	**228**	**228**

2	Brawl		9	31		
	Aultivullen		4	18		
	Strathy Point		46	173		
		Total	59	222		
3	Strathy East		29	97		
	Baligill		13	50		
		Total	42	147		
4	Strathy West		22	70		
	Bowside		1	4		
	Dalangwell		1	6		
	Loch Strathy		1	2		
		Total	25	82	451	679
5	Portskerra		86	337		
	Melvich		50	160		
	Kirkton		3	24		
	Bighouse		5	13		
	Golval		1	9		
		Total	145	543	543	
6	Halladale	Total	77	310	310	
						1532

A census is of course a snapshot. It lists those resident in a particular place on a particular day: a total of 1,532 men, women and children in the east ward of Farr as a whole. Thus as Strathy's Bowside Lodge was unoccupied by either the Gilmours or their staff when the census was taken, the census shows at Bowside only the gamekeeper, George Macleod and his family. Similarly the single home at Loch Strathy is shown as occupied by Mary Ann Mackay, 'shepherd's wife', but without her husband. In this and similar cases, the presumption is that the shepherd himself was away from home on the hill, going about his work. On the other hand some temporary visitors were included in the numbers present on the day of the census: William Westmorland, for example, an engineer fitter from Leeds, was staying at the home of Hugh Gunn, Baligill. Perhaps surprisingly, though five visitors were recorded at the Melvich Hotel, none was listed at either of the other two hotels in the area: the Strathy Inn and the Forsinard Hotel.

Overwhelmingly, the population was Gaelic-speaking. Precise figures cannot be given, because the individual enumerators appear to have made slightly different assumptions as they completed the column recording whether each individual counted spoke Gaelic, or English and Gaelic; the return for Strath Halladale in particular contains an irritating number of blanks. Nevertheless, out of the overall total of some 1,111 adults, around 58 may have been primarily English-speakers – just over 5 per cent. Again, excluding 421 infants and schoolchildren, the number of Gaelic-only speakers was just nine (all female), leaving some 94 per cent of the adult population bilingual in Gaelic and English. If Gaelic was most often the language of the home, public education in the Highlands had been conducted in English for a century, and hence the bulk of the community could communicate in English. Public life, social and official meetings (but not worship) were in general conducted in English. Those with English as their primary language, however, had come from elsewhere: Donald Murray, for example, the hotel keeper at Forsinard, was born in Mid Yell, Shetland – though his wife came from Ross-shire and was bilingual. John Traill, shopkeeper and general merchant in Strathy West, was born in Cupar, Fife; James Storrier, crofter and clock-cleaner in Baligill, came from Glenisla in Angus – both John Traill and James Storrier, however, had bilingual wives from Sutherland.

One of the very few residents in Strathy who was not able to communicate in Gaelic was Rev. Alex Youngson. Certainly Gaelic was much more widespread in mainland Scotland at the beginning of the twentieth century than it is at the start of the twenty-first, but his native coastal Aberdeenshire was not part of the *Gaidhealtachd* in modern times.[2] Neither was Stroma, though the involvement of many Gaelic-speakers in the herring fleets would have brought the language to his notice while he was missionary minister there. At its meeting on March 1908, the Church of Scotland Presbytery of Tongue resolved that 'a knowledge of Gaelic is necessary on the part of the ministers of all the charges within these bounds' but faced with the shortage of applicants qualified to preach in Gaelic, the Presbytery soon modified its view and allowed that, while a knowledge of Gaelic was desirable throughout its area, it was necessary only in the case of the parish of Farr.[3] That Mr Youngson's Gaelic was rudimentary is shown by scribbled notes in his diary for 1915, where what appear to be three phonetic Gaelic phrases are accompanied by an English translation. So 'Ich Val' was set against 'Good night'. Correctly, this would be written in Gaelic as *oidhche mhath*. The implications for this gulf of language between minister and people we will explore later.

Of the 1,532 people counted in the east ward of Farr for the 1901 Census, 1,134 had been born in the Sutherland civil parish of Farr: almost 75 per cent. Of the remainder, a further 92 had been born in other parishes within Sutherland, and 87 had come from the neighbouring county of Caithness. Perhaps 15 per cent of the population had come from further afield: from other northern counties of Scotland – Ross, Inverness, Orkney, Shetland; some from Edinburgh, Glasgow and central Scotland; a very, very few from England, including Robert Robertson, the Land Steward for the Sutherland estates for Bighouse. There was also a handful of young people born in the United States and Canada, presumably the children of emigrants, sent back to stay with relatives for their education. The vast majority of the population of Strathy had strong roots in the area: that was where they and their families and neighbours had been born, educated, grown up and where, for the most part, they looked to live their lives; that was where they belonged because, there, they had access to land.

A population with strong roots in an area retains strong, shared memories. Of the Strathy residents listed by Alex Youngson in 1911, some twenty-three had been born in the civil parish of Farr between 1820 and 1835. Aged between seventy-seven and ninety-one, they were the last of the generation born in the later years of the period of clearance and settlement. On 24 October, the 1911 diary recorded the funeral of 'Angus Mackay's mother'. Betsy Mackay, then aged ninety-one, was already a widow at the time of the 1901 Census. Born in Farr in the year 1820, and formerly married to John, a crofter, the last decades of Betsy's life were spent with her son and his family in Strathy Point. Strathy was newly settled and 'improved' in her childhood; she was a mature woman of twenty-three at the time of the Free Church Disruption and, at sixty-six, elderly when the Crofters Holdings Act was passed. Even as late as the 1980s, there were old folk still living on the north coast who could remember their grandparents telling the story of the Clearances from their own personal experience. In Mr Youngson's day, such stories came from the immediate past and from a living generation.

The economies of the households of the east ward of Farr were almost entirely based on crofting: small-scale farming of rented land and shared common grazing, with labour undertaken personally, perhaps (but not invariably) with the household's income supplemented by some other work, income or employment. To have land meant the opportunity to seek self-sufficiency in food: growing potatoes, oats and vegetables, keeping hens, perhaps a cow or more and a hay crop depending on the size and quality of the arable land of the croft. Sharing in the common grazing meant being able to keep sheep and hence earn cash twice a year by selling wool and lambs. Fuel came from the annual round of cutting, drying and stacking peat. Of the forty-two households identified in Strathy East and Baligill in 1901, for example, thirty had a head of household described as a crofter and another six were cottars – smallholders without the heritable security of tenure belonging to a croft after the Crofters Holdings (Scotland) Act of 1886. The remaining six houses were the temporary manse of the United Free Church and the homes of a ghillie, an army pensioner, a road contractor, a mason and a farmer/general merchant. Of the forty-six families of Strathy Point, thirty had crofters or farmers at their head, while in only six was the householder a fisherman. Donald Mackenzie, innkeeper at Strathy Inn, was described as crofter and innkeeper. Larger households showed diversity of employment. For example, Hugh Macintosh of Strathy Point was a fisherman, as was one of his sons. His other son, however, was a mason, and his brother-in-law, a labourer (road man). In Armadale, occupations apart from crofting included shoemaking, shepherding and that of telegraphist at the Post Office. Seven men in Armadale were also registered by the census as employed in the herring fisheries – typically, they were the sons of active crofters and hence not required to work the land, but free to bring home an income.

Portskerra, however, was undoubtedly the fishing centre for this section of the north coast. Fifty-nine men there were registered in 1901 as either fisherman, retired fishermen or fishermen and crofters, and forty-nine households out of eighty-six had connections with the sea. Of these men, some will have worked away from home, sailing with the itinerant fleets that followed the shoals of herring round the coast of Britain. Others will have crewed small inshore boats sailing from the mouth of the

Halladale, fishing with baited lines for cod, haddock or flounders, or doing the rounds of lobster pots. Catches brought into
Portskerra itself, though (as with those landed at Strathy Point or
Armadale) will have had only the limited market of the north
coast communities themselves, as these settlements lacked any
fast or bulk means of transport for cargo to the cities of the south.
Fish preserved in salt brine was part of the general diet along the
north coast.

In many respects, British society was male-dominated in the
years that Alex Youngson was minister at Strathy. Both his own
lists of households in the parish and the official Valuation Rolls
for the County of Sutherland[4] commonly refer to, for example,
'Widow Angus Mackay', where the householder was a female
whose husband had died. For UK Parliamentary elections,
women (over thirty) did not receive the vote until 1918. While
women could hold crofts in their own right and thus head a
household, most women in the area were listed in the census
either as the wife or daughter of a crofter, fisherman, etc., or as a
domestic servant – even when this meant no more than helping to
keep house for a relative. Such wives and daughters of crofters
shared with the men in working their land as well as performing
their own tasks of raising a family and keeping house. Water
came not from a tap but from a well, or was collected rain; most
homes lacked bathrooms and toilets. Life was a constant struggle
to retain dignity and achieve more than bare subsistence. Accident, injury and old age all threatened. In the census, widows
were occasionally described as 'annuitants', where a deceased
husband had had the foresight, discipline and income to sub-
scribe to a life insurance policy or perhaps when the Parish
Council offered poor-law support. Crofts, of course, not being
owned by those who worked them, could not be sold and hence
crofters (and cottars even more so) had no land or business
beyond their stock to sell up to fund retirement – but then, stock
could not both be sold and handed on to an inheriting son. Old
age could therefore be a time of poverty for those no longer fit to
work land and without family to provide for them. Unmarried
women were particularly vulnerable. Largely denied access to
whatever income might come from employment, single women
even less than single men had few opportunities to save for the
future and they had no children or descendants to take them in.
Men without land could at least work as fishermen or on the

roads, or as farm labourers, ghillies, etc. Five houses in Strathy Point were homes in 1901 to single, elderly women for whom no occupation was recorded. Such might well have been classed as paupers, dependent on the poor-law functions of the Parish Council.

Families and Employment

Of all the men, women and children living in and around the district of Strathy, whom do we meet in its minister's diaries? A brief answer is, the whole of society: crofters, craftsmen, fishermen; the storekeeper; spinsters, wives, mothers and children; the poor and the rich; members of the family of the Duke of Sutherland; the MP and the proprietor; the doctor, the schoolmaster and his family. People came and went to and from the manse for a variety of social, domestic and business reasons – though in a small community such distinctions of purpose were not easily maintained. In the diary of a minister one might expect to find pastoral concerns, and perhaps matters of concern to the community: we will look at some examples of all of these. Other occasions for meeting local families, however, arose from the fact that with the manse of the parish church came both an extensive garden and a glebe – fifteen acres of land set aside for the minister of the day to farm, and to provide an important supplement to his cash stipend. Strathy manse's garden and glebe, in fact, comprised more land than an increasingly elderly minister could cultivate himself. Besides pastoral occasions, therefore, Alex Youngson's diaries also list the men and women who were engaged to assist with the potatoes, with the hay crop, with the corn.

Often, Mr Youngson's concern in keeping a diary was as a farmer to record who did what, so that they could be paid appropriately. In the extract below, three men had been engaged to cut grass in order to make hay, important for winter feed for cattle. The investment in September was worth making as over the winter the minister was able to supplement his income by selling hay to neighbours. From the point of view of the workers concerned, the cash paid by the manse for their time would have been a useful bonus in a self-sufficient economy where cash was in short supply.

September, 1919

Friday	12	*Cutting grass – J Campbell, Findlay, Malcolm McLeod*
		Set up coles
Saturday	13	*Grass cutting finished set up coles*
[weekend notes]		*Paid J Campbell £1; Findlay 14/-;*
		Malcolm 8/-:
		tot. £2/2/-

John Campbell, Findlay Mackay and Malcolm Macleod were adult neighbours of the Youngsons; John and Findlay were also active members of his congregation and he baptised several of their children.

Another member of the congregation who assisted Mr Youngson with his farming enterprises was John Gunn of Strathy West.

September, 1912

Sunday	22	*Fine Summer day*
Monday	23	*Preparing for taking in hay*
		Sent word to John Gunn
Tuesday	24	*Parish Council Meeting 11am*
Wednesday	25	*Taking in hay – two stacks*
		John Gunn & Hugh McLeod

At the time of the 1901 Census, John Gunn was a weaver, aged thirty-seven; married to Betsy, and with a family of three sons at school: Murdoch (thirteen), Donald (ten) and Robert (eight). All five were born in the parish of Farr but only John and Betsy were recorded as speaking 'G&E', Gaelic and English, in the census: their sons are entered as English-speakers. This perhaps indicates an ambition of the Gunns that their sons might be able to make their way anywhere in the English-speaking world. Most (though not all) of the boys' contemporaries in Strathy West were shown as bilingual. Betsy died, however, in 1908 and John remarried two years later. His new wife was Jacobina Wallace, a cook; the wedding took place at Bowside, conducted by Alex Youngson.[5] In 1914 John Gunn was ordained an elder of the congregation: Mr Youngson sought his assistance on a number of occasions, both on church business and for help with the glebe.

Apart from the physically small diary of 1919, Mr Youngson's diaries contain the lists he kept of all residents of townships within walking distance of his manse. As might be expected, there was substantial continuity between the Census of 1901 and these lists – though his lists, being of names only, obviously contain less information. In Strathy Point, for example, continuity of occupancy can be seen in some thirty-five homes out of forty-one then inhabited; the figures for Strathy East are twenty-one (out of twenty-three homes in 1911) and for Strathy West, eighteen (out of twenty-three). In some cases, a husband had died in the decade since the census. James and Angusina Maciver had farmed a croft in 1901: Alex Youngson's 1911 list shows 'Widow James Maciver' in the same house. Where in 1901 George Mackay (aged eighty, retired fisherman) had shared a home with his wife, Alexina (aged eighty-two), their unmarried daughter Christina, two granddaughters and a grand-nephew, all three diary lists show simply 'Christina Ann Mackay'. Clearly, the census gives the full names of all in the house while Mr Youngson mainly listed the householder. Hence a home occupied in 1901 by John Mackay, crofter, with his wife Hughina and his daughter Jessie, Mr Youngson listed as 'John Mackay & wife & dau[ghter] (Piper)'.

Distinguishing between multiple families with the surname Mackay presents its own difficulties. In Mr Youngson's visiting list for 1911, covering Strathy East and West, Strathy Point, Brawl, Baligill, Bowside and Aultiphurst, a full half of the 121 households had 'Mackay' as their surname. The use of bynames was therefore common for further identification. These could be geographic: Sandy Mackay, living in Aultivullen or Millburn, a small settlement on the west of Strathy Point, may have been known locally as Sandy Millburn. In Strathy West, where Mr Youngson listed 'Hugh Gunn & Mrs, Alex & Hector, Riverside', Mr Gunn was probably known as Hugh Riverside for most purposes. Similarly, on Sunday 24 September 1911, a diary entry reads: 'Sent for to see Mrs Mackay Riverside'. Bynames could also be formed in other ways. John Mackay Piper we have already met: his son Donald was known as Donald Piper from the family's traditional facility with the bagpipes.

In a few cases, bynames appear to have become somewhat more formal and to have been used to distinguish a related group of Mackay families. The names Gow and Cooper in particular were used almost as additional surnames, even in official documents. So when Angus, son of Donald Mackay Cooper, married Barbara Morrison in 1894, the Register of Marriages recorded his name as 'Angus Mackay (Cooper)'.[6] Mr Youngson made use of these bynames in his daily diary entries. In 1915 for Monday 28 June he wrote: 'Visited Point (Gow)'. The next day, 'Mrs W. Gow died, 2pm'. More formally, this referred to Alexanderina, Mrs William Mackay, whose funeral took place on 1 July 1915. For 13 November 1911 we read 'Covered turnips by J. Cooper' and there are numerous similar entries. Further to complicate matters, Mr Youngson also appears to have invented his own bynames for some of the families with whom he had most dealings. 'Doan's boy' (2 August 1918) was his shorthand for the son of Donald and Annabella Mackay. A number of men appear in the diaries under the Old Testament names of Samson, Job and Noah. 'Paid John Mackay (Job) 5/- for cows' reads the diary for 9 November 1911 and 'Lifting potatoes, Mrs Samson' on 2 November 1912. 'Mrs Samson' was in fact the Barbara Morrison who had married Angus Mackay (Cooper). Her husband thus appears in the diaries in any one of a number of options: Angus Mackay, Angus Cooper and Angus Samson, the second being his 'official' local byname, and the last probably Alex Youngson's private pet name for him – we do not know that it was ever actually used outside the manse.

People appear in Alex Youngson's diaries for a variety of reasons. One major cause was that they had been visited for some particular pastoral reason: an illness, a death – or perhaps a baptism or forthcoming wedding. 'Visited Melvich, D. Henderson' – 23 January 1912. 'D. Henderson died', 1 February; and then 'Funeral D. Henderson, 12noon' – 3 February. There are many sequences like this, where visits to named people – children, the elderly – end with a death. Sometimes the parallel entry in the statutory Register of Deaths shows 'cause unknown: no medical attendant'. This was the very beginning of National Insurance and the Old Age Pension, and before the National Health Service – doctors and medicine cost cash; but the parish minister was available to all to offer care and prayer, consolation and hope. In February 1911, for example, Mr Youngson called frequently at the home of Angus and Barbara Mackay (Cooper): their fifteen-year-old son, Angus, had meningitis and died from it, after ten days of illness.[7]

February, 1911

Friday	3	*Visited Angus Mackay Strathy Point*
Saturday	4	*Visited Angus Mackay*
Sunday	5	*Fine day*
		Visit of Doctor 4pm
Monday	6	*Visited Angus Cooper*
Tuesday	7	*Visited Angus Mackay Cooper*
Wednesday	8	*Visited Angus Mackay*
		Alice took cakes to them
Thursday	9	*Do/*
Friday	10	*Went with Mum to P[or]t Grant*
		Visited Angus Mackay
		Concert at Armadale
Saturday	11	*Samson's Angus died 6.30pm*
Sunday	12	*Fine day*
Monday	13	*Visited Samson's*
Tuesday	14	*Angus Mackay funeral*

Following this contact with the minister came the baptism of Angus and Barbara's third child, Hector Angus Morrison Mackay, on 16 April 1911. Hector Angus had been born earlier that year, on 3 January, and was baptised together with James Robert Malley Mackay, son of John and Christina Mackay (Roy), the Coopers' near neighbours in Strathy Point.[8]

Mr Youngson's connections with the Mackay Coopers and the Mackay Roys continued. In June 1912 Angus and Barbara's daughter Catherine also died as an infant of only a few days: 'Samson's baby died 11am.' There had been no medical attendant. A further and later child of theirs was baptised, however, in November 1920: James Gibson Mackay, born 18 July 1920. Mrs Barbara Mackay Cooper was to become a communicant member of Strathy Church in 1925. John Roy and Christina Mackay had already had their son, Alexander George Gordon Mackay, baptised in 1908; Finlay Cook Gunn Mackay was also baptised by Mr Youngson in December 1916.

A number of brief entries in the diaries relate to girls who were employed by the Youngsons as domestic servants, boarding in the manse, and something of their histories can be followed. The diary entry for Wednesday 10 March 1915 – besides recording a visit to Brawl – reads 'Jessie Shearer left'. Jessie was the daughter of Daniel and Louisina or Lucy Shearer, Portskerra crofters with three acres of land and an 'old worn thatched cottage and byre'.[9] Mr Shearer, according to the census, was from Caithness and an English-speaker rather than bilingual like his wife and daughter (their only child). Aged sixty-four in 1901, he was already a member of Strathy Church when Mr Youngson compiled his first communicant roll in 1910; and he was ordained an elder of the congregation in 1914. Those selected to assist domestically at the manse appear to come from families with close ties to the Youngsons. Jessie was perhaps pleased to win second prize for her crowdie at the local Mod at Tongue in 1911.[10] In 1915, aged twenty-nine, she left to marry a somewhat older man, David B. Henderson, a joiner then aged fifty-eight. Their marriage certificate gave her address as The Manse, Strathy. Sorrow followed, however. Her uncle, William Sutherland (a retired fisherman of Portskerra) died the next month on 20 April: 'Funeral Portskerra, Sutherland uncle of Jessie Shearer'. Next, her father died in November 1918 and her mother's death followed, in August 1919. Her husband died in an Inverness hospital in 1922, and Jessie herself was found drowned in Portskerra harbour in February 1924. It must have been with much sadness that Alex Youngson baptised Jessie's orphaned son, on 25 May 1924.[11]

A tragic history also belongs to another of the manse's domestic helps, Lizzie Gunn. Baptised Elizabeth Ann Mackay Gunn, she was the daughter of John M. Gunn, Strathy School's headmaster, and so the schoolhouse was her home. Schoolmasters held a key position in local society. John M. Gunn, like Daniel Shearer, was a communicant member of the Church of Scotland at Strathy in 1910: he had had local responsibility (under the Presbytery) for the arrangements for electing a minister that had brought Mr Youngson to the parish. Indeed in 1912 he was listed among those described as 'northern notables' who followed the Duke of Portland in subscribing 'An Appeal to the People of Scotland on behalf of Church Union'.[12] The diaries show that John M. Gunn was an occasional social visitor to the manse – so, too, were his children: 16 March 1911, 'Mr Gunn's children at manse'; 8 January 1915, 'Visit of Mr Gunn, Schoolhouse'. Another competitor in the 1911 local Mod, Lizzie had come third in the Gaelic Learners' Competition, third in a solo singing competition (Gaelic Medley with English words) and first for her piano playing of Gaelic Song airs. Clearly she was an accomplished young lady, aged thirteen, a credit to her parents.[13] Lizzie must have briefly replaced Jessie as the manse domestic help, for on 16 September 1915, 'Lizzie Gunn left'. The cash-book also shows that she received 5s. that day from Mr Youngson.

Unfortunately Lizzie's father had run into serious trouble with the local School Board. In 1914, two families complained that his discipline was unduly fierce and physical; and then in 1915 a complaint of his own against his assistant was not upheld. Finally, in August 1916, the Schools' Inspector discovered major failings in his keeping of the School Register and in September the Board gave him three months' notice. As the next head teacher, Miss Munro, already lived in the area, the Gunns were allowed to stay on in the Schoolhouse but not to use the school garden, which was needed for agricultural classes. Both Lizzie and her younger sister, Mary, followed their father's path to become teachers, one of the few options then open to bright girls, and it may be that she left the manse to begin her own vocation. Lizzie also joined the Church of Scotland, taking communion at Strathy in July 1917, at the (for that place and time) most unusually young age of nineteen. She must have had both courage and personal conviction. While teaching in the parish of Latheron and unmarried, however, she succumbed to influenza and died on 26 November 1918, and Alex Youngson removed her from the communion roll. Her death was registered by her father who gave his address as the Inverasdale Poorhouse, Ross-shire, presumably his new place of employment. John M. Gunn and his wife were to remain on the Strathy communion roll until 1919.[14]

Besides the teachers and the ministers, the other professional in the parish was the doctor; and the doctors, too, feature in Mr Youngson's diaries. The local doctor was employed by the Parish Council as its Medical Officer and Vaccinator and with that appointment came a tied house at Armadale: of stone and lime, slated, and enjoying eight rooms and hot and cold water in its bathroom, it offered some of the best accommodation in the parish.[15] The doctor's official duties included, besides an annual vaccination programme, providing the Council with medical reports on those seeking poor relief. Given accommodation and a salary from the Council, the doctor could then practise on his own account in his remaining time. The Highlands, however, as an area where cash was in short supply, had difficulty retaining doctors. In January 1913, a Committee of Enquiry set up by the Chancellor of the Exchequer recommended a new authority to bring together the various interested parties, which included the National Health Insurance Commission, the Scotch Education Department and the General Board of Lunacy. More funds from the Treasury would be needed to offer all Highland doctors a minimum of £300 per year with a travelling allowance, provided a fixed tariff of low fees was agreed.[16] A Highlands and Islands Medical Act followed, and a new Board was created later in 1913. Disputes over travelling expenses had cost Strathy at least one doctor. The Parish Council, meeting in Armadale on Saturday 24 October 1903, declined to pay the doctor's £2 16s. invoice for expenses for his visits and reports in connection with poor relief. The councillors believed that such travel was part of the contracted duties under the Poor Law Acts for which he was paid; instead, it was moved and agreed to give him three months' notice and to advertise for a replacement.[17]

The coming of war disrupted the plans announced in 1913, but by 1915 the new Medical Service Board for the Highlands and Islands had a budget of £32,000 to give in grants to medical practitioners. It was reported that:

> The Board's aim is to bring an efficient medical service within reach of the crofter and cottar class. The doctor receiving the grant must be prepared to give systematic attention in all cases and act as officer of health for schools. Grants will be made where the income derived from patients is entirely inadequate as a fair recompense for work involved. The Board's grant therefore will aim at raising the income to a fixed sum . . . assistance may also be given in housing. The Board will require to be satisfied as to the entire efficiency of the service.[18]

It is clear from these aspirations that 'an efficient medical service' was *not* at that stage wholly 'within reach of the crofter and cottar class' – which meant, of course, the vast bulk of the population. Even low fees were too high for some. Incurable disease, unexpected and early death were part of normal Highland life.

Three doctors make their appearance in Mr Youngson's diaries. When the diary for Thursday 2 February 1911 reads: 'Doctor sent for and visited in eve[ning]', this refers to Dr John Grant Macgregor MB ChB. Presumably someone in the manse was ill and needed a home visit – the doctor returned to check on the patient the next Sunday afternoon. Happier occasions would have been those of Wednesday 3 May 1911 and Saturday 15 July 1911: 'Visit of Dr and Mrs Macgregor'. Next we read 'Baptism of Dr Macgregor's child', Wednesday 9 August 1911. The Register of Baptisms for the congregation shows that John Clark Macgregor had been born on 27 June 1911, so presumably the visit of the doctor and his wife Dorothy to the manse in July was also an occasion to plan for and talk about the baptism.[19] Within weeks, the doctor was back at the manse and on serious business: Alex Youngson's wife died on 26 August 1911.

The last death recorded by the Strathy Registrar that was certified by Dr John Macgregor took place on 12 October 1911. By 18 October, James Silver MB ChB was the doctor in Armadale.[20] Though as we shall see he had had a hand in the new doctor's appointment, Mr Youngson made no reference to this change in his diary: indeed, the first mention we find of the new doctor is not until Saturday 17 August 1912, 'Visit of Dr and Mrs Silver'. Mrs Silver and a Miss Day were back at the manse on a social call in December that year. We lack the diaries for 1913 and 1914, but the doctor's wife was still calling socially at the manse in February 1915. Doctor and wife came round together on Friday 2 April, and James Silver took Alice Youngson to Bettyhill in May. 'Visit of Mrs Silver and Miss Day' was repeated on 19 August, while Dr and Mrs Silver called on Saturday 2 October and on Friday 24 December 1915. Perhaps the doctor was initially cautious about developing social connections when he first arrived in the area, but a friendship of some warmth appears to have been built. The doctor's wife and the minister's daughter may well have particularly valued each other's company, knowing that each would respect the confidences of the professions of their respective homes. Dr Silver also assisted with the scout troop that Alice led. New Year, 1919, was celebrated at Dr Silver's: Thursday 2 January, 'Dinner at Dr Silver's 11.30'.

This was, however, to be the Silvers' last New Year at Armadale. The *Northern Times* of 6 March 1919 reported that a meeting of the Parish Council of Farr had received his resignation with great regret. Dr Silver was asked if he might reconsider if he was granted a considerable holiday, but he affirmed his intention to leave on 15 May.[21] Covering the entire population of Farr meant being the sole doctor not just for Strathy and its immediate area, but also for the western section of Farr (Bettyhill itself and the entire length of Strathnaver) as well as Portskerra, Melvich and Strath Halladale as far as Forsinard. James Silver was obviously conscientious (otherwise he would not have attracted such support from the Council) but the strain of lengthy travel and being constantly available and on duty had become too much. On 13 May, Alex Youngson recorded 'Dr Silver's sale': it was easier to hold a displenishment sale on leaving a home than to arrange for large amounts of household goods to be transported. The diary entry for Wednesday 14 May read: 'Dr and Mrs Beard arrived; Dr Silver left'.

Alex Youngson's relationship with Dr E. A. Cameron Beard MB ChB began much more quickly than that with James Silver. By this stage, however, Mr Youngson was occasionally chairing the Parish Council, the doctor's employer. The two men needed to work well together from the beginning. Scribbled notes in the back of the diary for 1919 list Dr Beard's name along with a further three doctors and give an address for him in Dunbartonshire; and on the next page 'Beard Robroyston Hospital'. These notes may well have been made in connection with the selection process. Then in advance of his appointment to Armadale, the diary shows that Dr Beard arrived at the manse on Saturday 3 May and departed again the next Tuesday after a final meeting with the Council to establish mutual satisfaction before the contract began. 'Visit of Dr and Mrs Beard' occurs quickly after their arrival, on Sunday 25 May, and again on Friday 29 August. Alice visited the Beards in Armadale on 6 October, and Mr Youngson called himself while visiting in Armadale on 6 November. Clearly a working relationship had been established, but perhaps without quite the warmth of friendship that had been enjoyed with the Silvers.

One final component of Strathy society to feature in Mr Youngson's diaries may be mentioned at this stage: the local shopkeepers, John Traill of Strathy West and Hugh J. Gunn of Baligill. The motor car and the motor van were just beginning to have an impact on Highland communities at this time. Most people went about on foot, by bicycle, or by pony and trap or horse and cart. Mr Youngson was delighted to acquire a dogcart in 1912. Bringing goods in quantity from afar was not an easy matter, though that was the business of both the railways and coastal shipping. Christopher J. Uncles tells the story of Robert Garden, who – though originally from Aberdeenshire – built up a northern trading empire from the port of Kirkwall in Orkney. An entrepreneur of vision, he financed and supplied by sea a string of franchised general stores across Sutherland, including those at Melvich, Bettyhill and Tongue. Groceries, clothing, crofting tools, building materials – Garden's steamer the *Cormorant* could carry them all.[22] Shopping, however, was not for most people an everyday activity. Once again, the self-sufficient nature of crofting and its lack of capital resources limited all sorts of economic activity. People did not have the money to buy goods, either in quantity or regularly. Besides, the townships still had their remaining craftsmen: John Gunn, for example, the weaver in Strathy West. The census showed two shoemakers in Armadale and a travelling draper visiting Baligill. Nevertheless there was to be sufficient business for John Traill's store in Strathy West and for Hugh J. Gunn's shop at Baligill during Mr Youngson's time. He appears to have had little trade with the latter, described in his residents' lists for 1911 and 1912 (but not 1915) as 'Gunn baker'.

Mr Traill, according to the census, was aged thirty-seven in 1901, a general merchant from Cupar in Fife, with English as his native language. His son Thomas (aged sixteen) worked with him as a shop assistant. When the Traills first appear in Mr Youngson's diary, their relationship is a trading one and the manse had an account with the local store: Tuesday 10 January 1911: 'Paid Traill'; Tuesday 6 February 1912: 'Paid Traill £1 6s 5d'; 6 July 1915: 'Bag of poultry food, Traill'. Other calls in 1915, however, were obviously pastoral. On 12 April 1915, the minister visited Mrs Traill. Her sister, Catherine Macleod, who lived with her, had died the day before. The entry for 14 April then reads: 'Funeral Mrs Macleod (Traill)'. There was a further visit to Mrs Traill on 20 April, and next we read 'Funeral Mrs Traill, 12noon' on Tuesday 4 May. Frances Traill had died on Saturday 1 May – the doctor attending her had come from Thurso.[23]

John Traill remarried in 1919. Mr Youngson's diary entry for Friday 21 February 1919 reads: 'Marriage John Traill' and his Register of Proclamations of Banns shows that Mr Traill's second wife was a neighbour in Strathy West, Margaret Mackay. On 27 December 1921 a daughter was born to them, and Catherine Frances Macleod Traill was baptised by Alex Youngson at Strathy West on 21 February 1922.[24] Once again, relations between the manse and its neighbours were made up of a mixture of interests – commercial and pastoral went together; and the baptism shows clearly that the Parish Church was John Traill's congregation of choice, though he was entered simply and untypically as 'Traill' in the minister's visiting lists.

4

Congregations and Community

Adherents and Members of the Church

From a minister's diaries we expect to find information about his congregation, and it is to the congregation of the Church of Scotland in Strathy that we turn next, and to those of the other churches active in the district. Determining the make-up of a Highland congregation of this period is not, however, straightforward – if, indeed, such analysis can ever be clear-cut. The religious connection or allegiance of particular families was well understood at the time by all who needed to know, and hence did not require to be written down. Affiliation to a denomination, moreover, was an enduring loyalty not to be discovered by simply counting those regularly at Sunday worship or entered on the communion roll. In the Highlands of Scotland, though people were well prepared to walk considerable journeys, sheer distance from the church building might prevent regular Sabbath attendance. Attendance was, of course, understood to be desirable, but non-attendance due to youth, age, illness, sheer distance or even apathy did not break the connection. Families with no intention of hearing a sermon would still have a denominational loyalty. Even in the very different social climate of 2004, a report to the General Assembly suggested that many parish ministers would be:

> . . . wary of the danger of making hard and fast distinctions between those who occupy the pews and those whom they encounter as they go about the parish. These latter may feel they have a significant relationship with the Church through the minister or through the varied activities which the Church promotes or supports, and may even feel an allegiance to a particular building or denomination.[1]

Loyalty is in the end a frame of mind.

Since 1835 the Church of Scotland has counted its membership with the help of its congregations' annually revised communion rolls. To take communion has meant to join the Church, and vice versa. Other denominations have taken a different approach, the Roman Catholic Church, for example, sometimes giving a higher priority to baptismal status. In the Highlands, measuring membership by counting those eligible for communion had its own particular difficulties, for the Highland tradition was not to come forward 'to the tables' for communion but simply to attend public worship. Taking communion was judged to be most appropriate for those who had advanced some way along the spiritual journey; and considerable numbers believed they were unworthy of the sacrament. Most of those most regularly at church were thus not counted by the offices in Edinburgh as having joined or become members, and were described as 'adherents'. Only when it came to establishing the current composition of the congregation for the purpose of voting for a new minister were communicants and adherents counted equally. Adherents, however, had to claim their entitlement during the vacancy as no annual count of their names was made, and neither Presbytery nor Kirk Session retained information gathered at a vacancy once the new minister had been called. As a result, the most relevant statistic for establishing families which looked to Mr Youngson's kirk has not come down to us.

From the surviving communion roll that Alex Youngson maintained during his years at Strathy, this minimal and formal measurement suggests that there were no more than nineteen communicant members of Strathy Church in 1910; and of these, Mr Youngson's own family accounted for six. By 1917, the total had increased to twenty-six, of which only three belonged to the manse – the minister himself and his unmarried daughters Alice and Nellie. The year he demitted, 1930, saw the communicant membership at twenty-two, of which three were at the manse. Of course the number of families represented by these numbers was even smaller. Apart from the manse, in 1910 there were only nine households: Mr and Mrs Robert Robertson, Mr and Mrs Daniel Gorrie, John Gunn of Strathy West, Mr and Mrs John M. Gunn (Strathy Schoolhouse), Mrs Barbara Mackay, Mrs Margaret Mackay, Daniel Shearer, James Storrier, Mr and Mrs David Sinclair. Moreover, the Gorries and Sinclairs lived in homes at Bighouse, while the Shearers lived in Portskerra and the Robertsons in Melvich – all technically outside the parish of Strathy.

Hearing the Gospel

Several of those who were communicant members of the Strathy congregation we have met already: it is significant that they include some shown by the census to speak, primarily, English. Thus while Robert Robertson, the Melvich Land Steward, though from England was recorded as confident in both Gaelic and English, his wife Isabella was an English-speaker as were both Daniel Shearer and James Storrier. At the Strathy School-house the Gunns may well have understood Gaelic, but we have already seen their daughter Lizzie competing in the Gaelic lear-ners section of the Mod and succeeding with her Gaelic songs, as sung in English. The children of the Gunns of Strathy West were recorded as English-speakers. Mr Youngson undoubtedly preached and conducted worship only in English, and his was therefore the obvious congregation for the tiny proportion of the population of Strathy that was not at home in the language of the area. Alex Youngson's people heard the gospel in English.

By contrast, Strathy's other local ministers were Gaelic speak-ers. At the United Free Church, Rev. Ewen Fraser (minister at Strathy and Halladale 1903–12) was actually one of the judges for Gaelic at the 1911 Mod at Tongue.[2] His successor Rev. Neil Mackay (1913–20) was of a local family and had been educated at Armadale School and so certainly was as comfortable in both languages as 94 per cent of the population. For the Free Church, Rev. Hector Macaulay (minister at Strathy 1909–40) also preached in Gaelic: he was chosen to do so for the Free Presbytery in 1911 at the induction of a colleague to the neighbouring charge of Farr.[3] His gravestone is inscribed in both languages. The rhythms of worship and preaching in the UF and Free congrega-tions thus reflected the linguistic tradition of the community in a way that the Established Kirk could not attempt. The UF congregation in Strathy, for example, held their main Sunday morning service in Gaelic, while the afternoon service was con-ducted in English.[4] Similarly, for the UF communion in Strath Halladale two sacramental services were held, one in Gaelic and one in English.[5]

Gaelic was still the language of home of the people of the north in the early twentieth century: Gaelic had been the language of those who deserted the landlords' church in the aftermath of the Clearances to form their own congregations and to support their own ministers. There was a strong association in the Highlands between the evangelical faith and the use of Gaelic.[6] Even if English was the language of education and for public occasions, in such a society with such a background a minister capable only of English laboured at a grave disadvantage, quite apart from his inability to understand his neighbours when they gathered together and spoke to each other!

Alex Youngson was minister of a small congregation: few attended the Sunday worship that he led. His own diaries confirm this. Entries for Sundays during the summer months of 1911, week after week, read 'Few in Church'; 'Small attendance'. For Sunday 12 January 1913, the entry reads '9 in Church'. It must have been more than disappointing, in an age when city churches could gather many hundreds for both morning and evening worship. In the front of his diary for 1911, Mr Youngson wrote

> How to adorn a church:
> Two things to be observed.
> Let the church officer keep it clean
> and the minister keep it full.

His Telford-designed church, with its fifteen to twenty-five communicants and 'Small attendance', cannot be said to have been full. Ministers of presbyterian denominations are ordained to a ministry of 'Word and Sacrament'. It was as well for Mr Youngson's balance of mind that he found other ways of expressing his ministry apart from the round of Sabbath worship with his few loyal hearers.

Singing Praise

During Sabbath worship, the traditional Scottish presbyterian congregation sang praise to God unaccompanied by an organ or other musical instruments. Setting the tune, giving the note, and dictating the tempo of singing was the responsibility of a male lead singer, the Precentor. In Highland kirks the significance of this position (which might be salaried) was shown architecturally: the Precentor had a desk of his own positioned immediately below the pulpit, like the minister, facing down the centre of the church so that his face could be seen and his voice heard by the congregation. Before roughly 1870, praise in Scottish worship was selected only from the metrical psalms supplemented by metrical paraphrases of passages of Scripture. By the 1880s both the Free Church and the Established Church had published hymnbooks of their own, and in 1898 the jointly agreed *Church Hymnary* had been published.[7] Nevertheless the people of the northern Highlands continued to sing the psalms and paraphrases in the old style and the words and tunes were taught to new generations in their public schools. This singing came, over a number of decades of slow northward infiltration, to be accompanied by a harmonium rather than led by a Precentor; but such changes did not come without controversy. The subject of 'hymns, organs and instrumental music' could cause 'hot discussions' in a Highland village in 1909, though the Parish and the UF churches were considered 'progressive'.[8]

Praise in Strathy's Church of Scotland was led in 1911 by a Precentor, John Mackay Cooper of Strathy West.[9] Daily diary entries mention: 'Visited Precentors' [3 January 1911], and the Precentor also assisted the minister with work on the glebe: 'Precentor and John cutting grass', 'Precentor and Post taking up grass' [1 and 4 September 1911]. The same relationship was still intact as the 1919 diary came to an end: 'Visited Precentor', 'Got venison from Precentor' [19 and 20 December 1919]. On occasion Mr Youngson also consulted the Precentor over pastoral or personal issues, such as the unexpected death in 1915 of a young soldier from Loch Strathy. 'At Precentor's about Jackson' [22 January 1915]. Before the lengthy and time-consuming journey inland to Loch Strathy, Alex Youngson wished to learn more about the newly bereaved family – and the Precentor was the man to ask.

John Cooper's family belonged to the Established Church. His wife Margaret, 'Mrs Precentor' or Mrs John Mackay, became a communicant in 1910. Their son, James A. Mackay (Cooper), was married by Mr Youngson to Christina Barbara (née Cameron) on 12 November 1915, at which stage the groom, who had been born locally, was a coast watchman and the bride a domestic servant, from Portskerra. Their married life began in his home community of Strathy West and during the 1920s moved to her family croft in Portskerra. James Angus Mackay

(Cooper) was also to become a communicant member of Strathy Church in the 1920s, as was his wife. Six of their children were baptised by Alex Youngson between 1916 and 1929. Yet other members of the Cooper sept of Strathy's Mackays were connected to Mr Youngson's kirk: Donald Cooper and his son Angus Mackay Cooper (Samson) of Strathy Point we have already met. When John Cooper led praise in the Established Church, many of the congregation in front of him may have been members of his own family.

Baptised into Christ

Besides the Mackay Coopers, further local families were adherents of the Parish Church. These can best be identified from the Baptismal Roll, as the choice of a minister to approach to request the baptism of a child clearly indicates denominational preference, and especially when repeated over a number of years. Alex Youngson baptised ninety children between 1909 and 1930. Of these, sixty-three belonged to twenty families. The four younger children of John Campbell, a fisherman of Strathy Point, and his wife Christina (née Mackay) were baptised by Mr Youngson between April 1910 and September 1917; the third – Alexander Youngson Campbell – being named after the minister. The earlier baptism of John George had been a major event: the only Sunday in the extant diaries when a *large* congregation was recorded. John Campbell, a Strathy Point householder, fisherman and crofter, was aged thirty-two in 1901; although married to a girl from Stornoway, he, his parents and both his children alive in 1901 were all born in the parish of Farr. The Campbells were a Gaelic-fluent local family, all of whom (we can speculate) attended morning worship with their friends at the kirk on Sunday 8 December 1912 before the 3 p.m. baptism at their own home. John Campbell, it should be remembered, was also one of those often employed by Mr Youngson on his glebe – the family connection with the parish minister once again had an economic as well as a religious side to it.

The Baptismal Roll identifies other local families, fishermen and others, as belonging to the Parish Church. Angus Mackay Cooper was a fisherman. So, too, were Dahl Mackay and his wife Isabella (née Mackay) of Aultiphurst; Donald Mackay and his wife Annabella (née Sutherland) of Strathy Point; and Findlay Mackay and his wife Barbara (née Henderson), of Church Hill, Strathy. Two families (accounting between them for seven baptisms) had ploughmen as the fathers of the children: Hugh Kennedy Mackay (married to Lizzie Mackay née Weale) and Robert Munro (married to Lizzie Munro née Mackay), both of Strathy West.

Two further groups of families can be identified in connection with the Baptismal Roll. Besides the locally connected families, also baptised by Alex Youngson were the daughter of an itinerant hawker; the families of the successive local policemen at Melvich, Constables Ross and Oliver; the son of Dr Macgregor; the children of two gamekeepers, of Robert J. S. Ross the Water Bailiff at Forsinain, of the Farmer at Armadale and of the Hotel Manager at Forsinard. In Northern society, we can say that these were outsiders, holding posts that separated them from the bulk of their crofting neighbours.[10] Further, a number of single-parent mothers also brought their children to Alex Youngson for baptism – or rather, he went to their homes. Some 10 per cent of Alex Youngson's baptisms have no father of the child recorded. There were also a number of delayed baptisms: a child born in 1895, baptised in 1911; an illegitimate child born in 1909, baptised in 1912; another born in 1897, baptised in 1913. This baptismal record suggests a ministry to outsiders in another sense: Mr Youngson offered a pastoral and sacramental welcome where others might not; he was a minister seeking out children and families, following a deliberate policy of outreach and inclusion.

Before leaving Mr Youngson's baptismal practice, it is worth briefly investigating whether the Baptismal Roll can give any indication of the size of the congregation or the connection of his kirk relative to the other denominations active in Strathy. Between 1900 and 1920 an average of twenty-one to twenty-two children were born each year in the area covered by the Register of Births for the District of Strathy – which for this purpose included Portskerra, Melvich and Strath Halladale. The lowest number in any year was twelve (in 1918) and the highest forty (in 1901).[11] We have seen that Mr Youngson baptised on average four children a year over the whole span of his ministry. As it happens, the Baptismal Roll of the United Free Church from 1901 to 1911 is available in the National Archives of Scotland.[12] This reveals that in 1901 Rev. Walter Calder conducted twenty-one baptisms for families spread across the entire district from Armadale to Forsinain. Incidentally, of these, three took place in church, six in schools and twelve in the homes of the parents; and all were of infants. Contemporary doctrine and practice nowadays urge that baptism is a congregational matter, conducted during public worship so that the people of God can welcome a new member to the wider Christian family. Early twentieth-century realities of transport and the fact that churches might be unheated both insisted that babies and young children were safest at home, and the ceremony was considered more as a family and less as a congregational concern.

Twenty-one was a high point for the number of United Free baptisms. Ewen Fraser replaced Walter Calder in 1903, in which year the total was thirteen. Thereafter the number hovered between twelve and fourteen and was eleven in 1911, the last year covered in the register. Taking the number of baptisms recorded in the UF Register against the known births in the District in the relevant years, overall the UF denomination was baptising some 46 per cent of the babies born.

Interpreting these figures cannot, however, be done with too much accuracy. No congregational records are available from the ministry of Hector Macaulay in Strathy Free Church (1909–40), or from the Free Presbyterian congregation. We may speculate that by 1911 the United Free congregation had inherited perhaps half of those in the tradition of the 1843 Disruption. Walter Calder's own history of the parish, entitled *Strathy,* records that the whole community, 'with trifling exceptions' had joined the Free Church by 1845 and, though hardly an impartial account, this may well have been correct.[13] The Free Presbyterian Church, however, which split from the Free Church in 1892, was sufficiently strong in Strathy to merit the building of a church even though its worship in the parish was maintained by local preachers and visiting ministers; it could not sustain a minister of its own. Nationally, the majority of the Free Church next joined with a denomination not represented in Strathy, the United Presbyterians, to create in 1900 the United Free Church. Many in the Highlands resisted this union, however, and under an Act of Parliament of 1905 they were entitled to retain church buildings, manses, records, etc. if it could be shown that at least a third of a congregation wished to continue as a Free Church. In both Strathy and Halladale the Free Church did indeed so continue, while those who supported the union left to build their own new UF churches and manse. Nevertheless the remaining Free Church congregation was not of sufficient size to find the resources to maintain its buildings in Strathy and Halladale in good order. The Strathy FC church still had an earth floor by 1912.[14] In an appeal for funds from outside, Rev. Hector Macaulay wrote that both churches had needed work for many years: the local sanitary inspector had actually served a notice of closure on the church in Halladale, and Strathy was just as bad: 'It is impossible, however, for us here in Strathy to worship any longer in our church in winter. One of the congregation, a hardy fisherman, said to me once that he would prefer to worship on the hillside in winter than inside the church.'[15]

Of an annual average of around twenty-eight babies born in the district between 1900 and 1911, we know that the UF Church baptised around thirteen a year, again on average. We might suppose that the Free and Free Presbyterian Churches taken together exercised a ministry of similar size, while the Established Church as we have seen welcomed three or four a year, albeit over the period 1909 to 1930. This speculation would suggest that almost all babies born in the district were baptised (whether in the year of their birth or thereafter) by one or another of the presbyterian denominations; and that would not be a surprising conclusion. The calculation, however, certainly confirms the small size of Mr Youngson's congregation; it was small both relative to its neighbours in the district and in absolute terms.

The United Free Church

The United Free Church of Strathy and Halladale was, as we have seen, the largest of the congregations active in the district. As it happened, its new church building in Strathy was opened in 1911, and the event was recorded by Mr Youngson: 4 July, 'Opening of U.F. Church'. We may presume from this that he attended. The event was also reported in the press and there were apparently large congregations present at the special services. The impressive sum of £22 was collected. The Very Rev. Dr R. J. Drummond, one of the UF Church's leading evangelical ministers, conducted the worship during which Ewen Fraser was presented with a gown and cassock. The manager of the Melvich Hotel presented a clock to the congregation, and a set of new psalm books was also donated. (Clearly the Strathy UF Church still chose its praise from the psalms.) At forty-two, Ewen Fraser was a younger man than Alex Youngson. Strathy was his first charge: he had been ordained and inducted as Walter Calder's successor in 1903. Arriving as a single man, in 1908 he had married Katherine Elizabeth Mackay from Coldbackie, Tongue, in the Free North Church, Inverness.[16] Besides his fluency in Gaelic, Ewen Fraser was thus related by marriage to Mackays of the north coast, though he himself was born in Stratherrick, inland from the eastern shore of Loch Ness. Before the new manse was completed, a croft house was rented in Baligill: a slated cottage with two rooms, a closet and garrets. Seven acres of land in Strathy East served as a glebe.[17]

February, 1912

Tuesday	6	*Visited Mr Fraser*
Friday	9	*John Gunn came for corn to thresh*
		One load of straw to Mr Fraser

Alex Youngson seems to have enjoyed a good working relationship with his younger UF colleague and neighbour. 'Visited Mr Fraser' occurs several times as a diary entry, and agricultural produce from the larger Established Church glebe also frequently found its way to the UF manse. On Sunday 13 October 1912, however, 'Mr Fraser preached his farewell sermon' and the diary entry for Wednesday 23 October read, 'Mr Fraser inducted at Tarbat'. The *Northern Times* reported: 'Expressions of deep regret are felt all over the parish of Farr. Mr Fraser was greatly esteemed all over the parish of Farr and the best wishes of his congregation and a large proportion of the people of Farr go with him and Mrs Fraser to their new home in Tarbat'.[18] In his time at Strathy, Ewen Fraser indeed made a mark on both congregation and community. He had been elected to, and also chaired, the School Board for the parish; and earlier in 1912 he had been secretary and treasurer to a committee of leading representatives of the area who had organised a public presentation to the Marquis of Stafford, heir of the Duchy of Sutherland, on the occasion of his marriage.[19]

After a vacancy during which Mr Fraser's brother, Rev. Duncan Fraser, acted as locum for the UF congregations in Strathy and Halladale (delivering 'powerful and impressive sermons' according to the *Northern Times*[20]), a call was given to Rev. Neil Mackay, aged forty-two, who had been educated at Armadale Public School. Strathy and Halladale was his third charge after ordination in 1895: he began in July 1913 a ministry in the parish that was to last until his death in January 1920.[21] As Ewen Fraser had been, he was supported by a UF missionary minister in Halladale, resident first in lodgings and then in the mission house-cum-church built by the UF congregation after it lost possession of the Strath's Free church to the continuing Free congregation.

The split between the Free and the United Free Churches obviously left some scars and at the time caused some bitterness. The union of the pre-1900 Free Church and the United Presbyterian Church had been accepted by due process of both their General Assemblies, and by clear majorities of all their Presbyteries across Scotland. A minority, however, had successfully challenged the union in the civil courts and won, gaining possession of the entire property of the Free Church on the grounds that in law the majority had broken its constitution by diverging from the principles on which the Free Church had been established. It took an Act of the Westminster Parliament in 1905 to reverse the judgment and to allocate congregations, church buildings and manses more in accord with the wishes of the people. Such controversial matters must leave hurts behind them, and a poem from this period was later published in the *Northern Times*, reflecting the pain of the division in the close-knit community of Halladale:

The UF farewell to the Auld Kirk in the Glen

Side by side they sat together,
Side by side, the 'grand old men';
Side by side they prayed together,
In the Auld Kirk in the glen.

Now they're parted frae each other,
And may never meet again;
'Happy they've been a' together'
In the Auld Kirk in the glen.

Oft times they crossed the hills to Strathy,
And never thought the journey long
While with the 'brethren' they were happy,
Sweetly singing Zion's songs.

Now cauld's the wind that bla's between them,
And cauld's the law that brought them gain;
'And caulder still' the hearts within them,
That sent their brethren to the plain.

No longer shall they meet together,
In happy crowds as we have seen;
For now they mean to leave each other,
And build a New Kirk on the green.

And it's down in yonder flowery dale –
Beneath the hazel and the birch –
There the people of Strathhalladale,
Intend to build the UF Church.

And on its steeple, shall be written,
'In letters of fine gold',
'Spiritual Independence
For young – and for old.'

So now the people are away,
To the New Kirk and their 'men',
And they shall no longer stay
In the Auld Kirk in the glen.

John Mackay, Chilsey, Halladale[22]

Having lost possession of the church to those they described, ironically, as the 'legal Frees' the Halladale UF eldership arranged for communion to be celebrated at Smigelburn and the mill until their new, steeple-less, corrugated-iron and wood-framed mission was completed.[23]

Perhaps the best picture of the UF Church in this period is given by the *Northern Times* report of the Annual Congregational Meeting and Social Entertainment held in March 1915.[24] The UF people of both Strathy and Halladale met in the Strathy Public Hall at 7 p.m. on a Thursday evening. Proceedings were chaired by Neil Mackay, their 'esteemed minister', supported by both the Halladale missionary, Rev. D. Findlayson and Mr Mackenzie, the UF minister of Thurso West. The platform party included, besides elders from Portskerra and Baligill, Hugh Gunn the congregational treasurer and Clerk to the Parish Council, with John Munro, then Chairman of the Farr School Board. These were leading and influential figures in the community as well as in the UF congregation; so, too, was Mr Roderick Mackenzie, the Strathy East crofter and officer for the Strathy Graveyard under the Parish Council, who moved the adoption of the financial report. Besides the platform party, the weekly paper also listed the acting committee responsible for arranging the evening (a total of five) and the stewards for the evening, a further eleven men and women in all. Two ladies, Mrs Macdonald, Brawl, and Miss Katie Gunn, Baligill, were in charge of the teas.

The programme for the Annual Meeting and Social began with an act of worship, the singing of the 100th Psalm and prayer, and then tea was served. After tea came the minister's review of the year. 'One of their oldest and respected elders, Mr Donald Macleod, Strathy West' had died during the year and the minister paid tribute to 'a man noted for his piety, his zeal, and devotion to the cause of the Master'. Mr Mackay next mentioned he was pleased 'to see so many young people present' as, owing to the war, there had been a question as to whether the event should be held at all. It had gone ahead 'for the sake of the young people'. Another mention of the war came with the minister's comments on the financial state of the congregation: 'There were many calls from time to time made upon them during these sad times of stress and anxiety.' Such social events were not complete without choirs and presentations by the children, and on this occasion the Melvich schoolmaster, Alexander Macintosh, had handled the necessary preparation. Following the adoption of the accounts came a 'bright and benefiting address' from a visiting minister, the National Anthem and a Benediction. The Strathy UF Church, even during wartime, was clearly able to mount a well-attended event, supported by key figures in the community. No similar event for his congregation is recorded in any of Mr Youngson's surviving diaries, but then its constitution as an established kirk did not require such a meeting of the congregation to approve the annual accounts.

Community and Co-operation

Mr Youngson would surely have been one of those parish ministers who would be 'wary of the danger of making hard and fast distinctions between those who occupy the pews and those whom they encounter as they go about the parish'. His baptismal policy certainly suggests this, as well as his practice of visiting. For the people of the parish, too, denominational choice was not normally an urgent concern. It was a reality, but not a reality to be pressed to extremes. Crofting households lived in close proximity to each other; mutual support and reliance were imperatives. Sheep were gathered from the hill in a collaborative exercise; wells were shared; help was given when it was needed. Certainly divisions existed but they could be allowed only within limits. Co-operation was integral to the well-being of the community.

While Messrs Youngson, Fraser and Macaulay, the three Strathy ministers, all clearly pursued their own courses, examples of co-operation between them can be found: there was certainly mutual respect, at least where civil matters were concerned. When in 1911 both Hector Macaulay of the Free Church and Ewen Fraser of Strathy UF Church were elected to the School Board for the parish of Farr it was Mr Macaulay who seconded the proposal to reappoint Mr Fraser as Chairman of the Board.[25] In 1912, all three Strathy ministers jointly conducted the Religious Knowledge examinations of their local schools: Armadale, Strathy, Melvich, and Strath Halladale's Dalhalvaig, and at Dalhalvaig they were also joined by the UF missionary minister for the Strath. Reported in the *Northern Times* in May, Alex Youngson's diary shows that the inspections had been scheduled over two days in March:

March, 1912		
Tuesday	*5*	*Rainy day* *Examined school, Melvich & Strath*
Monday	*25*	*Examining of Strathy and Armadale Sch* *10.30am*

The ministers were pleased with the standard of religious teaching in the schools: 'This school in the two sections showed excellent work' (Dalhalvaig); 'The three divisions of this school gave evidence of careful teaching' (Melvich); 'Accurate knowledge of the subjects taught was shown by this school' (Strathy); 'The answers given prove that this school is carefully taught'

(Armadale). From the report of the inspection of Forsinard's small school, we gain an idea of what syllabus might be followed in these public schools. There, the senior section were examined on their knowledge of Psalm 65 and Paraphrase 37, 'committed to memory'; on questions 1–80 of the Westminster Shorter Catechism of Christian doctrine, and on the history of Daniel. The junior section had learnt a psalm and two paraphrases, questions 1–10 of the Catechism and the history of Joseph.[26] So successful was the religious teaching of the local schools, in fact, that pupils from the district won prizes in the national competitions organised by the United Free Church on both Scripture and the Catechism.

On Thursday 21 October 1915, Mr Youngson's diary records that he visited both his Free and his UF colleagues 'about Harvest Thanksgiving'. No doubt the three ministers sought to agree between them which day would be appropriate for the annual Thanksgiving, given the weather and local agricultural conditions that year. On occasion, and between only the Established Church and UF congregations, this co-operation seem to have extended to a programme of joint Harvest services.

November, 1919

Thursday	27	*Thanksgiving for Harvest*
		Preached at noon
		UF Church 2pm
		Meeting in School 7pm

Mr Youngson's 1919 diary suggests the pattern for Harvest Thanksgiving that year. He preached in the Established Church at noon on the chosen Thursday – noon was also the normal time for Sunday worship. The community then met in the UF Church in the afternoon, and in the school in the evening: the day was given over to celebration.

A funeral was also an occasion for the whole community. After a service at (or outside) the home of the deceased, the men of the neighbourhood followed the coffin and cortège to the burial ground where a further service of prayers took place. There were three burial grounds in the district, of which that at Strathy (on the headland above the Bay) was the largest, serving Armadale and Portskerra besides Strathy as more narrowly defined. An old, small burial ground at Kirkton lay to the south of Melvich, and to the south of the main crofting area of Halladale was Bunahoun. The Register of Deaths for the District of Strathy covered the entire area, and recorded in 1911 a total of twenty-six deaths. The figure for 1912 was twenty-five; for 1915, twenty-eight; for 1919, thirty-two. Some funerals were reported in the *Northern Times,* and from these we find that the ministers from different churches sometimes co-operated. Where members of the extended family had different denominational associations, the involvement of both ministers in the stages of a funeral avoided invidious choices and showed due respect. At the funeral of Mrs George Mackay of Strathy East in May 1920, for example, those leading the funeral at the house included Rev. Hector Macaulay of Strathy Free Church, while the graveside service was led by Mr Youngson.[27] The service at the house for John Mackay Chilsey's nephew, Roderick Macleod, was led by the UF missionary minister for Strath Halladale, while Mr Macaulay led worship at the grave.[28] When Angus and Barbara Mackay Cooper's son Angus died in 1911, the 'touching services were held in the house in English by Rev. Alexander Youngson, parish minister, and in Gaelic by Rev. Hector Macaulay, F.C., and at the grave by Mr Youngson'.[29]

Alex Youngson, in fact, attended the funerals in the district whether or not he was invited to take part as one of the officiating ministers. On 2 May 1911, we find in the diary 'Funeral at Forsinard Calder'. In a minister's diary nowadays, such an entry would undoubtedly mean that the diarist had conducted the funeral. It happens, however, that the *Northern Times* printed a notice of this occasion, which was for the fourteen-year-old son of the Station Master at Forsinard. We are told that the service at the house was 'feelingly and impressively conducted by Rev. Mr Fraser UFC Strathy'; and that worship at the grave at Kinbrace was led by the UF missionary stationed there.[30] On another occasion [9 January 1919], Mr Youngson's diary records 'Funeral of Mrs McCallum: notice sent too late for attending'. Clearly the family were not expecting him to conduct this funeral and the note sent round the neighbourhood gave him insufficient time to make arrangements to attend as he would otherwise have done. Part of his ministry was to be part of the community, and he went to mourn with his neighbours when the community gathered in mutual support. On 15 September 1919, his diary mentioned: 'Funeral Mrs Gunn, Melvich 12noon.' The *Northern Times* later reported that Mrs James Gunn had been the daughter of James Macdonald of Portskerra, who had been ordained an elder of Strathy Free Church in 1865. The article continued that Mary Gunn's

> mind was richly stored with reminiscences associated with the lives of Godly men and women of the preceding generation, many of whom she had known intimately and esteemed and loved in her early youth. In striking contrast with those days, only a generation removed, Christian women of Mrs Gunn's stamp are, it is to be feared, a sadly declining number, which makes the demise of such worthy persons an irreparable loss, not only to their immediate relatives and friends but to the community at large.[31]

Such funerals were indeed major occasions for the community irrespective of denomination.

5

The Regularities of Life

The Crofting Year

The survival of four of Alex Youngson's diaries provides just sufficient evidence to allow us to distinguish the normal flow of life, taken month to month over the year, as against those incidents that just cropped up: to see both the general pattern and the events that happened. It is to the regularities of life that we now turn. In a crofting community, this means looking first at the working or agricultural year, and closely linked with it, at north coast weather. The church year, too, had its distinctive patterns; and both of these contributed to a social round of events and entertainments that marked the passage of time.

When the Sutherland estates had acquired a Parliamentary church for Strathy, land was provided on which the church and manse were built. From the maps of the period mentioned earlier, it seems that this land may have included the original garden that had belonged to the Strathy laird's house.[1] By Alex Youngson's time, a fifteen-acre glebe was also set aside for the minister, just south of the manse.[2] Further, the minister shared with the crofting community in their use of the common grazings, and of the peat banks in the area. Mr Youngson's farming interests were therefore quite time consuming and they occupy a good deal of space in his diaries. Being an elderly man, he was unable to undertake heavy work himself and so in order to make best use of the land he had to find time (in those days before the telephone) to visit neighbours to make the necessary arrangements. Cutting peat in the 'mosses', spreading it to dry, bringing it home and stacking it were among the hard physical tasks Mr Youngson paid men to undertake for him. In 1919 it took nine days, forty loads and sixteen men to bring the year's supply of peat to the manse, and he noted the details in a 'Peat Account' at the back of the diary. As the months passed, he visited the peat banks himself to see how the work was going and noted with pleasure and relief: 'Peats almost home' [6 September 1919].

May, 1911

Thursday   11   *Visited moss all peats cut less bank at near road*

Like its neighbours, the manse relied on the land for fuel, for its basic and regular food supplies and to add cash supplements to annual income. By sharing in the annual round of farming work, the minister also participated in the essential regularities of life of a crofting people.

Alex Youngson began his diary for 1915, as was his practice, by inking in essential information from the year before. That year he was using not a clerical but a general professional pocket diary, and so he had to enter the household lists of his neighbours under the heading 'Memoranda from 1914'. The same page recorded, also in ink, the dates at which his two cows ('Rosy', 'Bessie') had been served by the district's bull, and the dates between which the tup (ram) borrowed from Armadale had visited and impregnated his own flock of sheep. Between the agricultural and the ministerial sections of the page, he wrote the words: 'Text: "The Lord is my shepherd"'. In retrospect, it is difficult to decide whether this text was entered in all seriousness, or with a touch of ironic humour.

Caring for his sheep certainly was a priority for Mr Youngson and their economy can be followed round the year. The tup visited late in the year, between 6 November 1914 and 9 January 1915 according to the 1915 diary. The flock was then 'put to the hill' for rough grazing until it was time to bring the ewes down to enclosed lower ground for lambing. Lambs began to arrive by the middle of April and each was carefully entered in the diary: 'First lamb today', 'four lambs today – twins'. '11th lamb today – ewe'. In 1919, we read: '3, 4 twins ee one given away' and that was shorthand for the arrival of the third and fourth lambs of the year, twins and both ewes; and that he had given one away. Deliberate breeding for twins was not as developed as it later became, and a double birth was viewed more as a bonus. To

assist a neighbour, one of a pair of twins might be given away to
suckle on a ewe that had lost a lamb; it would be expected that
the gesture would be reciprocated as necessary. 'Dead lamb'
occurred in the diaries for 1911, 1915 and 1919: 1919 was in
fact a particularly bad year, with the thirteenth, seventeenth,
eighteenth and nineteenth lambs all dying. Once into May, the
flock was ready to be 'cut and painted' and then 'put out'. This
was shorthand for castrating the male wedders and docking the
tails of both genders, seeing that each sheep was identified by
marking with the manse's own colour (blue in 1911), and sending
them back to the rough grazing of the hill. For this sort of work,
of course, the minister needed assistance, often provided by John
Gunn of Strathy West or by the Precentor and his family.

May, 1911

Monday	8	*Seen J Gunn about lambs*
Tuesday	9	*Lambs cut by John Gunn*
Saturday	13	*Given J Gunn two bags potatoes*

In some communities driving sheep back to the hill was a
collective exercise, so that the whole local flock could be moved
at once with the assistance of numerous dogs. In 1915, the manse
put eighteen sheep and thirteen lambs to the hill and retained
three sheep and three lambs for further feeding.

By late June or early July it was time for the wool harvest – the
sheep clipping/shearing. This was the last week of June in 1912,
and the manse had twenty-one sheep clipped and marked four of
them for sale, with the twelve lambs for that season. Twenty-one
sheep were also clipped in 1915, and twenty-six in 1919. Next
came sheep dipping, in August in 1911 and October in 1915,
against infection. By that stage, however, in both 1915 and 1919,
Mr Youngson had sold his lambs to Donald Henderson, the
farmer tenant of Armadale Farm: nine wedders and two ewes in
late July 1915 and four wedders and six ewes in August 1919.
The farm account kept separately in the 1911 diary shows the
income and expenditure on this small flock. Selling a sheepskin
earned 2s. in March 1911; later, 47 lb of wool brought in £4 7s.
The sale of seven lambs at 9s. each, and two lambs at 7s., earned

£3 17s. in August, and selling five ewes, a further £3 15s. in September. Against this, sheep dipping cost 6s., and 2/6d. was paid to Armadale Farm for the services of their tup in the late autumn. Gratuities and fees paid to men for their services also needed to be taken in account – but these were not shown in the diaries as specifically for work with sheep as distinct from payments for all forms of assistance in and around the glebe. The manse may also have enjoyed mutton from their own flock.

By selling its sheep to Armadale, the manse traded convenience against the opportunity of a better price.

July, 1915

Saturday	31	*Mr Henderson took away 9 wedders 2 ewe lambs*

While local sales took place at Bettyhill and Melvich, sales attended by buyers from the south took place at rail heads like Forsinard and Lairg, to which the flocks had to be moved via sheep walks over the hills. No doubt Mr Henderson sold on the Youngson lambs at a profit later in August. At the lamb sales at Forsinard in August 1911, the top price for a wedder was 16/3d., gained by Forsinain farm.[3] As with most relationships in this small community, Alex Youngson's connection with the Hendersons of Armadale Farm was not just one of the business of sheep and cows. Both men worked together for a time on the Parish Council for Farr. As minister, Alex Youngson baptised children of Donald Henderson and his wife Georgina (née Mackay) in the years 1915, 1918 and 1920.

Unlike north coast crofting today, land was used not just for sheep and cattle grazing but also for crops and vegetables from the one, two or three acres of arable land belonging to each croft. A routine of planting, weeding and harvesting took place through the year. At the manse, strawberries were planted in November 1911, and the gooseberry bushes cleaned out. The manse also had blackcurrant bushes. After the winter, Mr Youngson started planting onion sets in March 1912; as the month progressed, he moved on to parsley (two rows) and peas. Cabbage was planted in April, and in other years cauliflower, Brussels sprouts and onions from seed were also noted in the diary. Plants might come by mail-order ['Plants rec'd' – 11 April 1912], following the visit of a seedsman ['Call of seedsman from Inverness' – 30 August 1915]. Potatoes, of course – Ashleaf Kidney, Duke of York, British Queen – were regularly cropped. In May, parsnips, carrots, lettuce, turnip, radishes and parsley ('Parsley Dobbies') were sown, as well as more potatoes: 'potatoes planted today – 20 drills'. Later in May, it was time for the 'Swedish turnips'. May was also time for the corn crop of the year to be sown. Thereafter the diary shows men and women involved with hoeing, earthing up the potatoes, 'working in turnip land', 'cleaning strawberries', manuring the ground.

While, heavy snowfalls excepted, sheep can look after themselves over winter on rough grazing, cattle need the extra feeding of hay. The grass harvest of later August and September was therefore a busy time of the year: it needed to be cut, turned as it lay in the field to dry, and then (in the older Scots term that Mr Youngson used) 'set up in coles' – small haystacks. The whole process could take two or three helpers two or three weeks of fairly constant activity. The table below shows the process as it took place in 1912. John Gunn of Strathy West appeared at the final stage, the making of the coles/stacks. Before then, three helpers had done the work in the glebe: John Mackay, Hugh Macleod and John the Post(man). John Mackay was the Precentor. John the Post was his eldest son, John G. Mackay (Cooper), brother to James Angus, whose marriage was mentioned earlier. John G., aged sixteen at the time of the 1901 Census, was already the Post Letter Deliverer at that date. No doubt his round left him time to work with the manse hay in the afternoon. Payments to all three men were recorded in the glebe account for 1912.

September, 1912

Tuesday	10	*John Mackay cutting hay 10.30am*
		John Postman ditto 1pm
Wednesday	11	*John Mackay half day*
Thursday	12	*Cutting hay*
		Hugh McLeod day
		John Mackay Post half day

Friday	13	*Cutting hay*
		John Mackay day
		Hugh McLeod day
		John Postman half day
Saturday	14	*Cutting hay*
		John Mackay day
		Hugh McLeod day
		John Postman half day
Sunday	15	*Very wet day*
Monday	16	*Turning hay*
Tuesday	17	*Turning hay*
Thursday	19	*Turning hay*
Friday	20	*Turning hay*
Saturday	21	*Turning hay*
Sunday	22	*Fine Summer day*
Monday	23	*Preparing for taking in hay*
		Sent word to John Gunn
Wednesday	25	*Taking in hay – two stacks*
		John Gunn & Hugh McLeod

Once the hay crop was in, by October it was time to secure the corn crop: cutting and binding, and then putting into screws: 'Put corn in screws'. Alex Youngson was here using an older Norse/Scots term from Shetland and Orkney for a stack of corn or hay. Perhaps he had learned the word in Stroma.[4] November saw the potato crop being lifted and stored in a pit; the Harvest Thanksgiving followed at the end of the month, or even into December. The winter months were also the time when corn was taken for threshing, sometimes at Armadale but also sometimes at the Melvich Hotel – which, with its own sixty-three acres of land, employed its own farm workers and no doubt had the relevant equipment. Bags of threshed corn finally had to be sent to a mill to be turned to oatmeal for use in the manse kitchen for making porridge, oatcakes etc. And the year had returned to its beginning.

January, 1915		
Saturday	9	*Got load of corn threshed at Hotel*

February, 1915		
Friday	26	*Sent off three bags of corn to mill*

Because Alex Youngson had to employ local people to assist him, in money terms his farming of the glebe just about broke even over the year: cash left over once payments had been made was sufficient to pay for the labour involved in cutting and bringing in the peats: a full £7 10s. in 1911. He had enough land to have a surplus of some crops beyond the manse's own requirement. Eggs from the manse hens were posted off to friends in the south during the war years: Thursday 14 January 1915, 'Sent off eggs to Musselburgh'. Quite frequently he sold hay to Rev. Ewen Fraser, whose small croft/glebe obviously did not have much of a grass crop. Barrels of potatoes could be and were sold at 2/6d a barrel. Women like Jessie M. Mackay Cooper (of Strathy West, aged twenty-six in 1911) and 'Mrs Samson' (of Strathy Point, aged thirty-nine in 1911; wife of Angus Mackay Cooper), however, had been paid to lift the potatoes. Moreover, the glebe did not produce everything the manse needed by way of food supplies. A short entry entitled 'House Account' showed payments in October 1912 to the butcher, the fishmonger and the baker: 'bread, butter, cookies'. Fresh milk, eggs, vegetables and fruit, however, were available in season, with home produced potatoes, mutton and oatmeal. Beyond the economics, the diaries reflect genuine interest, satisfaction and pleasure in the year's work in the garden, the glebe and the hill.

All outdoor work on the north coast was weather dependent. Mr Youngson's work as a minister, as well as that of his crofting neighbours, benefited from fair weather as he, like most people most of the time, went about on foot from place to place on local business. Occasionally the weather meant he stayed at home, as he wrote in his diary: 'At home today, slippery roads' [Tuesday 12 January 1915]. At a neighbourhood level, parish councils had authority to pay for repairs to minor roads. The main road along the north coast, together with such local roads that were of sufficient quality to be adopted, was the responsibility of Sutherland County Council. Road engineering, however, was still largely unmechanised and not as yet tarmacadamised. Thus the County of Inverness-shire in 1908 sought the support of the other northern counties in making an approach to the Secretary for Scotland to obtain an 'imperial tax' on motor cars to help to pay for the damage this new traffic was doing to the broken stone surface of northern roads.[5]

Bad weather resulted in slippery roads, and roads Mr Youngson described as 'heavy': thick with snow. 'After heavy snow, clear sky but heavy road' [Sunday 1 December 1912]. Mid-November was by no means unusual for a snowfall. November 1912 had had a 'storm of wind and sleet' [Monday 11], 'wet and stormy day' [Tuesday 19], a 'severe storm of wind' [Wednesday 27] followed by 'storm of snow' [Thursday 28] and 'heavy snow' [Friday 29]. Both Sunday 1 and Monday 2 December saw more snow, but Tuesday brought rain and by Wednesday, 'snow disappeared – wet day'. That year, Harvest Thanksgiving was late, on Thursday 5 December. As the winter went on, the diary (which continued for two weeks into 1913) recorded that Sunday 15 December was a 'very stormy day', though Sunday 22 was fine. Sunday 5 January 1913 was a 'fine frosty day'; but then the storms returned: throughout Wednesday 8, Thursday 9 and Friday 10 January, 'fearful gales' blew. On Sunday 12 January 1913, Mr Youngson recorded: 'Very stormy day: rain and sleet. 9 in church'. In 1919, the cold continued until late April: Sunday 27 – 'Storm of snow – cold north wind'. Life on the north coast, of course, also included fine, sunny days under wide skies: quiet days, in an age before power tools and regular motor traffic, when the sounds of wind and sea predominated. Cold and storm were ever-present possibilities, however, and drove the imperatives of work and life.

The Church Year

Mr Youngson's calling to Strathy, of course, was not primarily as a crofter or farmer but as a minister; and this life, too, had its regularities. The primary pattern was week to week, Sunday to Sunday, but other strands can also be identified. Besides Sunday worship there was also the Sabbath School, following its course over the year. Moreover, presbyterian parish ministers are not simply called to a parish; they also compose (with elders and now deacons) the courts of the church. Alex Youngson had responsibilities beyond Strathy to the Presbytery of Tongue, to the Synod of Caithness and Sutherland, and to the General Assembly of the Church of Scotland. Each of these institutions had its own place in his life, occasionally demanding time, more often giving way to the priorities of parish life.

Sabbath Worship and the Communion Season

Sunday worship, and within that the Sunday sermon, was the first priority of a Scottish minister's life. The Reformation in Scotland cut away much that had seemed to clutter the life of the church, seeking to clear the accumulation of the centuries. The chief motivation was to allow the Bible to speak clearly, and that came to mean giving freedom to ministers to preach as each found best suited to the needs and capacity of his congregation. In consequence, the presbyterian tradition abandoned the cycle of saints' days and major festivals that in the Roman Catholic and Anglican disciplines determined so much to do with worship, from the readings set for each day to the colour of the vestments worn by the priests. The Scottish Church believed that there was no basis in the Bible for the celebration of some days as more important than others, and so the entire round of the seasons of the Christian year ceased to determine parish life. The spiritual year no longer began in Advent, nor moved through Christmas to Lent, Easter and Pentecost. The special days of the host of major and minor saints were abandoned, together with the images and altars of the saints. The radical tradition of John Knox considered that true worship was only that rooted in Scripture; that any man-made additions could only, idolatrously, detract.

By the beginning of the twentieth century this white clarity had begun to diffract and new colours were emerging. In part from reaction (some ministers preached week after week on the different and detailed doctrines to be found in a single verse of Scripture) and in part by assimilation from England, the major Christian festivals that built the year's pattern round the life of Jesus (his birth, crucifixion, resurrection and the giving of the Spirit) were being restored. The Highlands were conservative in doctrine and practice, however, and indications of how Strathy's Established Church minister approached Sunday worship are few. Did he structure his preaching around readings that built up to Christmas, or that assisted spiritual preparation for Easter? It is very unlikely that he did so.

Alex Youngson's diaries for 1911 and 1912 were, as has been said, designed for clergymen, especially of the Church of England. On each Sunday, therefore, the diary displayed the day's place within the cycle of the spiritual year and, basing itself on the Church of England's Book of Common Prayer, printed appropriate Scripture lessons. Most likely Alex Youngson ignored this information as he ignored other pages in these diaries that did not relate to Strathy. Or perhaps he did on occasion select his texts from these set passages, rather than choose his own. He was under no obligation to do so, however, and his congregation – ignorant of the English Prayer Book – would not have known the source of their minister's inspiration. The weekly sermon and text were the minister's responsibility: whether each sermon related to any further pattern or series was again his individual choice and there was no expectation of sharing in an ecumenical experience. Alex Youngson's diary entry for each Sunday typically included a note of the weather that day, of the collection taken and of attendance. Only once in all the Sundays in all four years that have come down to us is there a note of the topic on which he preached: Sunday 19 March 1911, 'Text: Shall not the Lord of all the Earth do right?' This text, Genesis 18:25, was not one of those set for that day in the printed diary.

There is certainly nothing in Mr Youngson's own entries in his diaries to suggest that Good Friday and Christmas Day were any different from the other days of the year. Scotland as a nation did not celebrate these days as public holidays: work continued as usual. The minister's work, his visiting, continued as usual: Wednesday 25 December 1912, 'Visited Point'; Saturday 25 December 1915, 'Visited Katie Mackay'. These were the only entries Mr Youngson made in his diary for those two days. Similarly, there is nothing in the diaries to indicate that an Easter Sunday was celebrated in any way differently from other Sundays. Whereas a series of preparatory Easter Week services in today's churches often traces Jesus' story through cross to resurrection, Strathy knew nothing of such innovations. On Sundays celebrated in England as Easter Day, offerings in Mr

Youngson's Strathy were the same size as usual– as the day had no special significance in local culture, his congregations on those days were no larger.

The church year in the north of Scotland revolved not to any denominational, ecumenical or catholic patterns but to that of the communion seasons. Each congregation in the district of Strathy celebrated communion once a year, an event that extended to a series of special services over most of a week. In Strathy's Established Church, communion Sunday was the second in July. In the Strathy UF congregation, communion was the third Sunday in February. In the Free Presbyterian congregation, it was the second Sunday in September, and for the Free Church in Strathy, the third in September.[6] Each of the congregations' celebrations followed the same basic pattern.[7] A series of preparatory sermons might be preached. Thursday was the Fast Day, for self- and collective-preparation; and a noon and an evening service might be held. Saturday saw a further service of preparation at noon; and the communion itself was celebrated at the Sabbath's services. A noon service on the Monday concluded matters with an act of thanksgiving. Friday being left free in this schedule, it had also become customary in the north to hold a formalised preparation on the Friday evening, in which the men of the congregation (and their neighbours) discussed practical and doctrinal issues of spirituality. Though Mr Youngson made no mention in his diary of such Friday gatherings in any of the Strathy congregations, Sandra Train certainly recollects Friday meetings at the Free Church communion in Halladale held annually in later July.[8] The UF congregation at Bettyhill also held Friday men's nights; at that in June 1912, eleven of the men spoke to the text Zephaniah 3:12: 'I will also leave in the midst of thee an afflicted and poor people, and they shall trust in the name of the Lord.'[9]

To assist a minister with such a number of additional services, the support of visiting ministers was expected. Rev. Dugald Carmichael, minister of Reay in Caithness, thus preached at Strathy's Fast Day on Thursday 6 July 1911 and also in 1919. In 1912 and 1915, he preached at the Saturday preparatory service. Mr Carmichael had been minister of Farr in 1909 when Alex Youngson came to Strathy, but in October of that year he was called to Reay, also an adjacent parish to Strathy but on the eastern and not the western boundary. Again from Caithness, Rev. David Lillie, minister of Watten, came to stay at the Strathy manse to preach at the Fast Day for 1912; the diary records that Mr Youngson and his guest walked out along Strathy Point on the Thursday, and that 'Mr Lillie left' on the Friday. Much the same pattern was followed in 1915, but in 1919 Mr Lillie was invited to preach for the sacrament itself on the Sunday. Mr Mackinnon, minister of Strathy's 'mother' church of Farr, preached at the evening service on communion Sunday, 1911, and at both the forenoon and evening services in 1912. In 1915, the minister of Latheron preached on the Sunday and a Mr Clark from Leith on the Monday; while in 1919 the difficulties of the aftermath of war meant that Mr Youngson 'preached self' at the services for both the Saturday and the Monday.

The minister of Strathy also received reciprocal invitations to assist with the sacrament in the neighbouring parish of Farr. In 1911 he preached for the Fast Day on Thursday 16 October – that day also saw a snowstorm, and his travel home on the Friday may have been uncomfortable. In 1915, he preached at Farr on the Sabbath itself, arriving home on the Monday. The same pattern held for 1919, though in that year Mr Youngson was leading the sacrament as the Interim Moderator for Farr, during a ministerial vacancy in that parish. In the meantime, there appears to have been no worship in Strathy church on Sundays when their minister was away assisting at Farr – after all, who else was there authorised to preach? As it was the practice for elders and others from neighbouring congregations also to travel to attend the celebration of communion, this absence from the pulpit was less noticed than might nowadays be expected.

The annual communion for a congregation was thus a major social event, with visiting ministers and elders to be received, members of extended families travelling from some distance and work in the fields ceasing not just (of course) on the Sabbath but also on the Fast Day. As a teenager, Sandra Train appreciated the opportunities of the season to meet with contemporaries visiting from outside Strath Halladale. In retrospect, she writes: 'As I look back now with an adult's eye, I see the true meaning of such a Communion Season so solemnly observed. All the best was kept for this time, our best clothes, new or more often renewed, our best food and dishes, our best hospitality to old friends.'[10]

Even though few actually received the bread and wine of the sacrament, numbers attending Highland communions could be so great as to exceed the capacity of church buildings and to require overflow congregations in the open air. As Strathy's population was divided into four congregations, each with their separate communion seasons, and with much coming and going to and from Halladale and the Strath's own sacraments, it was these occasions rather than the somewhat artificial divisions of the Christian year that must have dominated both the ministerial and the popular spiritual timetable of the months.

Kirk Session and Congregational Life

The diary of the Scottish minister of the late twentieth and early twenty-first centuries is often filled with entries such as 'Kirk Session', 'Kirk Session Committee', 'Congregational Board' – meetings of the bodies and groups that control the spiritual and business life of congregations, and have oversight of larger and smaller fleets of committees running congregational activities. There were no such entries in Alex Youngson's diaries. Strathy Kirk had a kirk session, yes, in form: the controlling body of all parish church congregations at that time was the elders met together in kirk session with the minister automatically in the chair as Moderator. But to ordain elders, there had first to be a reasonably sized pool of communicant members from which to select them – and in a male-dominated world, even those communicants who were female were as women *per se* ineligible to be ordained as an elder. At the time Alex Youngson was called to Strathy, there was no functioning kirk session; and that was the situation for most of his ministry. In effect, he ran the congregation in person with such unofficial advice as he might receive from intimates, the Precentor (who never became a communicant during Mr Youngson's ministry) and John Gunn, weaver, of Strathy West. Perhaps the experience of rejection by the elders of Newmill left Alex Youngson with an abiding distrust of independent-minded elders, but all the Established Church congregations of Sutherland's north coast had difficulty finding men prepared to be ordained as elders.

Such information as we know about Strathy's Established Kirk Session comes from its minute book, preserved in the National Archives of Scotland – this is in fact written on pages of the same, plain, exercise book that also served for the Communion Roll, the Baptismal Register and the Register of Proclamations of Marriages.[11] The first entry was for 10 June 1914, when Mr

Youngson (acting as both Moderator and Clerk of the Session) met with two assessors appointed by the Presbytery from outside: these were David Robertson (an elder) and Rev. Malcolm Mackinnon, minister of Farr. They agreed that three new elders should be ordained to office on 27 September 1914: David Sinclair, gardener, Bighouse; John Gunn, weaver, Strathy West; and Daniel Shearer, crofter, Portskerra. The ordinations went ahead as planned. The newly quorate local Kirk Session only met, however, annually on the communion Sunday in order to distribute to members intending to participate the small metal tokens that gave admission to the sacrament. According to the minutes, the assessor elder David Robertson and John Gunn, with the minister, performed this function, while David Sinclair and Daniel Shearer must have had other duties – the Communion Roll shows they were present. In 1921 the entry in the Minute Book said simply that 'tokens were given to intending Communicants, David Sinclair having left the parish and Daniel Shearer having died': in fact, Mr Shearer had died in 1918, the same year that Mr Sinclair 'left the district'. So, 1922 to 1924, instead of a formal record of meeting, a note of the celebration of communion was made. There were no entries in the Kirk Session Minutes after 1924 until, in 1930, Alex Youngson's intending retiral began a new round of formal vacancy proceedings.

This was as bare a minimum of activity as any Kirk Session could hope to get away with. The elders certainly played no formal part in the direction of the affairs and mission of the congregation that can now be perceived; there is no indication that they exercised spiritual oversight, whether of members or adherents; there is no suggestion, even, that they were involved in decisions about Christian education or the property or finances of the parish – though as a Kirk Session all such matters should have been their concern. The role, such as it was, was restricted to organising the communion. Of the elders, only with John Gunn, and that on an informal basis, does Alex Youngson appear to have had a sufficiently close relationship that we can imagine them consulting together on pastoral matters. Drummond and Bulloch, historians of the nineteenth-century Church of Scotland, noted that in that century many rural parishes had perhaps one elder or even none; that their ministers believed they could undertake personally all the work of ministry by themselves, assisted only by sabbath-school teachers. Writing of the 1880s and 1890s, they concluded of the Established Church: 'she was almost entirely dependent on her ministers, as sacerdotal as any Church could be.' However gracious the individual minister, the underlying assumption, common throughout the church, was that, whatever the issue, the minister would decide. Such an assumption I describe by the term 'institutional arrogance', though there is little doubt that it suited men reluctant to distinguish themselves from their neighbours as much as it suited their ministers. Alex Youngson's formative years and much of his adult life were lived in the nineteenth century; and his ministry at Strathy certainly fits the picture painted by Drummond and Bulloch.[12] Regular meetings of the Kirk Session played no part in Alex Youngson's yearly round, though the shared spiritual responsibility of elders and ministers was and is supposed to be at the heart of presbyterianism.

It also seems dubious whether Strathy Kirk had any Sabbath School teachers beyond the manse family. That there was an active Sabbath School is evident from the diaries. We also know that it was the only active congregational organisation, because the official *Year Book* of the Church of Scotland printed such details as the membership of all the Kirk's congregations, with the numbers of elders, of members of the Young Men's and the Women's Guilds, of the Bible Class and of Sabbath Schools. According to the *Year Book* for 1912, no congregation in the Presbytery of Tongue had a Guild (of either sort) or a Bible Class.

Alex Youngson's diaries for 1911 and 1912, as has been said, included his attendance register for the Sabbath School. Clearly, he took the roll in person each Sunday afternoon and so presumably also taught the class. He was, after all, a former schoolmaster. We can imagine that his daughter, Alice Youngson, who was accomplished on the harmonium, assisted; but one teacher of that time would expect easily to cope with classes of thirty or more pupils. The Sabbath School year ran from April to early January, being suspended during the winter months after the end of session January party. The 1911 Sabbath School session thus ended in January 1912 with the annual treat, and also a presentation reported in the *John O' Groat Journal*:

Parish Church Sunday School, Strathy
It is usual at this season of the year that Strathy Sabbath School should not meet during the months of February and March. On

Sabbath 14th inst before dismissing the children, Rev. Alex Youngson presented each of the children attending with a beautiful Bible as a New Year's present. This gift is much appreciated and shows the warm interest that Mr Youngson and Miss Alice take in the welfare of the children. It should be an encouragement to the children at Strathy to give regular attendance. The school meets again in the first Sabbath of April.[13]

January, 1912

Sunday   14   *Wind & rain*
                          Sabbath School dispersed till April

---

In 1912, the register shows that twenty scholars attended on 7 April when the school reopened, and fifteen others joined them during the weeks until Sunday 6 October – during which Sabbath School met without much interruption. School did not meet on communion Sunday, nor when Mr Youngson was away at the General Assembly or conducting worship at Farr Kirk. As he had run out of space, Mr Youngson began a new register on 13 October with thirty-four names and one, William Mackay, was added to these before the year ended.

Unfortunately it is rarely possible to determine who was who from the surviving class registers. To which family should Nellie Mackay, Gracie Mackay, Robert Mackay or Hugh Mackay be allocated? Neither can it be assumed that all the scholars were children. John Gunn's wife, Jacobina Wallace, was listed as attending Sabbath School in both 1911 and 1912: and the entry in the Register of Marriages shows her to have been aged forty-six in 1910 at the date of her wedding. Mrs John Gunn became a communicant member of Strathy Church in 1913, so presumably her presence on a Sunday afternoon was by way of preparation, following her marriage to one of the local Kirk's leading men. Younger teenagers, of school age, we do know were present. Lizzie Blank was presumably the daughter of George and Barbara Blank[14] of Strathy Point; she was aged one at the time of the 1901 Census and so was eleven in 1911. So too was John Campbell, son of John and Christina Campbell. Both Lizzie and John were also regularly at Sabbath School in 1912 as were Robert and Henrietta Gunn, children of Kenneth and Christina of Baligill. John Mackay Piper was registered as joining the Sabbath School only towards the end of the session in both 1911 and 1912. He may have been the John Alexander Mackay, son of Donald Piper, who had been baptised by Mr Youngson in December 1909; or more likely he was his older brother. Without the personal details of the 1911 Census, not yet released, we cannot know – and the same is true for most of the scholars listed in the diaries.

Clearly, though, the Sabbath School could be a multi-age affair, with both adults and children present to be taught Bible stories and Christian doctrine. Most scholars had a fairly regular pattern of attendance: Jacobina Wallace, for example, came twenty-seven times out of a possible thirty-four in 1912. Overall that year there was an average attendance of twenty, a figure brought down by three who joined late in the year and each of whom registered for only one Sunday. Attendance at Sabbath School was a regular part of life for children (and some adults) whose families belonging to the Established Kirk; and teaching the class was equally part of the minister's regular duties. I may add that one family who were children in Strathy soon after this time recollected attending the Sabbath Schools of all three of the congregations active in the community, moving from one to another as the day progressed. They were invited, they said, and so they went. Perhaps their parents were pleased to enjoy a quiet Sabbath afternoon. . . .

Presbytery and Synod

If Alex Youngson was away from home on occasion to assist with neighbouring communions, he also might be away from the manse mid-week to attend meetings or business of the Presbytery of Tongue. Six parishes comprised this Presbytery. Four were on the north coast with Strathy the most easterly of these; then came Farr, Tongue and Durness. Round Cape Wrath and on the west coast were Kinlochbervie and Eddrachillis. Properly, the minister of every parish together with an elder from each made up the membership of the Presbytery, but as the Kirk's congregations were chronically short of elders, frequently only one appeared at Presbytery, the ruling elder for Farr, schoolmaster and Justice of the Peace Mr Evander Mackay FEIS. Meetings took place twice a year in November and March as a minimum, and at other times

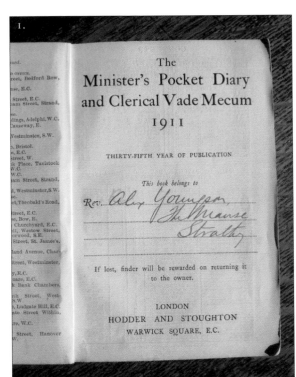

1. Title page, 1911

2. Week beginning Sunday,
1 January 1911

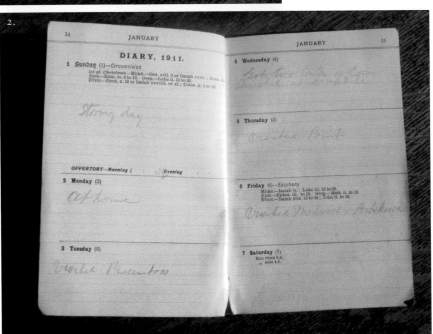

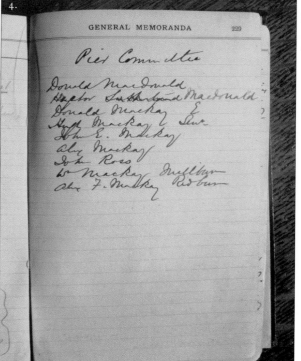

3. Visiting list,
Strathy West and East, 1911

4. Pier Committee, 1911

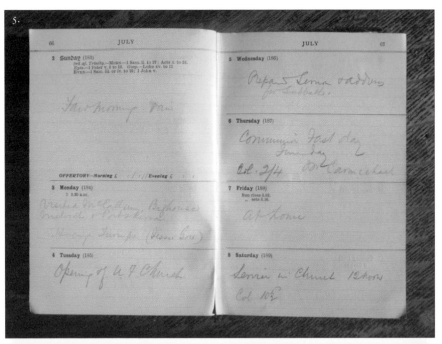

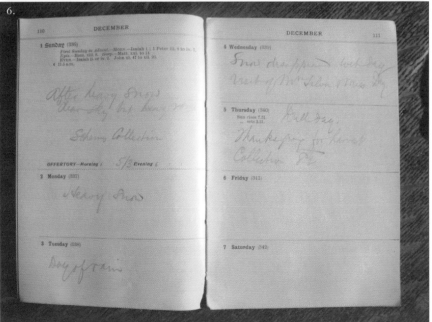

5. Opening of Strathy U. F. Church, 4 July 1911

6. Week beginning Sunday, 1 December 1912

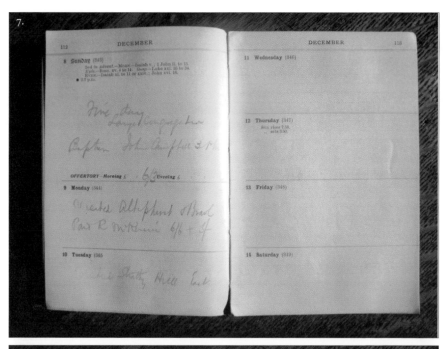

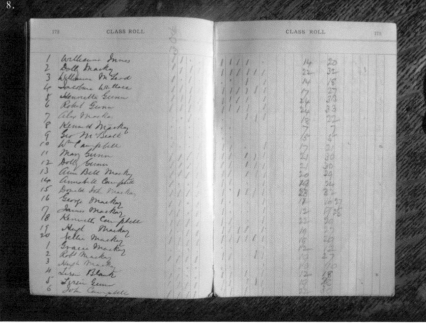

7. Baptism of John Campbell, 8 December 1912

8. Sabbath School Class Roll, 1912

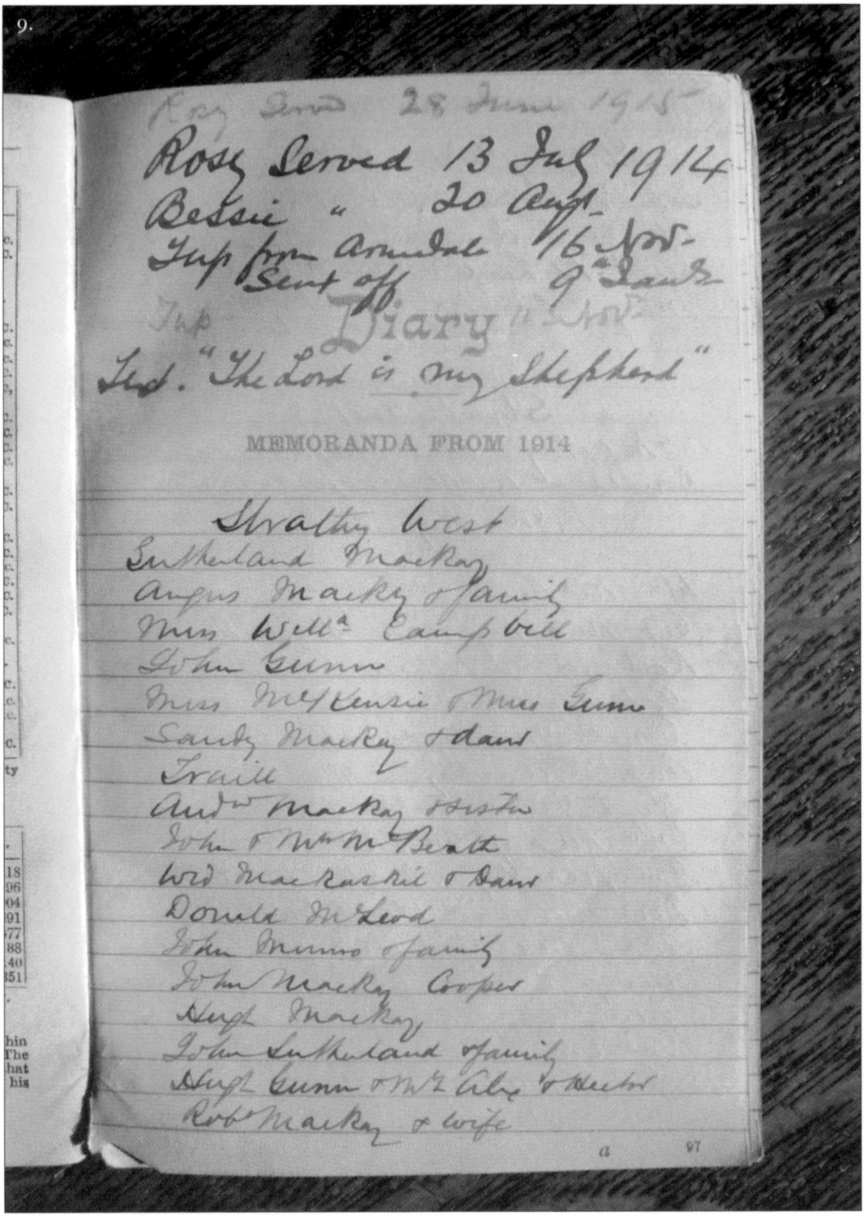

9. Opening Memoranda, 1915

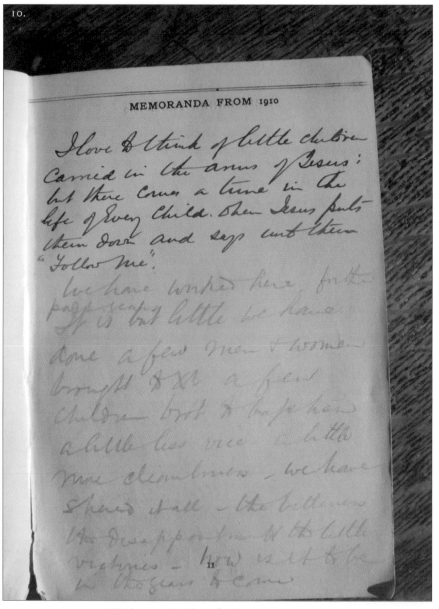

MEMORANDA FROM 1910

I love to think of little children
carried in the arms of Jesus;
but there comes a time in the
life of every child. When Jesus puts
them down and says unto them
"Follow me".

We have worked here for the
past years . . . but little we have
done a few men + women
brought to XT a few
children . . . but to hope how
a little less vice a little
more cleanliness . . . we have
shared it all — the bitterness
the disappointment the little
victories — How is it to be
in the ages to come

10. 'We have worked here for the past years . . .' (1911)

1. Strathy Parliamentary Church
2. Newmill Church
3. Old croft house and outbuilding, Strathy West

4. Strathy Bay
5. The Church of Scotland Manse, Strathy
6. Strathy Inn, School and Schoolhouse
7. The former Strathy U.F. (foreground) and Free Churches

as necessary. Additional meetings being called *pro re nata,* to deal with new or urgent particular business, those least affected by the business frequently did not attend. Presbytery met in the Church most relevant to the purpose of the meeting: if there was a vacancy in Eddrachillis, for example, then it met in Scourie, Eddrachillis's main settlement.

Apart from the two formal meetings for the year, Presbyteries were called by the Moderator or Clerk writing a letter to his colleagues to summon them. On receipt of such a letter, Mr Youngson might enter the meeting in his diary. 'Meeting of Pres. Farr, 10am' shows such an occasion, place and time for 22 February 1911. He did not, however, go on that occasion; the official Minutes of the Presbytery of Tongue do not suggest that he attended, and the Minute book with its neat writing and due form gives an appearance of accuracy.[15] Indeed the 1911 diary shows only three references to the Presbytery while the Minutes of the court record nine meetings. Of these nine, Alex Youngson was present only at those in March and November, the two regular occasions. During 1912 he was rather more active, being present at five of the ten meetings. The diary for Wednesday 3 January reads: 'Presb meeting Farr 10am, petition from Eddrachillis'; again, the minute of the meeting shows that Strathy's minister was not present when the Presbytery agreed to begin the process of appointing a new minister to Eddrachillis. He was present in March, however, and was chosen to moderate both that meeting and the subsequent ordination and induction of Rev. Alex Clark, from Markinch, Fife, to Eddrachillis, at which Mr Youngson preached on Psalm 103:1: 'Bless the Lord, O my soul'. Attending these meetings at Scourie meant an absence from Strathy covering three days.

March, 1912

Tuesday	26	*Left for Tongue 10am*
Wednesday	27	*Ordination at Eddrachillis 12noon*
		Officiated at ordination
		Retd to Tongue evening
Thursday	28	*Returned from Tongue*

Tongue was the parish of Rev. David Lundie MA, Clerk to the Presbytery, and no doubt Mr Youngson enjoyed the hospitality of the manse at Tongue on both the Tuesday and the Wednesday nights.

As far as the community and congregation of a parish were concerned, the annual round of Presbytery meetings can have meant little, apart, perhaps, from the temporary or longer absence of their minister. The jurisdiction of the Presbytery over its parishes, however, was in principle extensive and could have quite an impact on the lives of its ministers. Repairs to both church building and manse required the approval of Presbytery; so, too, did any absence from the parish beyond any normal holiday period. (Incidentally, none of Mr Youngson's four surviving diaries shows any absence on holiday at all – though some weeks were left blank.) So, for example, Rev. Dr George Henderson had been given permission to spend the last four winters of his ministry at Eddrachillis lecturing in Celtic at the University of Glasgow: the vacancy at Scourie in 1911–12 was due to his appointment to a permanent post at the University. During the World War, the ministers of Farr and of Eddrachillis were given leave of absence for war service. Such absences, of course, further reduced the number of ministers available for routine Presbytery business, besides placing Lay Missionaries or locum ministers in the affected pulpits. On 28 March 1917 when a Lay Missionary was appointed to caretake Farr, only two ministers arrived for the necessary meeting – which was hence inquorate. Alex Youngson was prevented from travelling to Farr by the weather but sent his consent by telegram, an ingenious but formally invalid gesture.[16] His attendance at Presbytery, never impressive, appears to have declined as the years went on: during 1915, he was present not at all.

Neither is there any evidence that Mr Youngson ever attended any of the committees of General Assembly to which the Presbytery appointed him. At that time, several of the central committees and boards of the Church of Scotland had a delegate from every Presbytery. In 1910, for example, Alex Youngson was appointed to three national committees: those on Foreign Mission, Colonial Mission and Small Livings – this last sought to raise ministers' stipends in some 270 parishes to a minimum of £200 p.a.[17] In 1914 he was appointed to the Committee anent Aged and Infirm Ministers, perhaps a pointed choice, as he was himself then in his seventy-third year. Attendance in Edinburgh would have been out of the question because of the time and distance involved, but such appointments would have brought agendas and minutes by post and hence news of a wider church. His diaries suggest that Mr Youngson shared some of this news with his congregation, inviting support by contributions and, no doubt, prayer. At this time, the central committees of the Kirk were supported financially as each congregation dedicated specific Sunday offerings to the projects of their choice; indeed, the General Assembly published a recommended rota to spread generosity evenly across what were known as the 'schemes' of the Church. In Strathy, the custom was to raise a Sunday offering for the schemes as a whole on the first Sunday in December and, when this was done, the sum raised was significantly larger than normal. 1 December 1912: 'Schemes collection – 5/3d'; 5 December 1915: 'Col for schemes – 5/6d'. In 1911, though, while Mr Youngson was associated with the central Mission committees, the entry reads: 'Collection for Missions – 7/6½d'. It is worth mentioning that in the Established Church the Sunday collection was additional to the minister's stipend unless otherwise directed and so normally went directly to his pockets, as Mr Youngson's cash accounts show. The other regular way of raising funds for the church was for designated collectors to pass a book around the community inviting subscriptions, and the Small Living Fund appears to have benefited in this way while Alex Youngson was associated with it: Friday 15 March 1912: 'Received from John Cooper £2 14s & sent off same to Glasgow, Smaller Livings Fund'.

Though it only indirectly affects Strathy, one story is worth telling from the minutes of the Presbytery of Tongue, for what it reveals of the conditions and social realities of the period. Early in his time at Strathy Alex Youngson obtained the necessary consents and grants for repairs to be undertaken, first to the church and then to his manse. In this, he was assisted by Strathy's proprietor, W. Ewing Gilmour Esq. This co-operation appears to have sparked some jealousy: for while Mr Gilmour had no formal duties to Strathy's Parliamentary church or manse, he did have responsibilities in the parish of Durness where he also held land. As the heritors of the parish, both the Duke of Sutherland and Mr Gilmour were legally required to maintain the fabric of the Established church and manse there. So (it appears) on hearing that Strathy's manse was to be improved and repaired with its proprietor's support, Rev. James D. Macdonald wrote in May 1913 to request Presbytery's intervention as he attempted to obtain similar work in Durness. He complained that his manse had as its water supply only collected run-off from the roof and he wanted piped water, a bathroom with a hot and cold supply and other repairs and alterations 'that it may conform to the standard of modern requirements, sanitary and otherwise . . . and to effect a few alterations to the internal fittings of the Church'. 'The sanitary condition of the manse is thoroughly bad. The walls also are damp and would require to be thoroughly overhauled and a part at least of the old portion of the manse would I fear require to be renovated', he wrote. It seemed that the Duke's Factor was willing to support the work, but Mr Gilmour's reply had not been satisfactory.

The Presbytery procrastinated, seeking advice from Edinburgh. It had authority in law to instruct the heritors to take action, and the civil courts could enforce such decisions; but in such a small Presbytery, both ministers and elders must have felt social and personal constraints against approving such compulsion against the Duke and a major landowner in the County. Alex Youngson's reluctance to challenge his benefactor can be imagined. By June, Mr Gilmour had volunteered to send tradesmen to the manse, while refusing to employ the architect needed for major alterations. The Presbytery ruled that the minister should deny the men entrance, as such work would be unauthorised. Next, the local Sanitary Inspector's report on the buildings, ruling the manse unfit, was sent to the heritors; as was (in 1914) a similar report by the County Medical Officer. By November 1913, Mr Gilmour had reluctantly agreed to the work, and plans were presented to the Presbytery in June 1914. By August 1915 there was agreement on the plans, but by then the country was at war. Many of the tradesmen had volunteered for the New Armies, and the price of building materials had risen. In consequence, and before work had started, Mr Gilmour refused to proceed and his agents suggested that, accepting that the manse was unfit for use, then perhaps an empty croft house in the area would suffice, temporarily? The Presbytery again sought the best legal advice open to them, that of the Procurator to the Church. On 22 June 1916 his advice was heard: he wrote that, despite the promises made previously, to compel the heritors to act would cause prejudice

against the church: 'every ounce of labour was required for
national purposes'. At such a time of national crisis, the Presbytery were advised, no sheriff in the civil courts would enforce a
judgment of Presbytery against the heritors. 'One may sym-
pathise', wrote the Procurator (from the comfort of his Edinburgh offices),

> with Mr Macdonald, though one may not quite approve of the
> language of his letter of 10th May, but even if he has to put up in a
> crofter's house, how much better is that than a dug-out in a
> trench, which is the only home that a war allows to thousands of
> as good men as he. War is war and we must put up with extra-
> ordinary conditions and it is vain to demand that there should be
> uniformity of inconvenience. Many burdens must just be allowed
> to rest where they light.

Presbytery thus agreed not to make an order against the heritors.
The work at Durness manse was not undertaken; and in spring
1917, Rev. James D. Macdonald left Durness for the parish of St
Oran's, Edinburgh, where perhaps he had the pleasure of making
the acquaintance of the Procurator in person.[18]

Social realities, indeed. The sad story of the Durness manse is a
reminder of the power of landed influence in early twentieth-
century Scotland, whatever the legal rights of a Presbytery of the
Church of Scotland. It is also a reminder that this was still a world
without piped water, without bathrooms, without flushing toilets, even in one of the larger homes of a parish. Half the Scottish
population lived in homes with no more than one or two rooms
according to the 1911 Census.[19] A manse roof was at least slated,
while (as we have seen) it was reported of Portskerra's homes in
1920: 'the buildings generally are of very poor description, being
small, drystone or clay built and roofed with straw thatch'.

If the Presbytery of Tongue played a minor part in the life of
both Alex Youngson and of his parish of Strathy, the Synod of
Caithness and Sutherland was even less relevant to daily life. At
that time, Synods met annually and reviewed the work of their
Presbyteries, coming between the Presbyteries and the General
Assembly in the hierarchy of courts. The Synod of Caithness
and Sutherland comprised the ministers of the Presbyteries of
Dornoch, Tongue and Caithness: over forty ministers in all with
an equal allowance for representative elders, had there been

sufficient willing to attend. In 1911 Mr Youngson was the only minister from his Presbytery who attended the Synod in Brora. In 1912 he was present when the Synod met in Thurso, one of only seven ministers attending out of a potential forty-two. Following an act of worship, business was entirely formal: inspection of Presbytery records; collating records of communicant membership and of attendance at Sabbath schools; totalling church collections and of other offerings.

It is illuminating to contrast the formal minutes of the Established Church with the account in the *Northern Times* of the meeting of the Synod of the United Free Church, held in Strathy on 12 April 1911: Rev. Ewen Fraser was Moderator of Synod that year.[20] The meeting heard a report from the Life and Work Committee of the Presbytery of Tongue: its tone was upbeat, reflecting a pervasive communal spirituality – or, at least, a pervasive religious observance, which is not necessarily the same thing. The Presbytery had had three vacancies in the last year, and all were filled. Its congregations (apart from one) now had buildings of their own to replace those retained under Act of Parliament by the Free Church. The 'means of grace' were well attended, especially Sabbath worship. Prayer meetings, too, were properly supported, as were joint district meetings. 'Family worship seems to be observed in most of the families so far as can be ascertained. The Sabbath is properly observed, at least outwardly, by young and old.' 'The morals of the community are good, and certainly compare favourably with the state of matters existing in former days.' The temperance movement was gaining ground. The visiting evangelists from the Faith Mission were doing good work. Sabbath Schools were well attended, with a good number of efficient teachers available; but the committee also wished to see the children attending congregational worship as well as Sabbath School. There was the regret that 'Each year, in increasing number, our young people leave us for the Colonies and the Capital and some of our large cities'. Even allowing for the difference in purpose between the formal minutes of the Established Church and the persuasive tone of a notice for the press, the UF Synod was engaging with the spirituality of its congregations and not merely handling business.

In the minutes of the Church of Scotland Synod of Sutherland and Caithness, the most obvious spiritual interest, beyond the various statistics, was the opening worship. Alex Youngson had been invited to preach at the 1912 Synod's act of worship, and he chose an appropriate text, Galatians 6:2: 'Bear ye one another's burdens'. Though, unfortunately, 'due to the inconvenient travelling facilities, there was an exceptionally small attendance of members',[21] the minute recorded the Synod's thanks for his 'able and helpful sermon'. Such thanks were, of course, as regular as the rest of the business, though when he preached in 1910 on Hebrews 2:10: 'For it became Him for whom are all things', the words of thanks 'for his thoughtful, appropriate and excellent sermon' do read a touch more warmly. Mr Youngson, however, sent his apologies to Synod in both 1915 and 1919; like those of the Presbytery, such meetings required absence from home over three days.[22]

April, 1912

Thursday	11	*Left for Thurso*
Friday	12	*Meeting of Synod 12 noon*
Saturday	13	*Ret'd from Thurso*

We, too, have been absent too long from Strathy on Presbytery and Synod business and need to return to yearly regularities of greater local import.

The Social Year

While Scotland's Reformed Church insisted on imposing its understanding of time largely on a weekly basis, emphasising each Sunday (apart from communion) as alike as the day for common prayers and preaching, the wider cultural patterns recognised for the year were more practical and social. But again, in a Highland culture in which the Christian faith played a leading part, no precise distinction should be made between the secular and the spiritual: even the communion season had its social aspects. Though the liturgical year was not observed and 25 December knew no special religious activity, as we have seen the annual day of thanksgiving for harvest brought the crofting communities to church, midweek. Harvest was of vital and practical importance – it determined levels of prosperity, perhaps even of survival. Harvest was also weather dependent, both as to timing and success. Without the means to transport large quantities of fresh and frozen food across continents, without local refrigeration, without preservatives beyond salt, the population looked to the near-at-hand land and sea for much of their diet and health. What humanity could not control, it was still easy to see the hand of God holding and withholding. Harvest Thanksgiving thus related to the world of work, in a way that 25 December totally failed to do.

With the working year determined by the patterns of the weather, the winter months of December, January, February and March provided time when people could get together socially. The regularities of life included a winter round of concerts and entertainments and, of course, the celebration of the turn of the year. The *Northern Times'* Halladale correspondent sent to the paper his account of New Year in the Strath, 1913. Perhaps a note of regret can be detected, with the 'quiet and orthodox' being equated (albeit at the remove of a long descriptive sentence) with the 'monotony of ordinary daily life':

Strathhalladale Entertainments

New Year's Day was ushered in in the usual quiet and orthodox way, many of the time serving customs of long ago have paid their last toll. Apart from the religious services held in the UF church during the day by Rev. Mr Findlayson, there were no public demonstrations, no banners furling in the breeze, no ostentatious revelry, no black bottle array, no pibroch sounding over the vale, no assemblies on the green to toss the caber, putt the stone or play the game of shinty. All was quiet and orderly and nothing beyond the monotony of ordinary daily life in the glen took place, except a few private gatherings late at night or rather early next day.[23]

Presbyterian social discipline has long been accused of being antipathetic to a more colourful Scottish heritage, and the article offers some support for this. Clearly the custom of first-footing survived, however, even when a sober moral tone was set by the special acts of worship promoted by the UF Church. And quite what was implied or concealed by the suggestion of the 'few private gatherings late at night'? In close Highland communities, what is not said can communicate as much as what is put into words.

Taken as a whole, however, the winter season was accepted as the time for a series of social gatherings, concerts and entertainments, held on a large scale; and these, too, were reported by the *Northern Times*. So the edition for 2 February 1911 reported the entertainment held at the public school of Dalhalvaig on 27 January, when the 'people of Halladale were ably assisted by artistes of high renown from the surrounding districts of Melvich and Portskerra'. A further such assembly was held in Portskerra itself on 16 March 1911 and was reported under the byline 'Concert & Dance at Portskerra'. The event was 'a brilliant assembly and enthusiastic proceedings, with entertainment of great excellence for a large and appreciative audience from surrounding districts' and was held in the Schoolroom. The committee had as its secretary Mr John Ross, son of James of Golval, 'who spared no efforts'. 'About 8.30pm Dr Macgregor, Armadale, who presided, entered the Hall amidst enthusiastic applause, and was accompanied on the platform by several ladies and gentlemen. The Chairman was greeted with a great ovation when rising to speak'. After these formalities, the programme included instrumental music, Gaelic recitations, songs and duets. A sobering note was struck by the purpose of the evening: to collect funds for the widow and orphans of the late Thomas Mackay, Armadale, who had died of heart disease on 13 January, aged fifty-four. Alex Youngson had noted his funeral: 'Funeral of Thos Mackay, Armadale 10am' [Monday 16 January 1911]. Amid the celebration and music was the possible destitution of a family.[24]

Public entertainments followed the same pattern as the benefit concert for the newly widowed Mary Ann Mackay née Macleod. There was a committee, a platform party of local notables and a chairman presiding as master of ceremonies for the evening. There were speeches beforehand and votes of thanks in conclusion. Very often the children of the community displayed their talents under the eye of their schoolmaster. The reports mention that 'after-assemblies' often followed such concerts – these were, simply, less formal dances often continuing to a late hour. Alex Youngson was delighted to be involved in the formal proceedings of public concerts. His 1911 diary shows references to three events in the winter months: a children's treat in January, a concert in Armadale on Friday 10 February and 'Concert at Strathy School', 24 March 1911. This last, the *Northern Times* reported in some detail:

Grand Concert & Dance at Strathy
A happy and enjoyable evening

Although Strathy Benefit Concert so happens to be the last on the roll of concerts in the parish of Farr for this season, it is by no means the least, as was fully evidenced on the evening of Friday last by the large and brilliant assembly which met in the Public School of the district, neatly and artistically decorated for the occasion. The day being fine and the roads being in good pedestrian order, it enabled many strangers to come from long distances to join in the evening's entertainment. The happy gathering was presided over by Rev. Mr Youngson, Church of Scotland, Strathy, who, on mounting the platform was received with great enthusiasm. In thanking the audience for the honour of calling on him to preside, he very briefly referred to the object of the concert, as being that of a benefit concert and in touching and pathetic terms, expressed his gratification at the hearty response given thereto. In submitting the programme for the night, he observed that the items largely consisted of vocal and instrumental music. He praised the young people of Strathy on their musical acquirements: and he also expressed the hope that they would long continue to take every opportunity of improving that talent. Music had an inspiring and charming influence, not only on nations and localities, but on individuals. It brightened and sweetened and cheered the life of every individual that intelligently took an interest in it. . . . The entertainment which followed was a most interesting one throughout, terminated with the usual votes of thanks. An after assembly was held, and largely patronised.[25]

Clearly Strathy's Established Kirk's minister had a place and acceptability in local society. His family, too, took part: his son Alex gave a recitation and Alice sang, though the 'crowning feature of the evening was the popular Gaelic songs beautifully rendered by Mr Donald Mackay (Strathy Point)'.[26] The people may not have attended Alex Youngson's church but they were happy to applaud him with enthusiasm at such a public occasion, recognising that by his presence in the chair he acknowledged a culture that others of his vocation sometimes denied. We may hope that Charles Maclean's description of Rev. John Mackay, Free Church missionary minister to St Kilda (1865–89) represented an extreme: dancing, all secular songs, traditional oral stories and even a draughts board were forbidden.[27] Neither did all ministers speak in such terms, which came close to the heart of Mr Youngson's ministry, of seeking to 'brighten and sweeten and cheer the life of every individual'. At the May 1911 meeting of the School Board for the parish of Farr, Strathy Free Church minister, Rev. Hector Macaulay, supported by his UF colleague, Rev. Ewen Fraser, successfully moved that dancing be prohibited in their public schools, though other Board members led by John Mackay, Chilsey, protested that the young people had (at that time) no other public buildings of sufficient size in which 'after-assemblies' might be held.[28]

One further report of a Strathy concert is of interest. The submission reached the *Northern Times* for its edition of 2 January 1919. Mr Youngson was again in the chair; the platform party also included his UF colleague, Rev. Neil Mackay, and people recognisable as leading members of their congregations:

Social Entertainment at Strathy
Pleasant and Enjoyable Proceedings

A very pleasant and enjoyable entertainment was held on a recent evening in the Public Hall Strathy, presided over by the Rev. Mr Youngson, Strathy. Promptly at the advertised time the doors of the hall were opened by courteous and competent janitors, and very soon after, the hall was well filled by an orderly audience. The Rev. Mr Youngson, who, on entering, was cordially received, was accompanied to the platform by the Rev. Mr Mackay, UFC Strathy, and Mr & Mrs Hector Mackay, Strathy School, Miss Robertson, Miss Youngson, Miss Sinclair, and Miss Lucy Gunn Baligill.[29]

The report continued with a précis of Mr Youngson's opening speech:

It was indeed a source of pleasure for him at all times to take part in any cause that had either the sacred, the social, or the intellectual good of the community at heart. (Cheers). The Public Hall procured by gifts of generous gentlemen of the neighbourhood was the object of these entertainments – and it was very soon to have a clean sheet. He then dwelt at some length on the charm, the influence and the grandeur of Highland music and Highland poetry. He deeply regretted he did not know the Gaelic language himself, but he was led to understand that Gaelic poetry contained the finest and the choicest of the genius of Highland sentiment . . . The music of the fountain and the rill, the echo of the mountain and the corrie, all contributing to the unspeakable inspiration of Highland sentiment, Highland poetry and Highland music. Needless to say that the Rev. Gentleman's remarks were very attentively listened to, much appreciated and loudly applauded.

The Vote of Thanks was proposed by Mr Mackay, UF manse, in eloquent and appreciative terms. . . . Mr John Mackay, Chilsey, moved the vote of thanks to the Committee under Mr Roderick Mackenzie, Strathy East. Mr Hugh Gunn, Inspector of Poor, Baligill, proposed the vote of thanks to the strangers.

Mr Youngson, in his thanks to the speakers, paid compliments to '. . . Mr & Mrs Mackay, Schoolhouse, Strathy, for their indefatigable energy always taken to get up a programme for any entertainment in the district (Prolonged cheers).' The evening ended with 'God Save the King'. The observer concluded his report by adding his own '. . . special mention of the graceful and efficient manner in which Miss Youngson acted as accompanist on the harmonium. Her gifted musical acquirements were much appreciated by the audience.'

As we read of an elderly minister 'speaking at some length' before the evening's entertainment can begin, we may perhaps raise an eyebrow of suspicion. But that Alex Youngson saw his participation in such an event as part of his ministry is not open to question. The schoolmaster turned minister had as his vocation the promotion of 'the sacred, the social, and the intellectual good of the community'; this was his goal as a minister of the Scottish Church. The success of his daughter, Miss Alice Youngson, as an accompanist on the harmonium meant that the evening was also a family occasion.

Before leaving the winter's 'social round' of concerts and entertainments, one diary entry needs particular attention. For Friday 13 January 1911, Mr Youngson wrote: 'Children's treat and Xmas Tree'. A Christmas tree – when we have insisted that the northern Highlands did not celebrate Christmas? While the churches of the north may not have followed the liturgical year, and while 25 December was not a Scottish public holiday, nevertheless the example of Prince Albert's royal Christmas trees had caught the public imagination. Children's treats during January were a well-established custom, in part for the closing of Sabbath School, and also as an element in the winter social round. However, 1912 in Portskerra and Melvich saw the addition of Santa Claus arriving to distribute gifts to children gathered around the tree. Once again, the *Northern Times* explains. The treat for that community was traditionally gifted by a benefactor, Mr Charles Swanson of Edinburgh, who also had a hand in the programme. Previously, 'tea and edibles were the predominant feature' of the entertainment, but

> ... the fête took the form of a Christmas Tree, a unique experience both to young and old of the district. This was the first occasion on which such a performance took place, and consequently the interest of the 'bairns' was excited to the highest degree. A tree laden with useful and costly gifts was got ready and many of the presents had to be given by hand which could not be accommodated on the tree. Mr Morrison [Manager of the Melvich Hotel] presided, and, after some songs by the schoolchildren, called upon Santa Claus to divest the tree of its contents. Each child received a gift.[30]

The rest of the evening included music and song, and a 'liberal supply of sweets', and the programme 'finished with Auld Lang Syne'. 'On leaving, each child was presented with an apple and an orange'. The programme was, in fact, very much like its predecessors: the Melvich/Portskerra treat in 1911 had included a hall lit by Chinese lanterns, a gramophone playing Gaelic and English music, parlour games, violin music, gifts of dolls for the girls and knives for the boys, a 'beauty competition' and crackers. When Mr Swanson had promised an 'even better treat next year', he clearly had had the tree and Santa in mind.[31]

Alex Youngson's diary shows a 'Christmas Tree' in Strathy in 1911 – we do not know, of course, whether that was the first for that local community or whether there had been earlier such 'Trees'. Neither do we know whether the innovations of 1911 and 1912 were repeated – though local treats in the 1980s were still called 'Christmas Trees', with Santa Claus costumes appearing in the village halls of the district. As Mr Youngson's diaries were personal documents, designed to help his own memory, he clearly had no doctrinal objection (such as some traditional presbyterians maintained through the twentieth century) to 'Christmas Trees', or else he would not have written the 1911 entry as he did. We may suspect that he had a soft spot for children and would welcome an opportunity to add to their pleasure. The 1915 diary, however, used the more neutral term 'Sabbath School treat' for Friday 22 January, and the cash-book contained in the diary for that year also shows that, on 21 January, he spent 3d. to buy the oranges needed for the treat.

Those who enjoyed the rights to hunting game on the hills and fishing salmon in the rivers had a social life that ticked to a different clock from the local communities: the arrival of gentry from the south for the hunting and fishing season was, in its way, also one of the regularities of life on the north coast. Thus in July 1919, the *Northern Times* reported 'Mr & Mrs Macandrew and party are at present residing on their Bighouse Estate and are obtaining excellent sport both on loch and river.'[32] Daily catches of up to fifteen trout on Lochs Strathy, Baligill, Ackron, on Loch na n-Eaglaise Beag, on Caol-Loch – Beinn Ruadh and others were reported in the Edinburgh papers, as was the shooting of grouse and snipe on the Melvich and Bighouse moors – ten brace of grouse represented an average day's shoot. The *John O' Groat Journal* reprinted from the *Sportsman's and Tourists' Guide* a list of who held which shootings in Caithness and Sutherland for the year: in 1912, Mr W. H. Fox was at Forsinard, Mr W. Ewing Gilmour at Armadale and Melvich, and Mr A. A. Delmege at Bighouse.[33] A. A. Delmege appears in Strathy's history like some exotic species of rare bird, blown in by the winds of the world. American citizens, he and his brother began their working lives with the steamships of the Mississippi, and made their fortunes running the blockade on the Southern States during the United States Civil War. Thereafter they left the USA and moved to Ceylon/Sri Lanka, then a British colony, creating a shipping and finance trading house that as Delmege Forsyth & Co. continues to this day.[34] A. A. Delmege was part of the international elite of his day, and his world was a universe away from that experienced by anyone living on Scotland's north coast – yet the success story that his life represented was part of the lure that attracted Highlanders to the United States and the Dominions.

W. Ewing Gilmour and his guests were based for the 'season' at Bowside, the hunting lodge for the Strathy Estate and run as part of Armadale Farm, with the permanent home for a gamekeeper near-by. Constructed of corrugated iron on a wooden frame, the lodge had eleven bedrooms and two public rooms, and so could accommodate a reasonable-sized, if perhaps spartan party.[35] So on 20 August 1911, Mr Youngson noted, 'Mrs Gilmour & family in Church'. The next year, the Gilmours appear to have visited their Strathy property later in the autumn: 7 October 1912, 'Dining with Mr Gilmour to 3pm'; 16 October 1912, 'Mr & Mrs Gilmour called to bid goodbye'.

In 1915 Strathy's lodge was let, but the minister went to call to greet 'the Bowside people'. An interesting set of transactions followed.

August, 1915			*Offering*
Thursday	5	*Visited Bowside*	
Sunday	8	*Bowside people in Church*	*13/5½d*
Monday	9	*Sent off B. currants to Bowside*	
Saturday	14	*Sent Black Currants to Bowside*	
Sunday	15	*Fine day Bowside people in Church*	*15/8½d*

The Parish Church was the obvious one for visiting gentry to attend, once they were reassured, by his visit, about the quality of the minister. It seems that conversation had turned to Alex Youngson's crops, and samples of blackcurrants found their way to the lodge. A haunch of venison travelled the reverse journey to the manse on 28 August. These courtesies were rewarding in another way, too. With the Bowside people in church, the offerings taken at Sunday's worship were markedly higher than usual: 13/5 ½d. and 15/8 ½d. in the first two Sundays in August as against a more normal weekly 1/6d. Those up for hunting and fishing were in a wholly different league of wealth from anyone normally resident in Strathy – 10s. notes might be *given away*. Offerings remained high throughout September 1915 until the first Sunday in October. Sunday 3 October saw 15/4d. collected: but on Sunday 10 October, only 1/5d.

Early twentieth-century Britain still knew a massive gulf of class distinctions, clearly demonstrated by the grouse, deer and salmon seasons in the north. The term 'society' tended to be

annexed to the wealthy, to the fashionable world into which
young ladies and gentlemen might be launched or 'come out'. The
accounts in the *Northern Times* of the winter season of concerts
in Strathy and district were designed, in their quiet way, to
subvert these assumptions. When he used such expressions as
'a brilliant assembly', the reporter from Strath Halladale was
modelling himself on court and county reporting of the doings of
people of much greater wealth. The parallel was even closer when
the paper published lists of people present at entertainments in
the Strathy Hall: 'Among those present we observed the following ladies and gentlemen: Mr & Mrs Angus Mackay, Strathy
West; Mr & Mrs John Munro, Strathy West; Misses Mackay,
Strathy West; Mr & Mrs Macdonald, Brawl. . . .' John Munro
and his wife lived in an 'old thatched cottage', with two rooms, a
closet and garrets.[36] Against the power of landed wealth there
was a democratic insistence that Bowside and Bighouse had no
prescriptive or exclusive right to assume the titles of 'ladies and
gentlemen'. Underneath the regularities of the social year were
tensions and grievances still to be resolved.

6

Service on the Public Bodies of the Civil Parish of Farr

The Parish Council

Of all the committees of which Rev. Alex Youngson was a member, the Parish Council for Farr and the local Pier Committee were those that he was most assiduous in attending; he was also successful in finding a place on the local School Board's successor, the Management Committee – though this took him longer. The Parish Council and the School Board were the means by which local people ran essential local services, having been elected to do so: care for the poor, health, education, and the public roads were all very local responsibilities. Looking back a century from these days of globalisation, the European Union and regulations from Brussels, the localness of local government before the First World War is astounding. In a civil parish such as Farr, covering Strathnaver, Bettyhill, Strathy, Portskerra, Melvich and Strath Halladale and with a population of some 2,500 in all, people knew each other well. Parish Councillors and members of the School Board lived next door, working in the open on their crofts, sharing in communal life, making their decisions in the public eye and unable to escape into anonymity if what they decided was unpopular. Public affairs, in consequence, could become heated with angry invective being exchanged both in person and in print. Local government could be responsive and knowledgeable government; it might also be petty and overbearing government.

A product of Gladstone's fourth Liberal Government, the Local Government Act of 1894 created parish councils; and, in line with the Liberal programme of extending grass-root democracy, it gave women householders the right both to vote for them and to serve on them. Regulated by the Local Government Board, parish councils raised their own local taxes, having power to adjust the local rates, a property tax. From this income they administered the Poor Law, employed the local Inspector of the Poor and made all the detailed decisions raised by individual applications for support. Because they employed a doctor as their Medical Officer, rural parish councils also in effect controlled medical provision for their area. Further, they had power to issue contracts to keep local roads and bridges in repair, and to maintain the local burial grounds. In the cash-poor society of the north coast, these contractual powers could give or withhold badly needed additional income. With its agenda dealing with delicate and sensitive personal matters, the Parish Council required discretion, fair play and a good ear to the ground if it was to be trusted and effective. This was still, of course, an authoritarian age: in looking at the Parish Council for Farr, we are looking at men exercising power. The right to vote was still restricted. Women did not in practice serve on these public bodies in the north: rather, they were often the dependants or needy about whom the decisions were made. Oral history suggests that some were unable to admit to neighbours that they needed help, preferring to starve.

When Alex Youngson first became minister of Strathy in 1909, Robert Robertson was Chairman of the Parish Council of Farr. Described either as Ground Officer or Land Steward, and resident in one of Melvich's larger houses (it had five rooms and seven acres), Mr Robertson held a responsible administrative position in the community. He was already aged seventy at the time of the 1901 Census, however, and must have relied heavily on the local knowledge of the Inspector of Poor and Clerk to the Council throughout this period, Hugh Gunn of Baligill. Aged forty-three and described as a mason and a widower in 1901, Mr Gunn had married again: Ewen Fraser baptised his son Angus in January 1911.[1] By 1915, Hugh Gunn's salary for his duties for the Parish Council was the not insignificant £76 a year, including expenses.[2] He also, of course, held a croft in Baligill (with eleven acres and a five-room slated house[3]) and had sufficient resources by 1896 to take a third share in tenanting the Duke of Sutherland's sheep farm of Kirkton, Melvich, with Hugh James Gunn and Murdo Macdonald, both also of Baligill.[4] Farmer, crofter and administrator, Hugh Gunn was a man of stature in the community and Treasurer of the United Free Church.

In 1909, 100 women and men were in receipt of poor relief in the east ward of Farr, between Armadale and Forsinard, out of a population of about 1,500.[5]

Admitted To Relief	Total	Women	Men
Armadale, Poulouriscaig and Lednagullen	12	10	2
Aultiphurst and Brawl	6	4	2
Strathy Point	16	13	3
Strathy	20	17	3
Portskerra	20	14	6
Melvich including Bighouse and Lower Bighouse	18	16	2
Halladale	8	5	3
	100	*79*	*21*

Significantly more women than men required assistance: roughly four times as many. Women, with few opportunities of employment, and particularly if unmarried or widowed, occupied an economically precarious position in this society. On assessment by the Inspector of Poor and if necessary also by the Medical Officer, applicants for support might be awarded a weekly income according to need: this ranged between 1/6d. and 3/6d. in 1912. In addition, and when personal circumstances required it, the Council provided clothing, blankets, shoes, slippers and flannel by entering into contracts with the local merchants. In 1910, these contracts were given on a specified district basis to the stores at Dalhalvaig and Baligill, to John Traill in Strathy and to Bettyhill. Further, fuel might be provided by giving contracts to neighbours to cut peat for those unable to do the work themselves: 12s. was allowed per 100 yards of peat bank, and both those who cut and those who received benefited. The Parish Council controlled a number of homes in the area, and these were let at £1 a year to those in need.[6] Finally, at death, the Parish Council paid for the coffin and burial of paupers, and attempted to reclaim its expenses by selling what household goods remained.

The Parish Council exercised an element of social control, both over those it admitted to support and more generally. In 1919 the Council officially called the attention of the local Police Constable to the fact that: '. . . large bands of young people congregate on the footbridge at Bighouse and cause damage to the structure by swinging and jumping to the detriment of said bridge.'[7] There are occasions in the minutes when neighbours complain to the Council about the behaviour of people supported by the parish. In November 1915, for example, Farr Parish Council issued an official warning not to be a nuisance, having heard that one of its annuitants was keeping a terrier dog that was disturbing sheep, and that she was also 'harbouring tinkers about the place'.[8] As we have said, this was an authoritarian age. A further case in 1915 concerned complaints about two elderly ladies who were in receipt of both medical and nursing care, and were unable to arrange for their sheep to be properly dipped. Noting that they had no friends able to undertake this for them, the Parish Council instructed that the sheep should be sold and the proceeds applied 'for the comfort of the parties'.[9] When old (or even young) people were beyond caring for themselves, perhaps due to a stroke, dementia or advanced age, the final sanction available to the Parish Council, on medical advice, was to declare them lunatic and to have them removed to an appropriate institution or asylum: in 1915, some twenty 'lunatics' or 'mental defectives' were in private homes throughout the civil parish of Farr, and nine had been removed to asylums.[10]

In December 1910 new elections were held for the Parish Council of Farr and the following were declared elected:

> Mr Donald Henderson, farmer, Armadale
> Mr Hugh Macdonald, crofter, Calgary Beg
> Mr Robert Macdonald, crofter, Achina
> Mr Donald Mackay, merchant, Bettyhill
> Mr James Mackay, cottar, Kirtomy
> Mr Hugh Mackenzie, farmer, Syre
> Mr Angus Morrison, hotel keeper, Melvich
> Mr Thomas Munro, crofter, Newlands
> Mr Donald Sinclair, crofter, Portskerra
> Rev. Alexander Youngson, minister, Strathy
> Mr Hugh Mackay, crofter, Trantlemore[11]

Very early in his ministry in Strathy, Alex Youngson thus joined the Parish Council. He was to retain his seat until he decided not to seek re-election in 1925. Indeed, even in 1910 he was nominated by Donald Henderson and Angus Morrison to chair the new Council, but unsuccessfully: Hugh Macdonald gained the majority vote. Alex Youngson and Donald Henderson, however, as the local members for Strathy and Armadale, were asked to work together on a number of occasions. The new Council delegated to them to inspect the state of the roads to Aultiphurst and Baligill before payments were made to the local contractors; they were also asked to report on the state of the Strathy burial ground.[12]

In May 1911 Alex Youngson and Donald Henderson were instructed to confer with Mr Gilmour, Strathy's proprietor, on the 'desirableness of finishing the road to Poulouriscaig as requested by a deputation of residents'.[13] Poulouriscaig was at that time a small settlement of three crofts in the hills to the west of Armadale; a road joining the communities had been a concern of the Council since 1903, when an application to the Congested Districts Board for a grant for construction was turned down. With the support of Mr Gilmour and the Parish Council, however, a start had been made. By 1911, concerns were growing that those holding the contract to do the work were treating their payments as a form of relief – and the road showed no signs of being finished. In August it was reported that Mr Gilmour had agreed to give £20 towards completion on condition that the Council matched his grant and that no further appeal for funds was made, and the Council agreed to this.[14] The next year, attention turned back to the existing roads to Baligill and Aultiphurst, maintained at the expense of the Parish Council. Here, the ambition was to have the roads adopted and their expense transferred to the Sutherland County Council. In February 1912, the County Roads Board heard the report of their Surveyor: he considered neither was up to standard. With Angus Morrison as the Melvich representative on the Board, a vote was carried to postpone a decision rather than not to adopt; and the Parish Council then issued a new contract for repair, again delegating to Alex Youngson and Donald Henderson to see that the work was in fact completed to the desired standard.[15] Such duties of Parish Councillors required both tactfulness and honesty. On one occasion Mr Youngson had to report that the contractor for maintaining the Strathy burial ground had failed to cut the grass. The man concerned was one of those who sometimes undertook work for the manse. An official letter of warning resulted.[16]

The responsibilities of the Parish Council as employer of the local doctor caused occasional anxiety. The doctor was officially employed as Medical Officer to the Council, responsible to it for duties under the Poor Law, Lunacy and Vaccination Acts. A house was provided in Armadale; and such fees as any private practice might bring were allowed. Indeed, all medical care (except to those admitted to relief) was available only for payment. Because of the small population of the area and its relative poverty, recruitment of doctors was only possible before 1913 because of the Parish Council salary – though the fact that this was guaranteed meant that posts sometimes attracted several applicants. Retaining the doctor, however, was harder: if an opening arose in a bigger and richer practice, then he was away.

A Thurso doctor, Dr Asher, held the contract before Alex Youngson joined the Council in 1910; but there were complaints that he did not base himself, as expected, in Armadale. In April of that year, Dr Asher offered the services of a resident locum, Dr Macgregor. By August Dr Asher had resigned and Dr Macgregor was appointed as interim Medical Officer, while the post was advertised at a annual salary of £194 for duties under the Poor Law Acts with a further £5 for duties under the Lunacy Act and £1 a year as public vaccinator, with a house and garden. As the only applicant, Dr Macgregor was quickly offered the post at £200 a year. The Council then asked 'as to the Medical Officer's ability to successfully overtake the work over such a wide area on his bicycle, and the Council resolved to offer Dr Macgregor an increase of £50 pa to his salary in advance to assist him to procure a motor car and its upkeep.'[17] Today, it almost beggars belief that a single doctor was expected to service the entire area of Strathnaver, Strathy and Strath Halladale on a bicycle without assistance and, moreover, had to approach the Parish Council to be allowed holidays away from his post. Further requests from the doctor saw the road to the house in Armadale being repaired at the Council's expense and a plumber instructed to install a hot water system in his house. By September 1911, however,

Dr Macgregor submitted his resignation and indicated that a Dr Silver would be his locum for his forthcoming holiday. Although fourteen doctors responded to the subsequent advertisement, Alex Youngson and Donald Mackay successfully moved that Dr Silver be appointed.[18]

Alex Youngson's handling of business was such that by 1915 he was asked on occasion to chair the Parish Council of Farr in the absence of Hugh Macdonald. These absences appear to have been increasing, though the Halladale crofter was only aged about fifty-one (he had been thirty-seven in 1901). December 1919 saw new elections to the Council and the results for the successful candidates in the east section of the parish were:[19]

Rev. Alexander Youngson, minister, Strathy	101 votes
James Munro, crofter, Strathy West	80
Donald Murray, merchant, Dalhalvaig	78
Sutherland Mackay, shepherd, Bighouse	69
Hugh Mackay, Dyke	65
John Mackay, Chilsey	63

A further three candidates were unsuccessful, so to top the poll was an achievement that must have brought pleasure to the manse. Alex Youngson had earlier been appointed by the old Council to represent it on the new School Management Committee for the parish. Now, on the motion of John Mackay, Chilsey, he was unanimously appointed Chairman of the Parish Council for Farr. John Chilsey explained: 'The Rev. Mr Youngson was a learned gentleman, and one who had considerable experience of public work, both in this parish and elsewhere, and his acquaintance with him in deliberating on public matters, was that he always did so with a calm and judicious spirit of justice and fair play.'[20] Besides, John Chilsey continued, their Chairman needed to be convenient to Baligill to liaise effectively with Hugh Gunn, the Inspector of Poor and Clerk to the Council, who wrote the letters, ran the administration and actually did the work. Alex Youngson served as Chairman until 1925.

It is notable that, while ministers of religion frequently served on school boards and committees in the Highlands, Mr Youngson was the only minister to be elected over many years to the

Parish Council of Farr. His diaries certainly show that this work
was a key priority of his. Checking the dates of meetings in the
minute books against his diaries, 'Meeting of Parish Council,
11am' shows that only on one occasion in the whole of 1911,
1912, 1915 and 1919 did he miss a meeting – he had flu in the
spring of 1919 and was in bed on Tuesday 1 April. Each year
there were seven or so meetings. Perhaps he viewed the work as
continuing the traditional Established Church ministry of offering support to the poor. Poor relief had been the legal responsibility of the Kirk Sessions of the Church of Scotland until the
Poor Law Amendment (Scotland) Act of 1845 and, although the
legal structures changed, the vocational duty of care continued.
Certainly the 1919 testimony to his work, that it was always
performed 'with a calm and judicious spirit of justice and fair
play' was one any Christian minister would be pleased to receive.
From the point of view of the parishioners, it was crucial that they
could have a confidence that essential local affairs, the issuing of
contracts and the granting of poor relief, were indeed handled
fairly, and that sectional, family or sectarian interests were not
improperly favoured. As between the different townships that
comprised such a scattered parish as Farr, suspicion of favourit-
ism could easily arise.

The School Board

If Mr Youngson found a place for himself in the Parish Council, it
was his Free and United Free colleagues who were elected to the
School Board for Farr. With the same area of jurisdiction as the
Parish Council, the School Board controlled all the public schools
in the civil parish of Farr: Skelpick, Farr and Kirtomy; Armadale,
Strathy and Melvich; Dalhalvaig and Forsinard, besides the side-
schools needed from time to time by yet smaller communities.
Regulated by the Scotch Education Department, the boards
recruited and employed the teachers, determined their salaries
and maintained the properties of the schools. As with the Parish
Councillors, their members were directly elected. Through education there was hope that the children of the area might obtain
wider opportunities than their parents had had. There was much
interest in these elections, as the following table of candidates and
votes shows.[21]

April 1909	April 1911		April 1914	
John Morrison, Factor, Tongue 180	Rev. Ewen Fraser, Strathy	294	Mr John Morrison, Tongue	258
Rev. Ewen Fraser, UF minister, Baligill 174	Mr Thos Munro, Newlands	258	Mr Thomas Munro, Newlands	253
Rev. George Mackay, UF minister, Altnaharra 164	Mr John Morrison, Tongue	245	Mr John Mackay, Chilsey	226
Rev. D. Carmichael, Parish minister, Farr 138	Mr Donald Mackay, Bettyhill	180	Rev. H. Macaulay, Strathy	202
Mr Hugh Mackay, crofter, Trantlemore 112	Mr John Macbeath, Bighouse	176	Mr Donald Mackay, Bettyhill	199
Mr John Mackay, crofter, Chilsey 112	Mr John Mackay, Chilsey	174	Mr Robert Mackay, Achneisgich	197
Rev. Alex Macleod, UF minister, Rhianchatail 86	Rev. H. Macaulay, Strathy	170	Mr John Munro, Strathy	197
Unsuccessful	*Unsuccessful*		*Unsuccessful*	
Mr George Mackenzie, crofter, Croick 69	Mr Robert Mackay, Achneisgich	165	Rev. A. Youngson, Strathy	165
Mr Alex Fraser Mackay, crofter, Craigton 24	Rev. Alex Youngson, Strathy	156	Mr James Murray, Forsinard	159
Mr Donald Mackay, Portskerra 12	Rev. H. G. Maclennan, Skerray	134	Rev. Neil Mackay, Strathy	139
	Mr George Macintyre, Altnaharra	68	Mr Angus Morrison, Melvich	124
	Mrs Alexa Kiddie	66	Mr John Macbeath, Bighouse	91
	Rev. M. Mackinnon	40		
	Mr Hugh Mackenzie, Syre	37		

A number of the candidates were, of course, active in other areas of public life: John Mackay, Chilsey; Angus Morrison, Melvich. Ewen Fraser was elected Chairman of the Board in 1909, but in a contested vote he was replaced by Colonel John Morrison in 1911. The Tongue Factor was himself replaced in 1914 by John Munro of Strathy West after a further contest, and these changes should be seen as an indication of the public interest in the Board. The School Board, even more than the Parish Council, attracted the public figures of the area to what was a popularity contest: all candidates at these elections stood as independent of political parties or programmes.

The role of ministers was significant, with first Ewen Fraser of Strathy UF Church and then Hector Macaulay of Strathy Free Church attracting considerable support. It is interesting to see that Ewen Fraser's successor, Neil Mackay, did not inherit Mr Fraser's vote, and that Alex Youngson was unable to secure election. Four of the seven successful Board members in 1909, nevertheless, were ministers. With this sort of popular support for a religious input to public education it is hardly surprising that, as we have seen, schools in Farr continued with a doctrinal and biblical syllabus, inspected by ministers, when education elsewhere in Scotland was becoming more secular.

The School Board habitually met in public and its affairs were not without controversy. Discussions could continue over six hours, with 'wrangling galore', as for example when an attempt was made to cut the salary of the Farr schoolmaster by £10 a year to make economies for the benefit of the ratepayers.[22] On 9 January 1919 the *Northern Times* reported on a meeting of the Farr School Board, held at Strathy Inn. It was

> . . . one of the stormiest on record, violent scenes being created, it is stated, through the action of two Strathhalladale public men, and at which it is alleged the choicest of Billingsgate was used. Were it not, so the story goes, for the intervention of a clergyman member of the Board the affray would have led to more serious results. The scandalous affair has created intense speculation, throughout the whole parish, and many rejoice in the knowledge that the School Board affairs of this parish will soon pass to other hands.

The next week, the paper carried a letter from 'a Halladale man' rejecting the 'hysterical outburst of frightful misrepresentations'.[23] No names were printed – but, of course, everyone would know who had said what. Education for the community's children was taken very seriously: teachers were usually held in high regard, and where children and educational issues were at stake, passions could be raised.

We have already mentioned the dismissal of the Strathy headmaster, John M. Gunn, by the School Board for Farr. This controversy ran in stages between 1914 and 1916 and must have caused much grief. In November 1914 the complaining parents, Mrs Macintosh and Mr John Campbell, both of Strathy Point, came in person to give evidence. Mrs Macintosh spoke in Gaelic:

> Mrs Macintosh in her evidence given in Gaelic, stated that her boy wasn't strong, and she gave a detailed statement of the injuries inflicted on him by Mr Gunn, by hitting him with a stick on the hands, head, and other parts of the body. Mr Campbell complained his statement given at former meeting that his child was badly bruised by Mr Gunn and in consequence afraid to go to school. He only wanted justice from the Board, and justice he would have.[24]

On hearing this evidence, the Board (after a vote) agreed to ask the headmaster to hand in his resignation – the implication being that it would lie on the table, to be activated and accepted if matters did not improve. 'Mrs Macintosh remarked that no matter what pledges Mr Gunn gave she would refuse to send her boy to school.' Only at this stage was the headmaster was called in

> . . . and the Clerk read to him the Board's decision. For order to take his evidence the case was reopened. His statements were mostly in contradiction of those made by his accusers. He denied there were marks or bruises on Mr Campbell's boy and as for Mrs Macintosh there was not a word of truth in her allegations. Mr John Mackay asked Mr Gunn if it were true that he went fishing during school hours. Mr Gunn said he challenged the statement.

In retrospect, the Board had followed a dubious procedure and had breached what we would now consider to be Mr Gunn's legal rights in coming to a decision before they had even heard his side of the case. That the Tongue Factor, Colonel Morrison, was party to this shows just how heated and difficult matters were, and how the sympathies of the elected members were on the side of the local parents. Nevertheless the Board again voted to require a written resignation from the headmaster, and continued to press for this into 1915. Free Church minister, Rev. Hector Macaulay, advocated leniency but stated he could not vote against the majority. The minutes do not make it clear how

Mr Gunn was able to retain his post – perhaps he simply called their bluff, perceiving that the Board had not determined to dismiss him.

The next stage of the dispute came when Mr Gunn brought allegations against his infant mistress, Miss Marion Mackay, herself a respected member of local society. The Board agreed that its Chairman and Mr Macaulay should investigate and that both parties should be present at the next meeting. John Mackay, Chilsey, now moved that that meeting be open to the public – to which the Chairman replied that all their meetings were open and it was agreed that if a special meeting was called, then it would be intimated in the district to give the public an opportunity to attend. It thus seems likely that the previous meetings in this sad story were also attended by the public. Though she chose to accept another appointment, Miss Mackay was in due course cleared by the inquiry: the Schools' Inspector's reports on her classes had always been favourable.

Finally Mr Gunn was dismissed after further reports from the Schools' Inspector established that the Strathy School register had been incorrectly and inaccurately kept, due to the Headmaster's unauthorised absences. On the one side, allegations of unduly forceful punishment amounting to assault and of unprofessional behaviour; on the other the likelihood of the unbearable stress of running a school for a tiny, increasingly hostile, community and the possibility of depression – and the action that was taken, was taken on the grounds of incorrect paperwork.

Public interest in these matters continued to run high. Once Mr Gunn had left and his new deputy, Miss Mary Munro, was appointed head at Strathy, a further protest came from local residents.[25] A petition was presented in January 1917 to the Board from fifteen residents of the Strathy School area, 'of which twelve are parents with children at the school, urging the necessity of appointing a headmaster for Strathy School, if disastrous results were to be avoided.' Once again, we are made aware that this was a male-dominated society: head teachers were expected to be men. The School Board allowed the petition to lie on the table, asserting that Miss Munro had been appointed for the duration of the war only – a clause that was literally inserted between the lines in the written minute of her appointment. Not surprisingly, Miss Munro left Strathy during 1917 and a headmaster was appointed, Hector Mackay from Skeld Schoolhouse,

Raewick, Shetland, a personal acquaintance recommended by the Board's Chairman.

In 1919, however, a new Education Act reformed the administration of education in Scotland, creating countywide Education Authorities comprising one elected member per parish to have responsibility for the recruitment, salaries, transfer and dismissal of teachers. Elections – in those enlightened times – were conducted by proportional representation via a single transferable vote.[26] The reform was opposed by many in Sutherland who regretted the loss of local control over their teachers: 'very few (with the exception of a few feather-headed teachers and the invective-croakers of society) rejoice . . . It is doubtful whether the new system will afford any greater measure of relief to the claptrap of the aforementioned critics.'[27] Some local powers remained. Below the Authorities, new nominated School Management Committees for each parish, with a substantial number of parent representatives, continued to look after such matters as building repairs.

Once the new Authority had decided on the composition of the local bodies, the new Management Committee for Farr met at Strathy and was reported in the *Northern Times:*

> The day was an ideal summer day: pleasant and warm, with vegetation of all kinds presenting a refreshing appearance after the recent moistening showers. Nature, in its mantle of green adorning hill and plain, lent a fascinating charm to the scene of admiration while the mighty Atlantic Ocean, overlooking the hamlets of the surrounding coast, conveying its ships of merchandise to and fro through the Pentland Firth, looked peaceful and calm, gently lapping its waves incessantly round its rock-bound shores or rolling them softly on the golden sands of Strathy.[28]

More practically, the article also gave the list of members nominated to the committee:

> Mr Hugh Mackay, Trantlemore, from the new Education Authority
> Mr John Mackay, Chilsey, from the old School Board
> Mr Thomas Munro, Newlands, from the old School Board
> Rev. Mr Youngson MA, Parish Church, Strathy, from the Parish Council

Mrs Calderwood, Kirtomy, teachers' representative
Mr Macintosh, Melvich, teachers' representative
Mr D. Murray, Dalhalvaig, parents' representative
Mr M. Mackay, Portskerra, parents' representative
Mr J. Loutitt, Strathy Point, parents' representative
Mr N. Mackay, Armadale, parents' representative
Mr N. Mackay, Bettyhill, parents' representative
Mr D. J. Mackay, Strathnaver, parents' representative
Mr Peter Spence, Halladale, Clerk

Mr Youngson was unanimously elected to chair the new School Management Committee. After the turmoil of the former School Board, his 'calm and judicious spirit of justice and fair play' would no doubt have been appreciated. Behind his brief (and technically incorrect) diary entry for 5 June 1919, 'Meeting of School Board', lay a lot of passion and local history. In the close communal life of the north coast, once public feeling was ignited the pressure placed on local representatives could be considerable. The Established Kirk's minister, however, had the luxury of some detachment and independence. Unlike his professional colleagues, the doctor and the schoolmaster, he was not employed by bodies responsive to local opinion. External sources guaranteed his stipend for life, so even a small church attendance and poor Sunday offerings did not threaten his financial position. Even so, if he had been a member of the School Board 1914–16, Alex Youngson might have found it difficult to cope with the crisis, which set two families of his small congregation, the Campbells of Strathy Point and the Gunns of the Schoolhouse, against each other.

The Strathy Pier Committee, Sutherland County Council and the Congested Districts Board

Beyond the civil parish of Farr was the authority of Sutherland County Council and, yet more remote, the imperial government's minister, the Secretary for Scotland, with his civil servants in both London and Edinburgh. Permissions and grants were available from these more remote levels of government, and both worked closely with the Congested Districts Board (1897–1912) and its successor, the Board of Agriculture for Scotland. The interaction of these various bodies is well illustrated by the story of the

Strathy Point Pier Committee, whose secretaries were successive ministers of Strathy's Kirk. First, however, some account needs to be given of the Congested Districts Board [CDB].

The history of the Highlands of Scotland in the nineteenth century was, at least in part, a history of conflict over land. Despite the granting of heritable tenancies and regulated rents by the 1886 Crofters Holdings Act, the population had not forgotten the Clearances nor had the cottars given up their claim to land. In response both to land raids and to public concern, and following the example of a precedent in Ireland, the Highland Congested Districts Board was established in 1897 with three particular remits: to encourage local economic development, to improve farming techniques and to acquire land on which to settle the landless. In this last and crucial task its success was considerably restricted by its limited budget and by the fact that it had no power of compulsory purchase. Nevertheless James Hunter, historian of the crofting communities, believes the CDB laid the foundations necessary for crofting to survive and, indeed, to thrive, through the twentieth century.[29]

When Alex Youngson grew turnips and other vegetables, and when he attended a lecture on potato cultivation given by an expert from Aberdeen, he was well in line with the official development policies promoted by the CDB.

Halladale Notes by Rusticus

Severe frost characterised the weather during the whole of last week, bare pastures being iced over to an extent that made the movement of stock dangerous. The uplands are heavily coated with snow and hill stock have to be hand fed. Last week, the monotony which at this season of the year hangs over the district like a pall, was enlivened with a lecture by Mr Macleod, of the Aberdeen College of Agriculture. Mr Macleod dealt with his subject – the potato crop – with more exclusive reference to the principles which govern the proper cultivation of the soil, seeding, manuring, storage, and last but not least, potato diseases, their prevention and remedies.[30]

For Thursday 25 January 1912, Alex Youngson noted: 'Lecture on Agriculture, 7.30pm'. Promotion of good practice had also been the objective of the Crofters' Show in Melvich in 1911, sponsored by both the Duke of Sutherland and the CDB. 'Besides livestock, exhibits to include home industries, dairy and poultry produce, poultry etc.'[31] The *Northern Times* and other local papers also published standard weekly articles on 'Poultry for all', on how to maximise income from hens.

Under its remit to encourage local economic development, the CDB gave grants towards roads, bridges, piers and slipways. Numerous files are still retained in the National Archives of Scotland containing letters to the CDB from Hugh Gunn of Baligill as Clerk to the Parish Council for Farr requesting grants for the construction of roads in Baligill (1901–04); for the extension of a road from Achridigill (Melvich) to the Kirkton Burial Ground (1910–11); for the construction of various peat roads.[32] Support to build or maintain public roads between settlements, however, was a different matter from making peat roads – as only existing tenants of an estate (and not the general public) had the right to cut peats on that estate. When the Duke of Sutherland sold Strathy to Mr Gilmour, Portskerra was cut off from its former peat banks. Portskerra crofters, still being tenants of the Duke, were refused permission to continue to cut on land now no longer part of the Sutherland Estates. The CDB, December 1901, despite the urgency claimed for the situation . . .

> . . . the new roads would have to be made and completed by the month of June at latest, otherwise it will be a serious matter for us, as the only way of procuring fuel is by constructing roads to the peat grounds without which the mosses are quite inaccessible in regard to vehicular traffic.

. . . turned down a request for a grant for a road to new peat banks, partly because no details of length or cost were given in the request, and partly because there were questions of law to be settled first.[33] Ten years later the Parish Council of Farr asked the Clerk to the County Council for legal advice to clarify whether it might fund new peat roads, and Golspie solicitor Mr Argo returned a reply 'considered favourable by some and unfavourable by others'.[34] The CDB's varying responses to requests for help must also have had an oracular character, their replies sometimes favourable, sometimes not.

On 13 January 1902, Alex Youngson's predecessor, Rev. Angus Macpherson, forwarded to the CDB correspondence requesting its assistance for a landing slip for Strathy Point.[35] Mr Macpherson added that 'It is supposed that between £300 and £400 would be required to rectify matters and make the creek fairly safe.' He believed that some thirty householders had promised £1 each and 'they hope the Board will be graciously pleased to consider favourably their appeal'. In the archived file is a copy of a letter drafted by the Clerk of the Board, instructing that the request should first go to the County Council, together with all the information required under statute, and that the County must also guarantee future upkeep. Also in the file is a comment by a Board member [initialled 'AS'] to the effect that he supposed costs would quickly grow to beyond £1,000: 'I know the place very well; and the impression I have is that nothing of any service could be done there unless at a very great cost indeed, the coast being very much exposed to the principal storm point. The number of boats in Strathy Point as per official return is 5, all under 18 feet keel.' The seven members of the CDB were the chairmen of the Crofters Commission, the Fisheries and the Local Government boards, a further two men nominated by the Secretary for Scotland, the Secretary himself and his Under-Secretary. With this response on the files, however, it is hardly surprising that the 1902 initiative came to nothing – the coast was apparently considered too exposed and dangerous for the expense to be worthwhile!

Next came a petition signed by twenty-three Strathy Point householders forwarded via the Member of Parliament and received by the Secretary for Scotland on 21 February 1907:

We the undersigned inhabitants of Strathy Point and district would beg to draw your attention to the necessity of a boat slip at a place locally known as Port Grant, Strathy Point.

The fact of there being six boats and thirty men now engaged fishing for Cod, Haddocks, Flounders and Lobsters during the year should be of sufficient importance to prove the necessity of such a landing place as would prevent any risk to life or property when at present there only exists a beach.

The situation of the place is very favourable to the construction of a landing slip and would not entail a great cost.

We also undertake to assist in forwarding such a scheme as would meet our requirements.

Trusting that you will endeavour to promote our interest in this matter,

Your obedient servants . . .[36]

This petition met the same fate as the 1902 letter: no action could be taken; they should write first to the County Council. What was needed was not just a letter writer but an administrator and facilitator to draw together the strands needed to get the consent and the funds for the landing slip. As it happened, Alex Youngson had had experience at Stroma of the successful campaign there to build a pier.

Mr Youngson's diaries contain lists of the ad hoc Pier Committee through which the Strathy Point project was managed at a local level; and the occasional meetings of the Committee were also noted in his daily entries.

The Pier Committee: 1911 and 1912
Donald Macdonald
Hector Macdonald
Donald Mackay E
Hugh Mackay Gow Snr
John E. Mackay
John Ross
William Mackay, Millburn
Alex F. Mackay, Redburn
Alex Mackay Cooper

The diaries also contained the crew lists for the small boats sailing from Strathy Point; clearly the Pier Committee contained senior members of these crews.

Boats and Crews Strathy Point (1911)

Lady	John Cooper, John Mackay Piper, Donald Mackay (son), Neil Mackay, Hugh Mackay (Brawl), and William Mackay, Millburn
Morning Star	Donald Macdonald, John Macintosh, John Campbell, Hector Macdonald, John Macdonald, Donald Macleod
Royal George	John Ross, Hugh Mackay, Hugh William Mackay, Charles Loutitt, Angus Cooper, Robert Mackay

Busy Bee	John E. Mackay, John Mackay, Hugh Macleod, Sandy Cooper, Hugh Macintosh, Donald Mackay E.
Vine	Robert Sutherland, Alex F. Mackay, Murdoch Mackay (Sandy's son), George Mackay (Millburn), William John (son of Hugh), George Blank

It can be seen that thirty men were, indeed, active as fishermen as the letter of 1907 asserted; the number of their boats, however, appears to have been five and not six.

In April 1910, the Parish Council of Farr formally approved the petition for a Strathy Point boat slip and wrote to both the CDB and the County Council to confirm this: the Parish Council, seeking to appease another of its component communities, added that a boat slip at Portskerra was also desirable.[37] By December 1910 the Port Grant project was under way. Sutherland County Council was in correspondence with the CDB, which was provisionally offering a grant of £395. Mr Gilmour, as owner of the site identified for the pier at Port Grant, had offered it as a free gift during discussions at the County Council – naturally, he was a Councillor. At its meeting of July 1911, Sutherland County Council gave the final approval and ordered the construction of the pier, having received consent to the plans from both the Board of Trade and the Secretary for Scotland, a grant of £423 (three-quarters of the approved estimate) from the CDB, a written gift of the site from Mr Gilmour, and a payment of £190 from Strathy towards the balance of cost (£65 raised locally, £100 from Mr Gilmour and £25 from Lord Stafford).[38] Alex Youngson's diary confirmed the details.

May, 1911

Monday	1	*Meeting Pier Committee*
		Sent off £65 to Mr Argo [County Clerk]

Notes at the back of the 1911 diary also show that Mr Youngson had acted as treasurer for the Committee, gathering in the funds as they were subscribed and forwarding cheques etc to the bank. Not all the £65 *raised* locally had been actually *given* locally, as the minister had used his shipping connections to solicit external donations. Banks & Son, fishmongers in London's Billingsgate, and a Manchester fish salesman, John Donaldson, each donated guineas towards the pier. James Coats Jnr, who gave £5, was a prominent philanthropist, of a family of Paisley thread manu-facturers:[39] perhaps half of the Committee's 'local' funds came from outside the area.

April, 1911

Saturday   *15*   *Rec'd from Miss Davidson £10 / Jas.*
                             Coats £5 for pier

Difficulties, over-runs and additional costs are nothing new in public works. The County Council's contractor was Thomas Munro of Wick, whose tender of £563 19s. had been the lowest. He began work in April 1912, landing over seventy tons of concrete at Port Grant.[40] By November the fishermen were agitating that, though the slip was nearing completion, it should be hurried on so that their winter sailings might be safe.[41] The work initially approved had not been completed when 1913 began, however; and yet there was now a request for an exten-sion. Mr Youngson, on behalf of the Pier Committee, wrote to promise to pay, as before, a quarter of the additional cost; and the County Council applied to the new Board of Agriculture for more funds. A further hitch came in 1914 when Mr Gilmour attempted to withdraw his offer of the land as gift and tried to claim a nominal rent instead; during debate at the County Council he was persuaded to stand by the original gift. The Council heard in October 1914 that a new grant of £64 had been obtained, and in September 1915 approved a tender of £90 for the work from a Strathy Point man, Hugh Macintosh.

September, 1915

Thursday   *23*   *Saw Engineers for Pier*

Mr Macintosh, however, entered war service with the Royal Naval Reserve in early 1916, and all work on the extension ceased. On return from the war, he submitted a new estimate of £166 for widening the pier and that, too, was approved.[42] In

September 1919, Mr Youngson still needed to take the opportunity of his chairing a public meeting with Sir R. Leicester Harmsworth, MP for Caithness and Sutherland ('Electors of both sexes are cordially invited to attend'[43]) to press the Member for his support for further work on the Strathy pier, 'which he readily promised to do'.[44]

September, 1919

Wednesday   24   Sir R. L. Harmsworth at Strathy School

Port Grant, *Port Ghrantaich* in the Gaelic of the Ordnance Survey, was the site of the pier for Strathy Point and a family with the surname Grant occurred locally there at the time of and after the 1901 Census. In retrospect, the name might also serve as a reminder of the grants obtained towards the work from the CDB, the Board of Agriculture, Sutherland County Council and individual donors both local and throughout Britain. The work of the voluntary Pier Committee had achieved some success. Proactive local democratic pressure, with Mr Youngson as an enabler, had reached to all levels of government, from the Parish Council and the County Council to the MP and the Secretary for Scotland in the imperial capital of London, seeking to achieve safer conditions of work for the fisherman of Strathy Point. Yet the work was *very* late, perhaps a century too late. Already by 1911 it was known in Portskerra that seagoing trawlers were destroying the economics of line-fishing: what future remained for Scottish fishing, in terms of making money, was with deep-sea harbours and not boat slips.[45] Further, the state of the Portskerra harbour remained a largely local concern despite the drowning of seven men there in 1918 as their boats were overcome by high seas. Portskerra, indeed, was a far larger township than the Point and fishing was even more important there than to the Strathy Bay settlements.[46] The Parish Council had indeed promoted development, but the gains achieved were very narrowly focused and, in retrospect, insufficient to retain a fishing industry of any size in Farr's east ward.

The remaining remit of the Congested Districts Board and the Board of Agriculture, to acquire land for the landless, remained an issue that would raise local passions in 1919 and 1920 when legal, democratic procedures appeared to be inadequate.

7

The Tale of Years

Against a background of normal life, of the regular flow of time from New Year to New Year, from winter to harvest, Alex Youngson's diaries also record particular events: the sort of happenings that make years memorable. The two later years, of course, contained the turmoil of the First World War and its aftermath. In Alex Youngson's own family life, however, 1911 was a painful time, though he no doubt saw the renovation of Strathy church in the same year as a significant achievement. In the years 1911 and 1912 the promotion of Gaelic culture was moving forward, as was the promotion of temperance as a lifestyle option; Mr Youngson was involved with both movements. Sponsoring much of the formal life of the north were the 4th and 5th Dukes of Sutherland; members of their family, Sutherland-Leveson-Gower, make their appearance in the diaries. At the height of British society was, of course, the monarchy, and 1911 saw the start of a new reign: the coronation of King George V. The new 'King of the United Kingdom of Great Britain and Ireland and of the British Dominions beyond the seas, Defender of the Faith, Emperor of India' was the formal head of the largest Empire in the world, a fact that enabled young men and women to leave north Sutherland seeking land and work and better opportunities than their own country offered. The struggle for land reached a new peak in the Highlands immediately after the First World War, and it is no doubt of significance that this was not reflected in the diaries of the minister of the Established Church.

1911 and 1912 – Emigration, Bereavement, Recruitment, Celebration and Temperance

March, 1911

| Thursday | 30 | Donald Macdonald left for Canada today |

It is not possible to identify with certainty the Donald Macdonald whose departure for Canada Alex Youngson recorded early in his diary for 1911, even though he attempted to keep in touch with Donald, noting his address ['Calgary, Alb[ert]a, Canada PO Box 151'] in his 1911 and 1912 diaries. Perhaps this was the seven-year old Donald Macdonald recorded by the 1901 Census as living with his uncle George Munro in Aultiphurst; he would have been eighteen in 1911, and it was men of his generation who emigrated from the north in these years. Why did such young men leave? There was a centuries-long tradition of departure from the Highlands, of course, voluntary and involuntary: the other side of the history of clearance. The Dominions were proactively seeking Highlanders before the First War: 'Canada wants men to till the soil' proclaimed notices in the press. With the British Empire at its height, sea travel across the world was secure and reliable; the Royal Mail offered communication with those left behind. Both employment and land beckoned, and families scattered. From Armadale, Donald A. Mackay went to Canada while his brother Adam successfully made a new life for himself in Australia.[1]

Local attitudes to emigration swung between encouragement and regret: encouragement for those enterprising enough to go, and regret that the opportunities they sought had to be across the seas. When another Macdonald left the district in 1912, a presentation and dance were held in the Melvich Drill Hall, with speeches by Mr Morrison of the Hotel and the schoolmaster, Mr Macintosh:

> Mr John Hector Macdonald, youngest son of Piper Hugh Macdonald, Portskerra was presented on Friday evening 5th inst. with a gold Double Albert chain with Masonic pendant and inscription, and a purse containing a handsome cheque on the occasion of his leaving for Australia . . . He left on Saturday morning for London, and sails to Sydney on Tuesday.[2]

John Hector, aged eleven in 1901, was the second son of Hugh Piper, a Portskerra crofter. Portskerra crofts were among the smallest in the area, and Hugh's eldest son Angus would expect to inherit and then fully utilise their family's interest in the land. With no opportunity for higher education, John Hector's prospects would have been limited; there could be no market in crofts (for they were rented) and the estates were slow to make new land available for smallholders to rent. Indeed in 1911 one observer reported jottings of conversations in Portskerra directly linking emigration with the land issue: 'We have been promised land for fifty years. Almost everyone who could go has gone. Last month, thirteen left within seven miles of here. Some married men have gone to Alberta, Alaska and British Columbia and are sending money back to their wives.'[3] One of these married men was Robert G. Mackintosh of Lednagullen, who went to Canada in 1911 and obtained employment as an armed special policeman for the Canadian Pacific Railway. Just as it seemed a future had been secured for the family and his wife and children were making preparations to join him, he was shot dead at Calgary while on duty in the rail-yards. He was thirty years old. The CPR returned his body to Scotland, and he is buried in Strathy.[4]

October, 1912

Thursday   10   Funeral Robt McIntosh 12noon

William Macpherson, son of Hugh, Melvich, had better initial fortune in Canada. Leaving home with a group of others around 1910 when aged nineteen, he was said to be energetic and pushing, bravely facing the hardships of the new country, becoming the possessor of a 'large extent of land' near Lafleche, Saskatchewan, that after four years' labour he was slowly bringing into cultivation. His death from the flu pandemic was reported in 1918.[5]

Sufficient numbers of young men were leaving north Sutherland in these years for the community to be very aware of their loss. One correspondent reported in May 1912 in the *John O' Groat Journal* that 'owing to emigration and the early fishing all the young men are away, there are few left but old folks, so it is a pretty hard struggle to get the peats cut'.[6] Not everything in the press, of course, needs to be wholly believed. More factual were the returns of the 1911 Census, showing that the population in the east ward of Farr had decreased by 126 or over 8 per cent since 1901. The paper commented: 'The main cause of the decrease in the population in this district is emigration. Quite a number of young men and women left during the last three years.'[7] Alex Youngson's diary entry on the departure of Donald Macdonald was simply the recording of one of many who, without access to capital, land or the professions, left because they could see no prospects for themselves in Scotland. In response, Rev. Hector Macaulay, Strathy's Free Church minister, supported by John Mackay, Chilsey, pressed the School Board to move towards continued and secondary education in Farr's schools, so that their young people were not left at fourteen with only a basic education that qualified them for little.[8] Looking back across a century that has seen the British economy transformed by science and technology, and by the growth of the communications and service industries, Hector Macaulay's emphasis on secondary education certainly has been vindicated.

Members of Alex Youngson's own family appear to have moved overseas in the years around the First World War. Saturday 18 February 1911: 'Emilie and family sailed from Liverpool by "Ayrshire"'. With her husband John Begg, Emilie, Alex Youngson's second daughter, emigrated to Australia on a ship of Scottish Shires Line, which sailed via South Africa to Australia and New Zealand. By the beginning of 1919, her address was 'c/o the Post Office, Stanthorpe, Queensland'. Similarly Mr Youngson's notes in his 1919 diary showed Katie's address as 'Mrs Martin – 1915 Lakewood Drive, Vancouver B.C.' The family kept in touch with each other. Letters from both Emilie and Katie arrived at the manse on 3 April 1911; it seems to have been Mr Youngson's son-in-law, John Begg, who wrote to say that Katie had had a daughter on 18 June; the letter arrived on 8 July 1912. Finally Nellie was recorded as sailing to Buenos Aires on 20 May and arriving 16 August 1919. Meanwhile Mr Youngson's only son, Alex, was following his career as a ship's engineer, with only occasional visits to the manse, though (aged thirty-five) he was as yet unmarried. In January 1911, for example, the diary records that 'Alex arrived 10.30am' on Tuesday 17 and that he left for Glasgow on Monday 23. Alex's visit in August 1912 seems to have encouraged his father to take a break: the diary has no work-related entries, apart from the two Sundays, for the ten days his son was at the manse.

August, 1912		
Saturday	24	*Alex arrived*
Sunday	25	*Fine day*
Monday	26	
Tuesday	27	
Wednesday	28	
Thursday	29	
Friday	30	
Saturday	31	

September, 1912		
Sunday	1	*Wet morning*
Monday	2	*New service of mails* *Hay secured in stacks*
Tuesday	3	*Alex left today, Alice going to For[sinard]*

In the Strathy Burial Ground stand two gravestones for Mr Youngson and his family. The same year that his daughter Emilie departed overseas, his own wife Elizabeth Catherine died. It was August and their daughters Alice and Nellie were at home.

August, 1911		
Saturday	26	*Mother died 7.50am.*
Sunday	27	*No service*
Monday	28	*Mother placed in coffin*
Tuesday	29	*All at home* *Callers*
Wednesday	30	*Funeral 12noon* *Service at Manse 11.30 in Church 12 at the Grave 1.30*

| *Sunday* | 3 | *No service in Church* |
| | | *Visited Church Yard – Nellie Alice & self* |

Alex Youngson erected a modest stone 'in loving memory' of his wife, the mother of his family, to which in due course his own name was added. Beside it stands a stone, topped with a cross, erected by his daughter Alice for her brother Alex (died 13 May 1938) and her unmarried sister Nellie (died 26 May 1960). Emilie and Katie, being married, are not commemorated in Strathy. Alice died in March 1961, and her own name was added to the gravestone. Emigration and death had separated the manse family across and beyond the world in the years before and after 1914. It was an experience the minister shared with many of his parish.

Mrs Youngson's death was obviously a heavy blow to her husband. Very likely, they had been childhood friends. They had been married for forty-one years, ever since he was schoolmaster at Skene. She had stood by him during his bankruptcy; they had raised their family together; and she had loyally supported his ministry. 'Every one can master a grief but he who has felt it', he wrote in his 1911 diary. Clearly the normal Sabbath services were cancelled immediately before and after her funeral. They did not in fact resume until Sunday 22 October 1911, after a break of eight weeks. This, however, was also due to another of 1911's major events, the renovation of Strathy church.

The first record in Alex Youngson's diaries of his intentions for his Telford-designed church came on Monday 9 January 1911: 'Sent off plans to Highland Committee'. The plans, drawn by Mr Gilmour's Thurso architect, Mr Sinclair Macdonald, had been given the blessing of the Presbytery of Tongue in November 1910.[9] On Friday 14 July, Mr Youngson heard that the General Assembly's Highland Committee had both approved the repairs and also awarded a grant of £250 towards the cost. Contracts were awarded to Thurso painters and carpenters, and to Hugh Macintosh of Strathy Point for masonry. The work was undertaken in August and September, and the church reopened on 22 October with guest preachers from Tongue and Reay.

October, 1911

Sunday	*15*	*No service*
Monday	*16*	
Tuesday	*17*	
Wednesday	*18*	*Cleaning Church*
Thursday	*19*	*Cleaning Church*
Friday	*20*	*Fitting up pulpit*
Saturday	*21*	*Preparing Church for opening*
Sunday	*22*	*Church reopened* *Rev. Mr Lundie noon* *Rev. Mr Carmichael eve*

The next edition of the *John O' Groat Journal* offered an account of the reopening services. Morning worship was well attended and in the evening the church was crowded – no doubt with members of the other local congregations coming to join the celebration and see the changes with their own eyes. The architect was congratulated by the article's writer on 'accomplishing with entire satisfaction what is always a difficult task of remodelling an old building to suit modern requirements': 'one could scarcely recognise the interior now who was acquainted with the old aspect'. The ceiling was painted white, while the walls were a lemon shade and the woodwork a light mahogany. The pulpit was now 'tastefully upholstered in a shade of coronation blue, with plated studs'. The anonymous correspondent concluded:

> We wish Mr Youngson's ministry every success. He is a great favourite here, and is always willing to say a kind word and do a kind deed to everyone, irrespective of denomination. It is to be hoped that the days of denominational acrimony are about to end, and that Mr Youngson will speedily require extensive enlargements to accommodate a returning people.[10]

While these aspirations for a crowded Established Church were not to be fulfilled, the sentiments of the press coverage and the success of the opening Sunday must have been pleasing to Alex

Youngson. Not everyone locally had been content that the old church was being altered; there had, in fact, been an attempt to burn it down (or at least to sabotage the work) earlier in October.[11]

No doubt the 'shade of coronation blue' had been chosen for the pulpit's upholstery because 1911 was coronation year. Westminster Abbey was itself decked for the occasion with new blue carpets and blue delphiniums, besides red tulips and white lilies completing the colours of the union flag. Without either television or radio to offer national coverage and participation, it fell to each community to arrange their own coronation events. Across Sutherland ad hoc committees had made plans for local celebrations. In Strathy Mr Youngson joined in a series of weekly meetings in the School from Wednesday 24 May leading up to Coronation Day itself, Thursday 22 June. No account of events in Strathy itself survives, but the *Northern Times* and the *Northern Ensign* printed accounts of the celebrations in the Sutherland burghs, and in Forsinard, Halladale, Melvich and Portskerra. The day, of course, was a general holiday. Flags and bunting were in evidence. In Brora, Dornoch and Helmsdale, united church services offered public thanksgiving. Forsinard, Halladale and Melvich/Portskerra held teas and children's games, with piper-led parades – to Bighouse Lodge, in the case of the coastal communities, where the games included flat races, egg and spoon, obstacle, needle and thread races; a sack race, a frog race, a stone and bucket race, skipping and a tug of war between the married and the single ladies, which the strapping married lassies won. Coronation medals and mugs were presented; 'customary toasts loyally and enthusiastically proposed'. In Strath Halladale, where earlier proceedings in the Coronation Park were led by the resident UF missionary minister, a midnight bonfire and dancing lasted until early the next day.

Although everyone might in any event be expected to enjoy a rare general holiday, the sentiments of the Coronation Day celebrations were reported to be patriotism and loyalty. At Bighouse Lodge, 'all joined most heartily in singing "God save the King" with resounding cheers'. Elsewhere in the Highlands and especially in the Hebrides, the unresolved issues of land ownership had already in the early twentieth century produced land raids, illegal and forcible occupations of farms and conflict with sheriff officers: 'deep and enduring discontent' and bitterness.[12]

Yet in north Sutherland, where similar grievances were also strongly felt, they coexisted with at least outward expressions of deference to those who stood at the top of the landowning tree. Cheers were given on the lawn of Bighouse Lodge not just to King George and Queen Mary but also to the Duke of Sutherland, his heir, the Marquis of Stafford, and their current tenants in the Lodge, Mr and Mrs Delmege. The forces that bound north coast society together were still strong and could be glimpsed in the coronation blue of the upholstery of Strathy Kirk's refurbished pulpit.

The Duke of Sutherland and the Marquis of Stafford did not just join with others to sponsor the Bighouse coronation party. Prizes were given for the first north coast Crofters' Cattle Show, held in Melvich in 1911 and co-sponsored by the CDB.[13] Owners of Cliveden House in Buckinghamshire and Trentham Hall in Staffordshire, the Sutherland-Leveson-Gowers also hosted 'brilliant parties and literary receptions' in London at Stafford House, 'then the largest and most splendid of all London houses'.[14] They were present at Dunrobin Castle, Golspie, for part of each year and took a personal interest in the various communities of the north. Alex Youngson recorded for Monday 15 May 1911: 'Visit of Duchess of Sutherland at Melvich 12.30pm'. Millicent, Duchess of Sutherland, wife of the 4th Duke, presided over the committee of the Sutherland Celtic Society that in 1911 arranged Mods to be held in Dornoch, Lochinver and Tongue. In May she was touring the county, visiting the various local committees, and encouraging them to make use of the services of a Mod gold medallist, Miss Margrat Duncan, who had been appointed by the Society to teach Gaelic singing.[15] Alex Youngson was chosen to chair a similar meeting in 1912. The commitment of the Strathy manse family to their local Mod, that at Tongue, was shown by the fact that Alice attended on Friday 25 August 1911 despite the fact that her mother must by then have been seriously ill, dying at 7.30 a.m. the next morning.

In May 1911 Her Grace the Duchess of Sutherland also attended a meeting to 'awaken interest in the Boy Scout movement'.[16] Born between 1907 and 1909, the Scouting movement was the product of General R. Baden-Powell's popularity after his celebrated defence of Mafeking in the Boer War combined with the runaway success of his *Scouting for Boys*, published in fortnightly parts. 'B-P' held the first scouts' rally in London in

1909, and by 1912 was touring the world to spread the ideals of 'being prepared' with newly formed troops and patrols. Duchess Millicent was therefore promoting in Sutherland one of London's fashionable crazes; and Alice Youngson caught the vision. By 1915, she had become the Scoutmaster for Strathy's Scouts.

Though the Duke of Sutherland was Lord Lieutenant of the County, the old Strathy Estate had not been the property of the Duke since its sale to W. E. Gilmour. The local communities of Strathy and Armadale were not therefore much involved in the next display of feudal loyalty, that of 1912, inspired by the engagement and marriage of the Marquis of Stafford, the heir to the duchy. The engagement was reported in the *John O' Groat Journal* in January. The Marquis, George Granville, Lord Stafford, was twenty-three; he had served in the regular army with the Scots Greys but was then a Captain in the Territorial 5th (Sutherland and Caithness) Battalion of the Seaforth Highlanders, and was a frequent visitor to Dunrobin. His fiancée,

> Lady Eileen Butler is the eldest daughter of Lord and Lady Lanesborough and made her debut the year before last. She was considered the most beautiful debutante of the season and is today one of the most admired girls in the social world. She is tall and slim with a graceful carriage, and possesses most charming manners. She will be twenty one this year . . .[17]

As Lady Eileen was of an Irish family, the wedding was heralded in the press as the 'Union of the Thistle and the Shamrock' and it was announced that the couple intended to make Dunrobin their main residence. A public meeting was held in Golspie of 'men from all over the county' to raise funds for a presentation. From Strathy, Rev. Ewen Fraser and John Mackay, Crossroads, attended; so, too, did Angus Morrison, the Duke's tenant in the Melvich Hotel. The day of the London marriage, 11 April, was a school holiday in both Melvich and Halladale, with night-time bonfires and dancing. After their arrival at Dunrobin by train, the couple set out on a car tour of the county, and were greeted by their tenants at each stage. At Dalhalvaig on 29 April the children from the school made up a guard of honour, a bouquet was presented, hands shaken and cheers called for. Similarly on Lord and Lady Stafford's arrival at Portskerra, they were met by the schoolchildren and two pipers, who 'played the children from

School to Hotel where they lined the road with a large gathering of the tenantry'. And again a bouquet was presented, and the hands of the tenantry shaken.[18] Lord Stafford in fact succeeded his father as 5th Duke of Sutherland in 1913. He continued his father's policy of selling off his lands. Perhaps we should again remember that in Portskerra, eight years after this high society wedding, 'the buildings generally are of very poor description, being small, drystone or clay built and roofed with straw thatch'.[19]

If the marriage of Lord and Lady Stafford passed by Alex Youngson's diaries, so too did another significant Portskerra/ Melvich event of 1912: the opening of the drill hall on 13 February. Faced with an increasing military threat from Germany, in 1909 the British government authorised part-time local battalions to join the regiments of the regular army. These battalions were raised on condition that they would not serve abroad. Men who volunteered for the Territorial battalions were obliged to parade locally for training and exercises under military discipline and to attend a fortnight's camp each year, and were paid to do so. To the Seaforth Highlanders, the regular regiment for northern Scotland, were added three Territorial battalions, of which one, 5/Seaforth, was designated to be raised in Sutherland and Caithness; the others were based in Ross & Cromarty and Morayshire. The Marquis of Stafford, while a Captain in 5/Seaforth, presided over the Sutherland Territorial Association. In February 1911, the Reay Company of 5/Seaforth laid on a recruiting 'concert' in Portskerra, with John Mackay, Chilsey, in the chair. Members of the Reay Company offered pipe music, rifle drill, club and sword swinging and various other 'evolutions of military discipline'. 'It is satisfactory to note', the report in the *Northern Ensign* concluded, 'that at the end of the concert, several young men of Melvich, Portskerra and Strath Halladale joined the Territorials.'[20] An alternative view was presented by another correspondent who believed that this recruiting was 'not very successful' with only about a dozen young men coming forward from Portskerra, Melvich and Strathy taken together, and only one from Halladale. 'Henceforth he could sleep soundly and with a profound sense of security against German invasion', a cynic in the Strath was heard to remark.[21]

However the 'spin' in the press went, the new section needed a hall in which to assemble and drill, and so the drill hall opened in 1912:

Opening of New Territorial Hall Melvich: Concert & Dance

The districts of Melvich & Portskerra have been long been famous for their social and enjoyable entertainments, but never in the history of the locality have they achieved a greater success or attained to a higher standard of excellency than that which they arrived at on the evening of Friday last at the opening of their new Territorial Hall.[22]

Under their Colonel, 'the young territorials of Melvich' were much in evidence on 13 February in 'their neat little building containing 3–400 people with a Morris Tube Gallery and ante-rooms attached. The colours of old England [*sic*] are much in evidence inside and out.' Territorial Colonel John Morrison, Factor to the Duke of Sutherland in Tongue, was to become the senior Factor to the Sutherland Estates, based in Golspie, later in 1912.[23] Others present at Portskerra in February included Dr Silver, Armadale; Mr James Murray, Forsinard Hotel; Mr Morrison, Melvich Hotel; Mr Rose, County Sanitary Inspector; and Miss Mackay, infant school teacher in Strathy, but not, apparently, any of the local ministers.

The Rev. Alex Youngson was, however, among a long list of patrons and subscribers to the Melvich Territorial Sports held in September 1911. A Gala Day was mounted by the new section, supported by 'A' Coy. from Golspie, and the aim of the event was further recruitment. Mrs Gilmour presented the prizes, which were donated by her son, Allan Gilmour Jnr, of Rosehall, the Duchess of Sutherland, Lord Stafford, Mr Delmege and many others.[24] Time was to show that the recruitment of these young men would indeed prove to be a significant event in the history of the community.

Though the clouds of war were darkening, in 1912 Alex Youngson was more immediately involved with the Sutherland Celtic Society and the local temperance movement. He also enjoyed a break in the south that year, attending the General Assembly of the Church of Scotland.

The Sutherland Celtic Society has already been mentioned: on 2 March 1912, Alex Youngson chaired the local committee to arrange for the annual tuition to be given by Miss Strachan of Barvas, Lewis. As it turned out, she was disappointed that none of the local schools had a piano – but, then, the psalms taught in the schools were sung unaccompanied.[25]

March, 1912

Saturday	2	*Meeting at Melvich*
Saturday	9	*Miss Strachan called Molly served*
Monday	18	*Visit of Miss Strachan*

The Dominions, the Territorial army and the temperance movement were all competing for the attention of the young men of the east ward of Farr at this time; and, of the three, it seems that the temperance cause was the most successful. In February 1912 the *Northern Times* reported: 'The temperance movement has been making steady process in Melvich and Portskerra townships ever since its inception about a year ago. Practically all the young men and women in the respective localities are on the roll of membership, and the proportion of lapses is very small.'[26] The particular organisation that the young adults joined was the International Order of Good Templars [IOGT], a branch-based movement that modelled its structure on Freemasonry, held both closed and open sessions and addressed its members as 'Brother' and 'Sister'. The Order was introduced to Scotland from the USA in 1869 when the first Scottish Lodge opened in Glasgow. The movement, with 'its uncompromisingly prohibitionist aims', 'spread like wildfire'.[27] Patriotic, with its ritual available in Gaelic and strongly supported by the churches, IOGT branches already existed in the east coast Sutherland burghs before it came, relatively late, to the north coast: a Temperance Hall in Brora bears the date 1893. A report of an open meeting in Dornoch gives a flavour of the movement, which borrowed elements from church worship, public concerts and political meetings. After a singing of the hymn 'Yield not to Temptation' came a talk, comparing the toll of Britain's annual drink-related deaths to those of the Battle of Waterloo. Various songs and solos followed, including 'Nae luck aboot the house' and 'True till death'. Then came 'a stump speech on Women's rights'. The meeting 'had to be cut short due to the lateness of the hour'.[28]

The speech on women's rights at Dornoch reflected the progressive ethos of the Good Templars. Not only did they sing hymns, but their office-bearers could also be female. Strathy's infant mistress,

Miss Marion Mackay, was elected the Chief Templar of the Victoria Lodge of Good Templars, Strathy. Similarly, the Chief and the Vice Templar of the Gladstone Lodge (Melvich and Portskerra) were both female when the Lodges were inaugurated in 1911.[29] It was Brother John Munro of Strathy West, however, who presided on behalf of the Victoria Branch at their open concert, 'a happy night of mirth and glee', in the Library Hall on Friday 20 December 1912. Bro. John was at the time also the Chairman of the School Board for Farr – temperance had the support of the community's leading figures. In Melvich, John Mackay, Chilsey presided over a similar IOGT winter entertainment, which included a Gaelic play and playlet, action songs, fiddle recitations and a new march composed in honour of the movement by the Portskerra piper, Alex Macleod.[30]

December, 1912			Col.
Sunday	29	Preach to Good Templars Collection for Royal Infirmary Edinburgh	£1/1/10

Templars' Church Parade

A Good Templars' church parade in full regalia is to take place in Strathy Parish Church on Sunday, 29th December, where the Rev. Mr Youngson is to preach a temperance sermon in the forenoon of the day. The aisle of the church is to be reserved for the Templars. Both Lodges, viz the Victoria Lodge IOGT, Strathy, and the Gladstone Lodge IOGT, Portskerra and Melvich, are to take part in the parade, when a collection for the Royal Infirmary, Edinburgh, will be taken up.

On the last Sunday of the year 1912, the two local IOGT Lodges held a joint church parade in Strathy's parish church, and it was surely a mark of respect that the office-bearers should have chosen Mr Youngson to host the event and to preach at it.[31] In the 'General Memoranda' section of his diary for 1912 is a page devoted to temperance-related jottings, perhaps notes for a talk on this or another occasion. 'Case of Jamie Newmill 3 bottles Gaffer to blame' suggests he recounted a warning example from his ministry at Newmill. 'Doctors differ Appeal to experience and observation' suggests that he was asking his audience to reject the obviously detrimental path of alcoholism. The tempting customs of society were not overlooked – 'Funerals bring a bottle' – and against the drink culture Alex Youngson offered an alternative lifestyle: 'Waste Young – Married – Family Self-denial in practice – temperance in language – parents look after children'. A saying from the noted millionaire and philanthropist, 'Carnegie: Be teetotal until you are a millionaire' concluded the pragmatic tone of the notes. That there was a social conflict over drinking was shown by a case in the Sheriff Court in Dornoch, November 1912, when Donald Mackay was convicted of assaulting Robert Mackay, both of Portskerra. On his way to a Good Templar meeting, Donald had met Robert; and Robert mocked Donald's intention to rejoin the Lodge. 'A quarrel took place between the two men.' The Sheriff found the charge proved and imposed a fine of 10s. or seven days' imprisonment.[32]

Concluding this review of Alex Youngson's memorable events in 1912, his visit to Edinburgh should be mentioned. He travelled by train as the minister commissioned by the Presbytery of Tongue to attend the General Assembly that year. This period, Monday 20 to Wednesday 29 May 1912, appears to have been his only extended period away from the manse in any of the four years covered by his extant diaries. He used the opportunity to visit his daughter Nellie, to stay with friends in Giffnock over the Assembly weekend, and to lunch (twice) and 'Dine with Mr Macpherson', the Edinburgh accountant who held an elder's commission to the Assembly from the Presbytery of Tongue. C. E. W. Macpherson Esq. CA was a member of the executive of the Assembly's Highland Committee, the committee that oversaw the fabric needs of Parliamentary churches and manses, and that had awarded the grant for the 1911 renovation of Strathy church. On Friday 24 May, Mr Youngson's diary noted 'Dine at Palace & Presentation': he had been chosen to be presented at Holyrood Palace to the King's Lord High Commissioner. He was back at the Palace, accompanied by Nellie, on Monday 27 May. By contrast, he took the opportunity while in Edinburgh to pay off his bookshop account for Bibles, and to buy an umbrella and a coffee mill, besides collars and shoes. (In the back of his diary for 1912 was kept a special cash account for these two weeks.) Nothing in the diary mentions any topics under discussion by the Assembly.

Perhaps Alex Youngson viewed his networking with Mr Macpherson as the key business he had to transact in Edinburgh. In November 1912, the Highland Committee received an application for approval and a grant towards £220-worth of repairs to Strathy manse, and no doubt he looked to Mr Macpherson to smooth the way.[33] Further applications to the Committee for work on the manse came regularly until Mr Youngson's retirement. Strathy's elderly minister was a practical man.

1915 – A Community at War

Historians have described the First World War as 'an iron gate separating the present from the past'.[34] By the time Alex Youngson began his 1915 diary, Europe had been at war for over four months. Corporal Benjamin Sutherland of the 1st Battalion of the Seaforth Highlanders, whose name is recorded on the Strath Halladale War Memorial, had already died in November 1914, as the Regular Army sought to stem the German advance into Belgium and France. All three Territorial battalions of the Seaforth Highlanders had been immediately called up on the outbreak of war and by 16 August 1914 were encamped for intensive training at Bedford, in England's East Anglia. A history published for the Regimental Association explains:

> The Territorials were not originally intended for service overseas but, within a few days of the outbreak of War, every Man on the strength of the three battalions with the exception of two or three elderly men, had volunteered for active service. Throughout the war their strength was, for the most part, maintained by men recruited in their Regimental district. It is on record that no part of the United Kingdom responded to the call to arms in greater numbers, proportionate to the population, than the Highlands of Scotland.[35]

With the Gaelic motto *Cuidich 'n Righ* ('Help the King') on their cap badge, the Seaforth Highlanders were eventually to comprise nineteen battalions: the pre-war Regulars and their Territorial partners were joined by New Army and War Service battalions, raised from volunteers for over a year after August 1914 and then by conscription from 1916 to meet the demands of the attrition of the trenches and the global nature of the war. Itself part of the 51st (Highland) Division, the Regiment's battalions saw severe fighting on the Western Front, in Palestine and the Near East. The sword drill and 'military evolutions' of the recruiting concert at Portskerra in 1912 were an unimaginable world away from what the young men then present came to experience.

The Seaforth Highlanders were not the only service in which the young men of the district of Strathy fought in the First World War. Privates and sergeants, cavalry troopers and artillery gunners, some found their way to other Scottish regiments and some to such new forces as the Machine Gun Corps. From the Strathy shop, John Traill's son Thomas was a private in the Army Service Corps, ending the war as part of the Expeditionary Force in Mesopotamia and as a holder of the British Army and Victory Medals.[36] Some men who had emigrated returned to Britain to volunteer; others served and died in the armies raised by the Dominion governments on whose behalf London had declared war. From the small settlement of Aultiphurst, by January 1915 four men had come forward from five homes: retired Sergeant W. M. Mackay's son, John W. Mackay, served in the RNR on a destroyer and his son-in-law, John G. Gunn, on HMS *Kent*, while his grandson, Donald Macdonald, was in 5/Seaforth together with William, son of Donald Mackay.[37] The *Northern Times*' Halladale column (also January 1915) remarked that 'Mr James Ross Golval and Mr John Mackay Trantlebeg have contributed to the Roll of Honour in having respectively four and three sons in HM Forces.'[38] At this point, the term 'Roll of Honour' referred to those who had volunteered; later, it was to obtain a more sombre meaning. Private Thomas R. Ross of Golval, serving with the Black Watch (Royal Highlanders) died in August 1918, aged twenty-two, during the 'advance to victory', having been awarded the Military Medal and the French Croix de Guerre for gallantry.[39]

Many men were not just crofters but also fishermen; numbers therefore also served in the Royal Naval Reserve (RNR). While the war at sea was not as prodigal of life as the trenches, and fleet engagements involving battleships were rare, nevertheless escorting military transports and convoys of essential trade placed sailors in the front line against submarine warfare as well as exposing them to danger from mines in addition to their normal risks of illness, accident and storm. Some 330 of HM ships of all grades were lost during the conflict that began in 1914. Men from the north coast found themselves in a whole range of wartime service. From Poulouriscaig, John Mackay spent four years in Scapa Flow, base of the Home Fleet, and returned in 1919 with plans to take up fishing.[40] Men buried in both the Strathy and Kirkton cemeteries died while officially attached to HMS *Victory*, Nelson's former flagship, still in service and flying the flag of the Commander-in-Chief. From Portskerra, Lieutenant R. Maclean was drowned serving on the battleship HMS *Hibernia* in September 1918; at the other end of the scale another Portskerra man had been lost with motor launch ML 403 the month before. Others served as seamen and deck hands in HM drifters, sloops, cruisers and light cruisers.

The first death to bring the war home to Strathy manse was that of Private David Michael Jackson, 5/Seaforth, aged twenty-two, of scarlet fever and pneumonia while recovering from measles, in January 1915 while his battalion was still at Bedford. Indeed the camp was swept that winter by a measles epidemic that too often proved fatal to those from the northern areas.[41] As one of the Melvich section of the 5/Seaforth, he had, like his colleagues, formally volunteered for foreign service: Private Jackson was the first of the section to die. Word had in fact been sent that he was seriously ill and his mother had left their home at Loch Strathy to go by train to be with him. A telegram with news of his death reached her at Inverness, so she turned back. Walking through the hills from Forsinard station in the dusk, she lost her way and was rescued by Donald Mackay of Dyke, who 'through the darkness of night and over bog and moorland' accompanied her back to the family's solitary shepherd's cottage.[42] Though David Jackson's funeral was to be at his family's former home of Lochcarron, after consulting his Precentor Alex Youngson spent Monday 25 January at Loch Strathy going to comfort the bereaved parents, sister and younger brother.

January, 1915

Thursday	21	*News of Jackson's death*
Friday	22	*At Precentor's about Jackson*
Saturday	23	
Sunday	24	*Fine day*
Monday	25	*Visited Loch Strathy Jackson's*
		Left 10am ret'n 6.20pm
		Nellie girl Duncan boy

The family rallied and the community offered its support. Finding consolation in her faith, Mrs Jackson became an active communicant member of Strathy's Parish Kirk in 1916. Meanwhile her daughter Nellie was the first choice of the School Board of Farr in September 1915 when a teacher was required for a side-school at Bowside. When in 1918 the Jacksons moved from Loch Strathy to Drumbasbie, Nellie was appointed an unqualified assistant teacher at Armadale School.[43]

The next death came yet closer home to Alex Youngson. His diary noted 'Notice of Murdo's illness' on 26 April 1915, and then 'Notice of Murdo's death' on 27 April. Murdo was the eldest son of John, the weaver of Strathy West and his wife Elizabeth; John Gunn was one of Alex Youngson's elders and his regular confidant. Murdo Macdonald Gunn, a Private in 'C' Company, the 8th Battalion of the Gordon Highlanders, was buried at Strathy at 6 p.m. on Saturday 1 May 1915 and his name is inscribed on the family memorial.

To encourage men to volunteer for the armies in the numbers needed on the Western Front, separation allowances were paid to their dependants in addition to the military salary offered. The men were also encouraged to remit a proportion of their pay to the families at home, so that the total weekly payments to a wife and two children came to 21s. in 1915, with a further 2s. added for all additional children. If it could be shown that unmarried soldiers had used their income before the war to support elderly relatives, then, again, an allowance might be offered by the government.[44] The very fact of the separation of the families of combatants, however, could lead to administrative confusion and worse. In March 1915 the *Northern Times* published a letter from the Recruiting Officer for Sutherland complaining about the severe approach taken by local councillors to those claiming separation allowances: one mother of a 1914 volunteer had been told straitly that she was a liar. 'I feel the German Chancellor has close relatives in Sutherland' wrote Major D. Sutherland.[45]

Alex Youngson's diaries show that he offered administrative support to those caught up in the problems of war away from the front lines, and in particular with the payment of separation allowances. In October 1915 he was writing to the Admiralty and the serviceman concerned 're separation allowance re Jessie'.

October, 1915

Saturday	16	*Written to Admiralty & Angus Gow re separation allowance re Jessie*

A note in the Memoranda section of the 1919 diary shows that on 19 March he wrote to the Accountant General of the Navy, Separation Allowance Branch, 4a Newgate Street, London SC1, on behalf of one Alice Mackay. Other entries show Alex Youngson tracking the careers of servicemen, often sailors, so that he could correspond with the authorities on their behalf. The details, of course, are sparse: we cannot, even if we wanted to, from the diaries alone fully identify those concerned. One Angus Mackay, for example, in no. 5 Mess of HMS *Europa*, a 1st class cruiser of 11,000 tons whose home port was Portsmouth, had a sixteen-year old dependant for whom Alex Youngson wrote in August 1915. In September he was writing on behalf of Angus Mackay RNR, in 44 Mess, HMS *Canada*, a battleship. He was still writing for Angus Mackay of HMS *Canada* in January 1919. Indeed a number of cases cover the early pages of the 1919 diary: Robert J. Mackay, John Angus Macintosh and William J. Macdonald, serving in naval motor launches, respectively HM ML 90, 205 and 486; Seaman Donald Sinclair, in 677 Mess Portsmouth Barracks; Alex Mackay in HMS *Prestatyn*; Malcolm Macleod in HM SS *St Cuthbert*; Private C. Mackay, No. 3 Troop, 'C' Squadron 2nd Dragoon Guards, The Queen's Bays, with the Expeditionary Force in Germany. More easily identified was Alex Williamson, whose address was given in March 1915 as 'Chrysea 626, Patrol Boat, Orkney', and in January 1919 as attached to the Cunard Line's cargo-ship SS *Phrygia*, at the Cunard Pier, Liverpool. Aged twenty-two in the 1901 Census, he was then single, from Coatbridge, Lanarkshire but living with his uncle John Macintosh in Strathy Point. A peacetime fisherman, Alex Williamson had signed the petition for a landing slip at Port Grant in 1907.

Demands continued in 1915 for more and more volunteers for the front. At the meeting of the Parish Council for Farr on 27 April, Alex Youngson, with the other members, committed himself to encouraging recruitment:

> The Parish Council had before them a communication from His Grace the Duke of Sutherland asking for their cooperation and

assistance in encouraging recruiting. The Council resolved to acknowledge His Grace's communication and to assure him of their entire sympathy with the movement and that they would do everything in their power both officially and individually to help on the movement.[46]

Already in January 1915, full-page notices had appeared in the press: 'Your King and country need another 100,000 men. In the present grave national emergency, another 100,000 men are needed at once to rally round the Flag and add to the ranks of our New Armies.'[47] The Duke of Sutherland now held the post of Honorary Colonel of 5/Seaforth, and in June he added to the pressure by asking the county for a further 1,000 men.[48] There was in fact some controversy in the Wick-based press as to whether the men of Sutherland were coming forward in sufficient numbers. The accusation was strongly rebutted by one who signed himself 'Pro Patria':

> The fact is that the men of the north and west of Sutherland including the men of Halladale have responded most loyally and punctually to the trumpet call of their King and Country in the day and hour of danger. Beginning at Halladale and all the way up along the north coast to Durness and round by Kinlochbervie and Lairg the young men responded in their hundreds and swelled the ranks of the Regulars, Territorials or Royal Navy or Fleet Reserve just as they were connected with either of these branches of the King's land or sea forces prior to the outbreak of hostilities with Germany. . . . The men of the north and west were never yet 'laggards' or 'shirkers' or 'cowards' or 'traitors' in the day and hour of danger and the remnant of those who are left in their native land kept tryst to the brave old tradition of the past when the war clouds suddenly darkened Europe in August last.[49]

Age shall not weary them, nor the years condemn.

In May 1915 the three Territorial battalions of the Seaforth Highlanders left camp at Bedford and, under newly appointed regular army officers who had seen service in France, wearing their uniform kilts and to the playing of the pipes, 5/Seaforth landed at Boulogne preparatory to deployment at the front. The battalion was involved with an offensive conducted by the 51st (Highland) Division on 15 June designed to straighten the line of trenches near Festubert. Colonel John Sym's history reports that they attacked 'with the confidence of veterans, but the operation failed through a total lack of artillery support. The division suffered 1,500 casualties.' Another history remembers that 'the outlook was hopeless, the wire was an insurmountable obstacle'.[50] The *John O' Groat Journal*'s pages filled with lists of name after name of Caithness men killed attempting to assault unbroken barbed wire in the face of machine-guns uncowed by artillery. At home the mood turned darker and controversy grew about the fairness of a national burden carried only by volunteers. The *Northern Times* had a weekly unattributed feature entitled 'What the Brora people are saying'. By 17 June this now included '. . . that farmers, shop keepers, and other local gentry would willingly join the colours if they were made officers, had a pound a day, and were not asked to take their turn in the trenches with the "common" folk like crofters and fishermen'; and '. . . that we all wish the war to end and to see our boys back from the Dardenelles and from France.'[51] In July, the paper reprinted a strongly worded article from the *Glasgow Herald* that criticised recruiting speeches made by 'distinguished clergymen and prominent citizens':

> An ornament of the pulpit or an eminent Justiciary may employ the not inconsiderable oratorical powers that are his in urging men to die for their country and offer their bodies to be torn by shrapnel in defence of the grand cause, and in stigmatising as cowards the lusty hangers-back. But the said hangers-back may be inclined to reflect that the silver-tongued gentleman who points the way to the trenches and the grave is returning, having made his appeal, to a good dinner, an easy chair, and comfortable bed. Now, Sir, why not bring over here some of our officers who have fought, who have suffered and bled, who have looked death and hell in the face . . . Get them to give recruiting speeches and if that fails, bring in universal conscription.[52]

Nevertheless, that July the figures showed that, of all parishes in the County of Sutherland, the parish of Farr already had the highest percentage of eligible men enlisted.[53]

In July 1915, Asquith's government passed the National Registration Act through Parliament. The Prime Minister denied that it was preparatory to conscription, and 'people in Brora' retorted:[54] 'that the Government are afraid to bring in conscription'. Nominally in connection with a census, the Act required the registration of 'all persons . . . between the ages of 15 and 65, not being members of His Majesty's Forces'. Under the authority of County Councils, papers required to be distributed and collected on a parish basis to all households. Sutherland County Council 'confidently anticipated that the whole task . . . will be done gratuitously by persons willing and anxious to take a part in a work of National importance'.[55] At its meeting on 27 July, the Parish Council of Farr allocated the visitation needed for National Registration in its east ward as follows:[56]

Portskerra	Alex Macintosh	Melvich Schoolmaster
Baligill	Hugh Gunn	Clerk & Inspector of Poor
Strathy East and West	Alex Youngson	Parish Minister
Strathy Point	John M. Gunn	Strathy Schoolmaster
Millburn, Fleuchary & Lednagullen	Donald John Macdonald	Crofter, Brawl
Armadale	Donald Henderson	Armadale Farm

Melvich schoolmaster Alex Macintosh's own son, Lieutenant J. Macintosh, was among the officers sent from training at Golspie to France to replace those the Seaforths lost in the 15 June assault.[57]

It took Alex Youngson six days in August to complete the task allocated to him in connection with the National Registration of those not engaged in war service.

August, 1915

Tuesday	10	*Delivering Reg'n papers East Strathy*
Wednesday	11	*Do/West Strathy*
Thursday	12	*Finished delivering West Strathy*
Monday	16	*Collecting papers forenoon*
Tuesday	17	*Collecting papers*
Wednesday	18	*Delivering papers at Baligill*

As the registration exercise was understood to be connected with the war effort, it seems to have been designed to allow local leaders of the community personal opportunities to bring moral pressure to bear on those who had yet to volunteer – a benefit quite apart from the detailed information it provided the government. Alex Youngson was again visiting the households in December 1915: 'Out with Recruiting cards, Strathy East and West' [8 December 1915] and 'Sent off Recruiting Papers to Inspector' [10 December 1915]. This was the government's last appeal for voluntary enlistment; on 6 January 1916 the House of Commons voted for conscription.

In his capacity as a Parish Councillor, during 1915 Rev. Alex Youngson certainly added his weight to the campaign to recruit ever more men for war service. The war was, of course, generally supported within Britain at this time. It is worth recollecting, however, that while the churches did indeed back the war their attitude was nuanced. At the beginning of 1915, Rev. Dr George Keith, Moderator of the General Assembly of the United Free Church, preached in Glasgow on 'What we pray for'. He began by insisting that 'this deplorable war is a call to recognize and confess our national sins, and to seek God's grace to renounce them.' He continued:

As we think of our relations to our enemies, we pray God in all good conscience to grant victory to our arms. Victory to Germany would mean unspeakable disaster to the world. There was a Germany once which many of us who shared its hospitality and knew it well loved and were proud of. There was a Germany once in closest alliance with Britain, an alliance determined by affinity in race and religion, and sealed by confederacy on the battlefield. That Germany will again reappear, and be, as in Luther's days, a spring of inestimable blessing to mankind. But it is not that Germany we are fighting against to-day. It is a Germany that aspires to lead, not by art or science or secular and religious learning, but by iron and blood – a Germany which is obnoxious to mankind, and must be brought to her knees. We pray for victory, not for self-exaltation, but for the interests of Truth and Righteousness, of Humanity and Brotherhood. Lastly, we pray for peace. As we try to realise the horrible butchery and the maiming of valued lives, and the anguish of innumerable homes and hearts, how can we help beseeching God to bring this cruel war to a speedy end![58]

Here was both a consciousness of the dreadfulness of the war and a vision for reconciliation beyond the conflict. Clearly the churches believed in the justness of the allied defence of Belgium, France and Russia and in armed opposition to aggression; and so they could pray, not just for peace, but for peace after victory.

Rev. Dr George Keith had been preaching at one of the special services held across Britain on the first Sunday in 1915, 'appointed by the King for united prayer, intercession and thanksgiving, and for remembrance for those who have fallen in their country's cause'. Large congregations attended these services in the Sutherland burghs.[59] At the UF congregation's communion in Strath Halladale later in 1915, the Friday men's night was devoted to 'prayer and supplication for the terrible world conflict raging in many lands'.[60] After the end of the war, the Halladale Memorial was to list sixteen men connected with the Strath, including Sergeant Angus Mackenzie of the American Expeditionary Force, Privates William J. Munro and Alexander A. Murray of the 44th and 28th Australian Battalions, 2nd Lieutenant Benjamin Macleod of the Canadian Field Artillery and Private George Mackay of the 10th Battalion of the Canadian Expeditionary Force. Hugh Mackay of Woodend, a private in the Black Watch, was to die in far away Mesopotamia (contemporary Iraq); he is commemorated at Basra. 'Many lands', indeed.

Meanwhile the weekly editions of the *John O' Groat Journal* continued to print the names of the dead: the man who had died of gas poisoning, who was killed in action at the Dardenelles, who accidentally drowned in Immingham Docks, or who died as a prisoner of war. In October 1915, it reported the death of Private William S. Mackay of Bighouse, Halladale, the first of the Melvich Company of 5/Seaforth to fall in action, while acting as sentry in a dangerous part of the line, fifteen yards from the German trenches.[61] The killing was to continue for a further three full years. William's brother Thomas had previously died in the camps at Bedford and had been buried in Kirkton on Monday 3 May.[62] Both men, 'rural workers', had been listed among the Halladale 'Roll of Honour' with eighteen others from the Strath serving in the forces by March 1915: a motor engineer, gamekeepers, foresters, shepherds, crofters.[63]

Other entries in Alex Youngson's diary for 1915 related to the First World War. The two Flag Days held in the autumn were recorded: the first, on Saturday 25 September, raised the grand sum of £48 'in aid of the comforts fund of the ten Battalions of the Seaforth Highlanders' and was observed across Sutherland. The next, on Saturday 23 October, was a Red Cross Scottish Flag Day and the district was one of over 600 towns and villages taking part. Ambulance boats had already been purchased and fitted out by Scottish donations to the Red Cross, and were then on their way to the ill-fated expedition to the Dardenelles.[64]

September, 1915		
Saturday	25	*Wet day*
		Flag Day for Seaforths

October, 1915		
Saturday	16	*Count Flag offering 11am £48*
Saturday	23	*Flag Day Red Cross*

That the then Duchess of Sutherland promoted General R. Baden-Powell's new movement in Sutherland has already been mentioned. While they wore a uniform and drilled, Boy Scout troops and patrols were designed for age groups too young to enlist in the armed services and, indeed, the movement was intended to enable young men to 'be prepared' whether for peace or war. By 1915 Strathy had a fully operational troop with Alice Youngson as its scoutmaster and several of her father's diary entries for that year relate to the Scouts. Dr Silver came from Armadale to offer first aid courses: 'Meeting of Scouts 2pm along with Dr.' [Saturday 30 January]; he was presented by the 1st Strathy Troop with a fishing basket by way of thanks.[65] To the annual round of entertainments and concerts was added a Scouts' Concert; that held in March 1915 was attended by the District Commissioner of Scouts for the County, Charles Heron Watson Esq, of Helmsdale.

March, 1915		
Friday	19	*Scouts Concert*
		Mr Heron Watson arrived
Saturday	20	*Mr Heron Watson left*

With society increasingly militarised, a wartime role was discovered for the Scouts. The Coastguard Service was under pressure as many of its men volunteered, and Baden-Powell offered the services of his Scouts to fill the gaps. By autumn 1915 some 1,800 Boy Scouts were doing Coastguard duty under the direction of the Admiralty, patrolling Britain's shores and sending in reports. Mr Heron Watson also held the post of Sea Scout Commissioner on Admiralty Service for the Watching of the Coast.[66]

June, 1915

Wednesday	2	*Visit of Commander Navy Scouts*
Saturday	26	*Visited Scouts*

Another connection between the Scouts and the war was made in June 1915, when the Strathy Troop were visited by Lieutenant Lord Alistair Leveson-Gower, brother to the 5th Duke of Sutherland. Lord Alistair was an officer in the Life Guards (Blues), an elite cavalry regiment, and (aged twenty-four) had been with the Guards at the front at the start of the war. He had had his horse killed under him, and was himself wounded early in 1915. By the summer he had been awarded the Military Cross and was recovered sufficiently to tour Sutherland promoting the Boy Scouts.[67]

August, 1915

Saturday	14	*At Scouts*
Monday	16	*Lord Alistair Leveson Gower visiting Scouts*

Alice Youngson, then aged forty, appears to have given a lot of attention to her Scouts; at least one picnic was held in 1915, besides the special meetings with official visitors.

For much of 1915, of course, life in Strathy manse continued as it had done before the war. Mr Youngson continued his round of visiting the settlements, attending the funerals of the elderly, supervising work in the glebe and looking after his vegetables. The work of the Pier Committee and the Parish Council continued; the congregations' annual communions and Harvest Thanksgiving took place as usual. Clearly, however, the war brought additional duties. Like so many others, when called upon, Alex Youngson rallied to the national cause. As part of the local establishment, both by reason of his vocation in the Established Church and as a leading member of the Parish Council of Farr, Alex Youngson supported the war effort and might well have been one of those 'ornaments of the pulpit' so criticised by the *Glasgow Herald*'s correspondent for 'urging men to die for their country' while themselves in no danger.[68] In mitigation, we need to remember that he was by now nearly seventy-five, and that he appears to have done his best to lighten the impact of the war on the bereaved and needy.

July 1915			
Thursday	15	*Alex & Margt arrived*	
Friday	16	*Visited Point*	
		{Christina Barbara Cameron	
		{James Angus Mackay	
Saturday	17		
Sunday	18	*Fine day*	*-/5/9*
Monday	19		
Tuesday	20	*Bettyhill*	
Wednesday	21	*Called Precentor's J Gunn Macaulay*	
		Cut lawn grass	
Thursday	29	*Alex & Margt left*	
		Went to Thurso returned eve	

On a positive family note, 1915 was the year that Alex Youngson's son, Alex William, married. The diary for July makes little mention of it, for the groom's father did not travel south for the occasion of the marriage. Alex Jnr and his new wife, however, arrived at the Strathy manse the day after their wedding, and their honeymoon was spent at Strathy while Mr Youngson Snr continued with his parish duties. His diary reads: 'Alex & Marg[are]t arrived' and 'Alex & Margt left – went to Thurso, returned eve[ning].' Alexander William Youngson married Margaret E. Gwynne (née Boffey), the widow of naval architect, David Gwynne, in St Bartholomew's Church, Gourock, on 14 July 1915 and their marital home was to be in Glasgow.[69] Now that he had a household of his own, Alex William's name was removed from the Communicant Roll of Strathy Church – the last year he is recorded as having joined in the annual communion was 1914.

Missing from Alex Youngson's diary for 1915 is any reference to the growing anger felt by many in the parish on the subject of the land. The hardships of the cottars and those holding small crofts had not been removed by the war. Indeed, the grievances created by the Clearances were returning to the fore as opportunities arose to return the land to the population. On the one hand, the Dukes of Sutherland were following a policy of selling off lands in Sutherland, 1891–1919; and on the other, the London government had, from 1912, replaced the CDB with a Board of Agriculture for Scotland. The Board had an increased budget and new powers to apply to the Land Court for the compulsory allocation to smallholders of land considered surplus to the large estates. The question, of course, was who was to benefit from these new opportunities? To which particular smallholders would the newly available land be granted?

At the foot of Strath Halladale, in 1915 the Duke of Sutherland owned the sheep farms of Bighouse and Golval, leased to Donald Innes, laird of the neighbouring Caithness estate of Sandside; and of Kirkton, run as a club farm by Hugh Gunn (the Parish Clerk of Farr), Miss Louisa Gunn on behalf of the deceased Hugh J. Gunn and Murdo Macdonald (all from Baligill) under a lease running since 1896. Both leases expired in 1915 and the year therefore saw a dispute as to who should succeed. The *John O' Groat Journal* as early as January reported plans to lease to five tenants new smallholdings 'of considerable size'. Such a division, however, would benefit the fortunate few who could afford to purchase and take over the existing sheep stock, and not the mass of small crofters in Portskerra and Melvich. Between seventy and eighty crofters put pressure on the Board to offer a scheme more generous to more people; and it refused. In July,

the angry applicants put their case before a visiting Commissioner of the Land Court, who replied that only the Board could
bring schemes before the Court – he was restricted to arbitrating
disputes concerning existing holdings and their common grazing.
Correspondents to the press argued the case, and the war service
of the Portskerra/Melvich applicants was brought into the
matter. One letter, signed 'A.M.' appeared in the *John O' Groat
Journal* in June:

> Several of those who applied are now fighting for their country on
> land and sea for land which they looked for but apparently now
> will never obtain. Is this the spirit of the Land Act? Is this the reward
> of the devotion and sacrifice of our men who are defending our
> land? Is this the best the government can do for our defenders? Is
> this an incentive to our men to defend a country where the land
> alongside them is disposed of in their absence? Is there any wonder
> that a feeling of indignation pervades the community?

In response, another letter argued that the popular campaign was
simply 'another effort to strengthen an otherwise untenable case
of a few about Melvich who profess to represent the people but
really represent only themselves.' To portray war service as
fighting for the country in the expectation of obtaining land
was an argument that was to be heard again. Indeed, in 1917 a
spokesman for the government explicitly promised, in a speech at
Inverness, that the Highlanders would be given possession of the
land at the end of the war; and other such pledges were made.[70]
In 1915, the Duke of Sutherland appears to have made a promise
to attend to the grievances of Portskerra and Melvich when peace
returned and when the absent servicemen were able to make their
claims personally. Kirkton Farm continued as a club, its resident
shepherd employed from Baligill, but on a tacit lease to the
shareholders from year to year.[71]

1919 – Peace, Controversy and Change

As we have seen, for Alex Youngson personally the year 1919
was the year in which he became both Chairman of the Parish
Council of Farr and a nominated member and Chairman of the
School Management Committee. His correspondence on behalf
of servicemen and their dependants continued. The regularities of

his pastoral duties, the garden and the glebe continued to occupy much of his diary space though he spent time ill in bed while the flu epidemic passed through Strathy. The war was ended and the men who had survived were beginning to return home. Those who had died were commemorated; those who still lived found themselves too often forgotten. Local society was divided on both matters – there was controversy about the right way to commemorate the fallen, and also controversy as to what was due to the returned. North coast men and women were again prepared to challenge the establishment. By 1919, revolution had overturned the monarchies of Russia, Germany and Austria-Hungary and the word 'Bolshevik' had entered common currency on Scotland's north coast. Here the land revolution that took place, took place lawfully, if not wholly peacefully. Looking back over the years of his ministry, Alex Youngson may well have seen 1919 as the year the old landed establishment of the district of Strathy abdicated.

Though New Year 1919 was (it was said) celebrated quietly – wartime restrictions on alcohol had yet to be relaxed – the winter round of entertainments was vigorous. The 1st Strathy Boy Scouts held a concert in the public hall on 31 December, collecting funds for the YMCA Huts for the forces still in France, with a silver collection for the Boy Scout Mission to Lepers.

December, 1918

| *Tuesday* | *31* | *Scouts' concert* |

Rev. Neil Mackay of the UF Church gave the opening speech and Alex Youngson presented prizes. The *John O' Groat Journal's* correspondent reported that:

> The success of the concert was due entirely to the perseverance of Miss A. Youngson, Troop Scoutmaster. Having taken over the management of the Troop when it was first formed in the commencing year of the war she has 'carried on' since then in a manner worthy of success. The Scouts, present and past, have a very high opinion of her and of the admirable way in which she 'carried on' the duties without the aid of her assistant, who is now a Cadet Pilot in the RAF.[72]

In Halladale, a Victory Ball had already been celebrated:

Victory Ball at Halladale

Christmas in the district was a red letter day through the indefatigable efforts of an energetic committee . . . by entertaining in
Halladale Public School in real Highland fashion, a gallant band
of khaki clad heroes on Christmas leave, fresh from the devastated
plains of France or Belgium, and likewise from captivity in
Hunland, crowned with laurels.[73]

Among those former prisoners of war now back in the district
was John William Mackay RNR, of Fern Cottage, Portskerra,
who had been a prisoner since the German raider *Moewe*
captured and sank the mail packet SS *Brecknockshire*, one
and a half days out from Rio de Janeiro on 15 February
1917. He was said to have arrived home in good health, thanks
to the Red Cross parcels he had received.[74]

There were, however, those who questioned whether celebration was appropriate in the aftermath of such a war and so recent
mourning. All six of the men named on the Portskerra War
Memorial, for example, died after December 1917. The Strathy
Memorial lists Lance Corporal D. A. Mackay, killed on 2
November 1918, days before the armistice, as a late assault by
the Seaforth Highlanders met strong resistance: aged forty-one,
he was a married man originally from Armadale, who had
returned from Canada in order to join up.[75] In December
1918, Donald Campbell of Portskerra had been buried in Kirkton
having died at Inverness from illness while on leave from his
vessel.[76] In all, thirty-four lives were to be commemorated on the
Strathy, Portskerra/Melvich and Strath Halladale War Memorials: by the end of 1918, four men besides Donald Campbell were
already buried at Kirkton, and three at Strathy itself.[77] From
Lednagullen, Mr D. Munro wrote to the *John O' Groat Journal*
in March 1919 to complain against Strathy's concerts and the
dancing that followed them:

In Strathy they held several of these gatherings under the pretence
of gathering money for the bereaved and needy people of the
district. It is grieving to those who have lost their dear ones to
think that the names of those heroes who fell in winning such a
glorious victory to our nation should be even mentioned at
gatherings where dancing and the singing of comic songs are

revelled in . . . Portskerra has lost heavily on sea and land. It is a disgrace that any of them should go to a dance headed by a piper, grieving them who have lost their all.[78]

Adding to his case, Mr Munro argued that the round of dances was helping to spread the influenza; he called on the local doctors to speak up in the name of public health, and in later correspondence he roundly criticised an unnamed Strathy minister 'seen driving a harmonium or organ to the hall to be played at the concert'. We may, perhaps, presume that this was Mr Youngson, with Alice's harmonium.

The correspondence continued in the weekly paper throughout March and into April 1919. Numbers of ex-servicemen replied, defending 'the delights of dancing in Strathy'. 'Surely those who were cheerful when things are dark and uncertain can still be cheerful though the 'flu is against us,' wrote 'Demobilised' on 14 March: 'Even though we have lost much in this war, we can keep our spirits up by being cheerful. One does not always mourn.' 'Demobilised' also defended 'our beloved old parsons' – surely including Alex Youngson. On 28 March, 'SB' accused Mr Munro of attacking ministers

> . . . more broad minded than the limits of his special dogma. The mobilised men have found [these] ministers real friends in time of need. Times innumerable they have had cause to ask their assistance regarding military and naval matters such as leave etc. To a man they will testify how willingly this has been given irrespective of church connections.[79]

The controversy degenerated: an ex-navy man himself, Mr Munro called the ex-servicemen dancers 'cork-headed idiots', and a group from Bettyhill threatened to demolish his house in retaliation.[80] Entertainments and dancing were mainly seasonal, of course, and the end of winter naturally took the heat out of the situation. The incident is worth recalling, however, in part because it shows the affection in which Mr Youngson was held, but also because it provides early evidence that, after the war, the dancing generations were prepared to challenge the older puritan disciplines defended by the correspondent from Lednagullen.

The Register of Deaths for the District of Strathy shows that five of the six deaths during March and April 1919 were considered to be (at least in part) due to influenza. Two of those who died were aged seventy-seven and one was a schoolboy of five; but the remaining deaths, of an unmarried man of twenty-three and an unmarried woman of thirty, do suggest that Mr Munro's concern that public gatherings could pose a health hazard was not as far-fetched as his opponents made out. Mr Youngson's diary records that he took to his bed on Saturday 29 March and did not get up until the next Thursday: worship on Sunday 30 was cancelled, and a fellow-minister assisted him the next week. Alex Youngson was not out of the manse again until Wednesday 9 April, but he retreated on the Thursday, faced with cold weather, and was unable to conduct worship on Sunday 13. Life returned to normal thereafter; he had thrown off the worst illness he caught in any of the four years covered in his surviving diaries. Across the world, the Spanish flu had killed millions between the autumn of 1918 and the spring of 1919.

Throughout 1919, Alex Youngson's diary records meetings of the 'Memorial Committee', a committee formed to create an appropriate War Memorial. He appears to have chaired the Committee, at least initially, in his capacity as Parish Minister rather than through the local Council.[81]

February, 1919

Monday	3	Meeting of Mem[oria]l Com[mitte]e 7pm
Sunday	9	Call meeting of Mem. Comte Monday 7pm
Monday	10	Meeting School, Memorial 7pm

Because it was important and emotional, the obvious need to commemorate the fallen was not without controversy. Memorials to the dead of the First and Second World Wars are so normal a part of British landscapes that it takes an effort to recollect that, once the First War ended, it still had to be decided how the dead should best be honoured. The YMCA movement, for example, argued that it would be more forward-looking to use the funds subscribed to build not memorials but further YMCA Halls.[82] In the Sutherland community of Creich, the Parish Council deliberated over a memorial, a cottage hospital or a fountain in the village square.[83] Public choice, of course, soon settled on memorials and names were gathered and funds collected. In May, the Duke of Sutherland offered £500 towards memorials to be built in the county.[84] Questions still remained to be discussed: which names should be included? Did deaths count that came after the armistice of 11 November 1918 but before the official signing of the peace treaty at Versailles, 28 June 1919? The General Assembly of the Church of Scotland thought fit to advise Presbyteries that War Memorials should be as comprehensive as possible, and the Presbytery of Tongue agreed 'to do their best to have a complete roll made up for each of the congregations within their bounds of all members, adherents and other parishioners unconnected with any church who have died on war service.'[85]

As we have seen, the parish of Farr was composed of many separate communities: its west ward – Bettyhill and Strathnaver – was distinct from the east, while the east ward, the Registration District of Strathy, itself comprised several settlements. Where, then, should a War Memorial be sited? Should there be one for the parish, or one for each ward, or several? In October 1919, a letter to the *John O Groat Journal* complained that as yet nothing had been done for a War Memorial for Armadale. The writer suggested that the current committee had lost momentum once Armadale refused to back a plan to put the funds gathered in the hands of Mr Gilmour of Rosehall, the proprietor, in order to build a memorial.[86] Mr Youngson, who had called the initial February meeting 'of the tenants of the Armadale estate . . . to erect a memorial to those belonging to the estate who have fallen in the war'[87] clearly had followed his normal practice of looking to the proprietor, whose land might in any case be required for a memorial. The letter writer, who signed himself 'Not a Rosehaller' nominated the local undertaker, D. J. Macdonald, and the Strathy schoolmaster, Hector Mackay, to take over the project. Mr Youngson's diary shows memorial committee meetings throughout 1919 and, besides further memorials for the war-dead of Portskerra and Melvich and of Strath Halladale, one memorial for the Strathy/Armadale estate was built. It stands outside the Parliamentary Kirk and includes at the head of its list of dead the name of Captain Allan Gilmour, of the 10th Battalion (Lovat's Scouts) of the Cameron Highlanders, who died in

Greece, 17 March 1917. This Allan Gilmour was W. E. Gilmour's son and would have been his heir: he had celebrated his marriage at the High Church, Inverness, less than two years before his death. Though his father was the proprietor of Strathy, and all the deaths were tragic, it was, perhaps, stretching a point to consider him as 'belonging to the estate', but Alex Youngson's involvement with W. E. Gilmour of Rosehall we have already noted and, besides, those responsible for other local monuments sought to be as comprehensive as possible as they compiled their names.

Not listed among the dead of the First World War on the Strathy Memorial was Hugh Mackay Cooper, who died of tuberculosis at Strathy Point on 28 August 1919, aged twenty-two, the youngest son of Sandy Cooper and Janet. While Hugh's occupation was given as 'fisherman' in Strathy's Register of Deaths, he had served in the RNR during the war, latterly as a deckhand on the depot ship HMS *Vivid*. At the time of his death on 28 August 1919 he was not long home: Alex Youngson had visited on 2 August. His grave at Strathy, however, is now considered to be a war grave: fatal illness was by no means the least risk common to both soldiers and sailors 1914–19.[88]

August, 1919

Saturday	2	*Visited Doan's boy*
		do/Hugh Cooper

September, 1919

Monday	1	*Hugh Mackay Cooper funeral 12noon*

The public opposition to their proprietor showed by 'Not a Rosehaller' and others within the Armadale Estate was a sign that the day of deference to the personal landlords of the north coast was drawing to a close. Already on 19 March 1914, under the leadership of William Mackay, 'the veteran Land Leaguer',[89] a group of Armadale crofters had written to gain the support of the Board of Agriculture to divide the lands of Mr Gilmour's Armadale sheep farm:

Dear Sir,

At a public meeting of the Armadale Crofters held on 18th instant, it was unanimously resolved to approach the Board with the view of breaking up the Armadale farm for enlargement of holdings and extension of hill grazing. The applicants are 15 and all residing in Armadale and within easy reach of the proposed enlargements.

The laird of Rosehall, like many other landowners throughout the UK, was after the war unable to sustain his investment in land: Strathy, Armadale, Eriboll and others were sent for sale by auction. On 10 July 1919 the Under-Secretary for Scotland received (at his offices in Whitehall) the news that his London agent on behalf of the Board of Agriculture had successfully bid the upset price for lot 7 of the Ewing Gilmour Estate Sale, there being no further competition. The Board had purchased the lands of Strathy and Armadale:

Land for Ex-Soldiers
Sutherland Estate Purchased

The Board of Agriculture for Scotland intimate that under the provisions of the Congested Districts Act 1897 they have purchased from Mr W. Ewing Gilmour . . . a grazing farm extending to 29,050 acres and 135 crofts extending to 10,900 acres. There are also included valuable salmon fisheries and shooting rights. The Board intend to utilise the grazing farm for the purpose of enlarging the holdings of the crofters many of whom have served with His Majesty's forces.[90]

Alex Youngson recorded Mr Gilmour's visit to the parish in December 1919 to collect rents from his Strathy tenants: this was to be the last personal visit of any proprietor to the district. The ancient Strathy Estate remains to this day under the control of the Scottish Executive's Environment and Rural Affairs Department.[91]

December, 1919

Saturday   6   *Mr Gilmour collecting rents*

During 1919 the Board had been in touch with the crofters of Armadale to determine how the Armadale sheep farm should be divided. Letters reached it on behalf of ex-servicemen insisting that they should have priority over applicants who already held crofts. In the event preference was indeed given to those who had served in the war, and also (by way of excluding more recent applicants) to those already connected with Armadale itself. All the arable land of the farm was to be reallocated, with most of the grazing. Fourteen men therefore benefited, choosing to run their new lands co-operatively, in runrig fashion, sharing fields between households rather than allocating them to individuals to cultivate. The Board also provided loans to enable the men to take over the farm steadings, mill and a proportion of the existing sheep stock. Ploughing began in February 1920, so that a crop could be secured later that year.[92] The *Northern Times* reported the 26 February ceremony by which the crofters occupied their new land: 'At 12 o'clock a procession comprising the principal men and children of the school accompanied by their teacher marched from the east end of the district, headed by a piper wearing Highland dress and who had seen much active service in Flanders.'[93] Two flags were carried in the procession, one a Union flag that had seen service at Land League meetings forty years before, and another bearing the words 'Back to the Land'. Refreshments were served, speeches made, a reel danced and symbolic furrows ploughed before everyone returned home. A spokesman was quoted as saying, 'We are entering on a new era and the wrongs of the past are being gradually wiped out. There is no fear of our being infected by Bolshevism.'

Meanwhile, in the autumn of 1918, the Duke of Sutherland had sold his Bighouse Estate by auction to Mr Vernon W. Macandrew, whose wife claimed some ancestry from the house of Mackay. Mr Macandrew also subsequently succeeded in purchasing the lands of Forsinard and thus owned the Halladale from mouth to source. In July 1919 the *Northern Times* reported, 'Mr & Mrs Macandrew and party are at present residing on their Bighouse Estate and are obtaining excellent sport both on loch and river. Recently they have visited all the tenants on their Bighouse Estate, and received a warm, a loyal, and cordial reception from all.'[94] Indeed, the Macandrews courteously visited Strathy manse on Thursday 5 June.

The new family at Bighouse diligently offered what they considered the traditional hospitality and social leadership that went with the lands they had purchased, and their generosity was carefully reported in the weekly press. A 'sumptuous repast and sports' were held at Bighouse in July to celebrate the Versailles Treaty and the official end of the war – the laird's own cars were sent to convey the children from Halladale. The cars were out again in October, offering lifts to enable the tenants to pay their rents to the new laird in person, in 'one of the spacious drawing rooms of the mansion', while in the dining room Mrs Macandrew served tea and cakes. The press notice, clearly written on behalf of the laird, asserted that this was the first time since 1817 that rents had been received in Bighouse itself. A further notice in December 1919 averred that Mrs Macandrew '. . . in her usual kind and generous manner has presented the deserving poor of Halladale, Melvich and Portskerra with very handsome Christmas gifts. Such gracious acts of kindness will ever remain a green leaf in the memory of the recipients.' These notices in the press suggest a campaign to win the hearts and mind of the people of Melvich, Portskerra and Halladale.[95] Contributions of £1 annually in Mr Macandrew's name were made to the Central Funds of the UF Church through the Halladale congregation's local collector for Golval, Kirkton and Bighouse.[96] Loyalty, however, is a frame of mind and cannot be purchased.

The times were unfavourable to the assertion of the rights of landowners in the north, however apparently gracious. Of all the ways in which service in the war was expected to be commemorated, the distribution of more land to the crofters of the Highlands held pride of place in the northern mind. The General Meeting of the Territorial Force Association for Sutherland (December 1918) considered that demobilised men who desired to acquire smallholdings and were otherwise suitable should be given preference; and that the government should provide the necessary capital.[97] The Free Church of Scotland's Association for the Betterment of the Highlands and Islands informed the Secretary for Scotland: 'The people regard the sacrifices they have made for King and Country as demanding for the returning soldiers, and for the friends of those who sacrificed their lives, a better share of the land for which they suffered.' Financial support for the fishing and other industries subsidiary to crofting was also recommended.[98] Speaking in the House of Lords, the Duke of Sutherland supported a new land settlement:

> We must look to these Bills which cover the broad terms of Land Settlement to establish a contented aftermath to the Great War amongst the mass of demobilised servicemen, to allay Bolshevism, unrest, and disorder in its many forms – to prevent the going out of our best blood to foreign countries, and for the well-being of the country itself to establish a class of contented and industrious people of the soil, in which they can themselves personally take an interest.[99]

Lloyd George's coalition government, faced with a national miners' strike, riots in Glasgow and land seizures in the Hebrides, for exactly the Duke's reasons planned to give the Board of Agriculture more funds and greater powers; in the meantime, however, officialdom's good intentions and as-yet-unfulfilled promises served to aggravate passions.[100]

With effect from 8 June 1919, the Board of Agriculture repartitioned the easterly sheep farm of Bighouse (located between Bighouse itself and Golval) into three smallholdings with two further sections of land granted to enlarge existing holdings. The new farms were 1,250, 1,383 and 1,565 acres respectively and caused outrage in Melvich and Portskerra, where crofts had an average arable size of 3.5 acres. The partition had achieved nothing for the bulk of the local population, had left the ex-servicemen's claims on the shelf and, because most of the only available land had now been allocated, appeared to offer little or no hope at all for the future despite the promises made in 1915. Public meetings were held and correspondence fired off to the Board, to the Secretary for Scotland and to the MP, who asked questions in the House of Commons. Threats began to be made: a public meeting at Portskerra on 7 March informed the Board that its failure to reverse its decision before it was too late:

> . . . may result in proceedings which they would deplore, and expressing to the Board their determination to have justice done to

their claims for a fair share of the land which is in their immediate neighbourhood and to which the men of the district have a just right in return for the sacrifice they made during the past four and a half years.

The community had a vision for its future, for which it was demanding the support of the state agencies, the Board of Agriculture and the Highland Reconstruction Committee. One part of the dream was the division of the lands of Bighouse, Golval and Kirkton between the 80–100 small crofting claimants, with ex-soldiers and sailors being given preference. Further, the harbour of Portskerra should be modernised to allow for greatly increased fishing activity; and a light railway should be constructed up Strath Halladale to the main line at Forsinard to allow catches to be sent south by rail. All of this programme had at one time or another been given official encouragement: the Duke of Sutherland had instructed surveys to establish the viability of the railway; County Council and CDB funds had been available for harbour works for some years. One correspondent summarised: 'More land with better transport facilities is the first essential in our case.' With the lands of Bighouse out of reach, however, attention turned to the club farm of Kirkton.[101]

Mr Macandrew wished to utilise Kirkton – the one section of land remaining at his disposal – as a home farm. He took action to bring to an end the unwritten year-to-year lease by which it had been run by the Baligill club. Moreover, he claimed that at the time of his purchase he had not been informed of the Duke's promise of 1915 to the servicemen and that, therefore, he was neither morally nor legally bound by it. Nevertheless the Board of Agriculture's local officer in July 1919 prepared a scheme by which the Board would use its powers to acquire Kirkton to be run as a club by forty-two local claimants. The stumbling block was the sheep stock on the farm: Vernon Macandrew had paid a high price for this to the Duke, and the Board foresaw that, if it had to lend this sum to the crofters, it would never be able to recoup its investment from the new tenants. Nothing therefore was done. Faced with the arrival of the new farming year of 1920, the local leaders negotiated with Mr Macandrew in person but achieved no satisfaction. He correctly stated that, of the 34,000 acres of the Bighouse Estate and the 36,000 acres of his Forsinard Estate, only the Forsinard deer forest and the 2,893 acres of

Kirkton farm remained at his disposal, the Board having already subdivided Bighouse and also created club farms at Craggie and Forsinain, with two further arable smallholdings at Forsinain. Given that the central section of Strath Halladale had remained under crofting tenure, it could therefore be said that: 'In probably no other part of the country can it be shown that almost the entire estate has been set apart for the purpose of the crofting community'.[102] Nevertheless, Portskerra and Melvich remained 'one of the most congested areas in the County of Sutherland'.[103]

In June 1920, twenty-three activists from Portskerra occupied Kirkton. Twelve had seen service with the RNR and five with 5/Seaforth. One had served with the Canadian navy, another in the Gordon Highlanders, another in the Engineers. Two fathers took part, one representing a son still to be demobilised from 5/Seaforth, while the other's son had been killed on active service. One raider was a widow whose husband had been killed.[104] The *Northern Times* reported under the heading: 'Portskerra Ex-Servicemen take Action (Contributed)':

> A scene unprecedented in the history of this north part of Sutherland was witnessed on Monday morning when the ex-servicemen and their parents and friends, having assembled with their cattle and sheep and to the strains of the bagpipes, the tune being that which was played on the 5th Seaforth's landing at Boulogne in May 1915, the piper being one of those who played on that memorable day, with flags flying drove them to the sheep farm of Kirkton, which fell into the proprietor's hands on the 28th ult, having previously been tenanted by a club of three, whose holdings are on the neighbouring estate.[105]

A dance was held that night in the Melvich Drill Hall to celebrate the occupation. Next, a sheriff officer formally served interdicts on fourteen of the men, following application to the court on behalf of Mr Macandrew; but the raiders refused to remove their stock, rendering themselves liable to imprisonment for contempt of court.

The Portskerra raiders received much support: the Rogart Post of the Comrades of the Great War 'strongly commended' the raid. Sir R. Leicester Harmsworth, Bt, the local Member of Parliament (supporting the coalition government), visited and interviewed the raiders: 'The solution, in his opinion, was that the

Board of Agriculture should enter into possession and make over the land to the people of the district in the manner arranged for under the Land Settlement Act.' In the House of Lords, the Duke of Sutherland laid the blame on the inaction of the Board. Sutherland County Council agreed – with only W. E. Gilmour dissenting – 'that the County Council ask the Board of Agriculture to redress the grievances of the Portskerra crofters and ex-servicemen in regard to Kirkton Farm now taken over by Mr Macandrew.'

Others crofters followed the initial raiders' example and letters were received by the Board respectfully threatening illegal occupations of the lands held by the Melvich Hotel, and of the club farms in Halladale:

> I have to say that if your Board still refuses to take action and assist me my only course is to take possession of one of the houses and a holding. Surely I am quite justified in fighting for a home in the country I have fought for the last three years, and as sure as I write it I will take forcible possession and let the world see how I have been treated . . . from our family two brothers and myself had been on active service for upwards of four years.
>
> I ask your Board to assist me in the case and if you do help me, good, and if not my only course is to fight it alone and with the other soldier boys.
>
> I am, sir, your obedient servant . . .[106]

Land already rented by smallholders, however, could not be redistributed and the officials of the Board continued to insist that the likely cost of acquiring Kirkton was too high. Privately, they suggested that 'drastic action' should be taken against the raiders, but no political support for imprisonment was forthcoming from the Secretary for Scotland. As time went on, however, the situation turned from black and white into shades of grey. Other claimants appeared, who had not participated in the occupation, insisting that their respect for legality should not be penalised. The existing shepherd at Kirkton and his son wrote to the Board, hoping their interests would not be neglected. Meanwhile, it seemed that Mr Macandrew's primary concern was for the fishing on the Halladale. In October 1920, a conference for all the parties was held at Melvich at which the Board's representative said he had instructions that, failing an amicable agreement, the farm would be taken for land settlement. Despite this, the Board never did obtain overall ownership of the Bighouse lands and Forsinard as it had in Strathy and Armadale. Its 1922 proposals to turn Kirkton into a club farm were rejected by a meeting in the drill hall and the affair petered out with no benefit to the generality of the ex-servicemen.[107] Mr Macandrew sold on his Bighouse Estate at the end of the 1920s.

In none of this – in the press coverage, the remaining government files or in papers derived from Mr Macandrew's agents – is there the slightest indication that any of the district's ministers were involved, whether to support the Portskerra raiders or to urge legality and an end to the occupation. The main action, of course, took place in 1920, after the conclusion of the last of our diaries from Alex Youngson, so that source of evidence is denied us. The Portskerra land raid serves to highlight the enduring undercurrents of grievance felt by those with small crofts or none, as well as the sense of bitterness and betrayal felt by those who survived the Great War. Richard Holmes, historian of the army's lower ranks, suggests that 'Many of those who came to look back upon the war as a waste and sham did so, not at the time of the armistice, but through the lens of penury and disillusionment that characterised the post-war years for too many of them.'[108] The minister of Strathy's Established Church, however, receiving courteous calls from the Macandrews and on better terms yet with Mr Gilmour, had little point of contact with those seeking to change the local patterns of landholding by illegal pressure.

With the plans for a better infrastructure for the north coast, for a better harbour at Portskerra and for rail connections to the south, Alex Youngson did have sympathy. In fact, memoranda at the back of his diary for 1911 show that he had solicited and collected donations from some twenty-four landowners and merchants across Scotland and the UK towards 'Help for Portskerra Slip'. An interesting note at the back of the 1919 diary was entitled 'Light Railway'. His own initials, 'AY' headed a list of Armadale and Strathy men: 'Mr McIntosh Laid[nagulle]n; Mr Munro Armadale; Mr McDonald, Point; Mr Jas Sutherland; Mr John Gunn; Mr McDonald, Brawl'. A press report of March 1919 had in fact predicted that, now that a railway connection from Forsinard to Portskerra was projected, 'it was expected that the adjoining districts will bestir themselves', and specific reference was made to a possible branch along the coast to Armadale.[109] Mr Youngson's diary is evidence that, under his chairmanship, a committee was formed to pursue the plan. No Strath Halladale railway was ever constructed to Portskerra, however, without which any connection to Strathy and Armadale remained a dream.

As a parish minister, Alex Youngson was on good terms with the local lairds and landowners. When he was able to use his connections to solicit funds and support that benefited the local community, good results followed. At the end of August 1919, for example, the Pilkingtons of Sandside, Reay, hosted an enjoyable tea and party for the joint Strathy and Reay Scout Troops: 'Alice with scouts to Reay' [30 August 1919].[110] In the circumstances of 1919, however, the separate settlements of the east ward of Farr sought to go their own ways with regard to War Memorials and to pursue their own quests for land and economic development. Associated most clearly with the communities around Strathy Bay, Alex Youngson – though a senior member of the Parish Council for Farr – was distrusted by some in Armadale and bypassed by Portskerra in its hunger for land. Indeed, part of the grievance of the people of Portskerra was the 1896–1919 lease of Kirkton to the Baligill club headed by Hugh Gunn, Clerk to the Parish Council; Baligill, they insisted, was clearly a separate settlement and not the closest to the farm. Not only his own reluctance to travel but also public sentiment could confine the Strathy minister to a limited sphere, as each settlement increasingly sought to speak for itself and to find its own voice.

One final entry in Alex Youngson's 1919 diary needs to be discussed. Wednesday 26 November, 'Meeting of Presbyt – storm of wind and rain'. The minutes of the Presbytery of Tongue show that Strathy's minister did not attend the meeting held at Tongue, though those that did appointed him to be their Moderator in 1920.[111] No doubt the storm prevented him from travelling. Alex Youngson, however, by telegraph added his consent to that of the meeting to the draft 'Articles Declaratory of the Constitution of the Church of Scotland in Matters Spiritual' sent down by the General Assembly to all Presbyteries. The possibility of a union between the United Free Church of Scotland and the established Church of Scotland had been discussed by committees of both General Assemblies since 1909. The UF Church Assembly had already passed an Act anent Spiritual Independence in 1906, asserting its right to independence in all matters of doctrine, worship, discipline and church government, to alter its own constitution and to unite with other churches. Now the Established Church, in its turn and after lengthy internal debate, was at the last stages of agreeing its own charter – one that declared its independence in matters spiritual from all secular authority. It was reported to the 1920 General Assembly that the Articles Declaratory had obtained the consent of an overwhelming majority of Presbyteries, besides that of Tongue. The United Kingdom Parliament in its Church of Scotland Act (1921) declared the Articles to be lawful, recognising the inherent divine authority of the Church's stance. The UF and Established Churches finally united in 1929 to form the Church of Scotland as it is known today.[112]

By the end of 1919, therefore, the writing was on the wall for Strathy's 'Auld Kirk' congregation. Any national union would inevitably see their small numbers swallowed by the larger and more vigorous Strathy and Halladale congregation of the local United Free Church. Their minister, aged seventy-eight, must increasingly lack energy for the sort of new initiatives needed to sustain congregational life. Further, a ministry that had enjoyed support from Strathy's proprietor, W. E. Gilmour, could not expect the same support from the secular, impersonal and remote Board of Agriculture that was the Strathy Estate's landlord after 1919. The ecclesiastical and civil structures that had underpinned the settled world of Alex Youngson's early ministry at Strathy were to change fundamentally after the Great War.

8

Retrospect – Minister and Community

At the union of the Churches in 1929, the UF congregation in Strathy became the Church of Scotland parish of Strathy East, while Alex Youngson's charge became the Strathy West parish. Such a division, however, was hardly viable and in October 1930 the Presbytery of Tongue accepted Rev. Alexander Youngson's decision to retire to enable the congregations to unite under a new minister and the new name of the Church of Scotland parish of Strathy and Halladale. Further: 'The Presbytery unanimously resolved to record their high appreciation not only of the faithfulness and efficiency with which Mr Youngson had discharged all the duties of his ministerial office, but also of his outstanding services on the public bodies of the whole civil parish of Farr.'[1] It is time to look, briefly, at this judgement. What light have the Youngson diaries shed on the practice of ministry in the 'Auld Kirk': the established Church of Scotland before the union? What successes were achieved? What were the weaknesses of this ministry in the scattered north coast settlements? How did Mr Youngson understand the 'duties of his ministerial office'? Is there any sense that his ministry typified that of the 'Auld Kirk', in its final years? And about the community itself, to which he ministered: what do Mr Youngson's diaries tell us of north Sutherland at the start of the twentieth century?

Among the notes recorded in Alex Youngson's dairy for 1911 is a paragraph, perhaps something said or written by someone else that had caught his attention, or perhaps his own thoughts:

We have worked here for the past years. It is but little we have done: a few men and women brought to Christ, a few children brought to baptism; a little less vice, a little more cleanlinesss – we have shared it all – the bitterness, the disappointment, the little victories: – how is it to be in the years to come.

This is a stark and realistic assessment of a ministry; it does not claim too much; it puts more emphasis on sharing in the life of the parish than on changing individual lives. Yet it does expect the Christian faith to change lives; its prime hope is that men and women should be brought to Christ. Again from the opening to the 1911 diary: 'I love to think of little children carried in the arms of Jesus: but there comes a time in the life of every child when Jesus puts them down and says unto them "Follow me".' Alex Youngson's ministry, from the records left to us, appears to have emphasised pastoral support and social involvement, but at its heart there was also an evangelical spirit that encouraged others to decide to follow Jesus.

Even bearing in mind the previously mentioned difficulties of using the Communion Roll to measure the health of a Highland congregation, it is worth noting that there was rarely a year when new members were not added to the communicant membership of Mr Youngson's kirk, for a time more than balancing those removed by death. For some, joining the church appears to have been a decision taken during or after a period of distress: the mother of Private David Jackson of 5/Seaforth; the parents of young Robert Calder, who died at Forsinard aged fourteen in April 1911; valiant Lizzie Gunn, standing by her father during his crisis with the School Board. At the risk of too strongly identifying a life's changed orientation with the sacrament, perhaps these few individuals may stand for however many were the 'men and women brought to Christ' by this ministry, whether or not they came forward to the Lord's Supper. In such matters, no historical evidence is adequate.

'A few children brought to baptism': Alex Youngson's baptismal policies have already been discussed. He took an open and welcoming approach that may have brought spiritual comfort, even joy, to the adults concerned. He sought through the sacraments to proclaim the redemption already achieved by Jesus Christ: 'Sin did not take God by surprise. He had foreseen it and had provided a Redeemer before it had led us captive. Man was left to his own free will – but fell – hence a Redeemer.'[2] We may imagine that such personal crises as the unexpected pregnancy of a young unmarried girl did not take him by surprise; rather, he would have emphasised the way forward offered by Christ. The 'tale of two jars', retold in the 1912 diary, explained his mindset in parable form: 'One jar said: "When we go from the well full we come back empty – is it not sad". Said the other: "But when we go back empty we come back full – is it not good that however empty, we come back full".' To emphasise that people could find fullness in Christ, however poor or weak in themselves, appears to have been a lasting goal of this ministry.

'It was indeed a source of pleasure for him at all times to take part in any cause that had either the sacred, the social, or the intellectual good of the community at heart.'[3] This reported statement of Alex Youngson's has already been noted in connection with his, sometimes controversial, support for the concerts and entertainments of the winter. Such an objective would also explain his support for the Sutherland Celtic Society and, indeed, his participation in the Parish Council and the educational politics of the parish of Farr. The formal business of the Presbytery of Tongue was less attractive to his practical mind than the essential realism of the Parish Council. His temperament was that of an activist, preferring participation and positive example to aloof condemnation. Moral challenge, though, was not lacking, as has been noted from his support for the temperance movement; it can also be seen in two simple verses jotted in the notes to the diary for 1911:

There is a little Public House which every one can close.
It is the little Public House that's just below the nose.

There is a little goodness plot
Which everyone can sow.
It is the little goodness plot
You are yourself, you know.

'A little less vice, a little more cleanliness' were objectives of this ministry, and Alex Youngson sought such 'social good' by contributing to north coast society and by engaging in its local political processes and structures. We have no means of measuring his achievements; he was, in any case, in these matters co-operating closely with the ministers of the other denominations active in Strathy.

This study has noted the difficulties of life on the north coast in Mr Youngson's time, especially for women, more than one of whom was found drowned in Portskerra harbour. 'We have shared it all – the bitterness, the disappointment . . .' Two funerals of babies were recorded in 1919 in the diaries: 'Funeral of . . . still born baby 2pm' [13 January 1919]. Neither the death of this child, nor that of the child that died in June, was recorded in the official Register of Deaths but their Christian funerals may have brought some comfort to the mothers. Also in 1919, Lexy Mackay was found, having hanged herself in her barn: 'Lexy found dead' [27 June 1919]. The Register of Deaths shows that Lexy was single and aged sixty-nine. Her unmarried sister, with whom she had shared a home, had died the month before from cancer of the stomach and had been buried at Strathy. It is clear from the record of those he frequently visited that Alex Youngson's pastoral priority was to offer comfort to people in distress, and to the dying. How far he could enter into the depression and blackness that afflicted some we cannot tell, though his own experiences of bankruptcy and bereavement may have brought him insight. 'Lift the eye', he wrote in 1919, 'to Him who is above the stars and who holds the sea, yea the sea of human thought and trouble, in the hollow of His hand'.

Alex Youngson's was a pastoral ministry, practical, and a ministry of presence: several of the comments recorded in the press noted his kindness and willingness to assist, irrespective of denominational loyalty. On public matters, John Mackay, Chilsey paid him the compliment of saying that he always brought 'a calm and judicious spirit of justice and fair play'.[4] Perhaps a saying in his 1912 diary reflects his ambition for himself: 'Gentleness is strength held in reserve and placed at the service of weakness.' The work of the Parish Council certainly enabled him to bring his administrative talents to the service of the weakest in the community. 'God is love', he wrote on a spare page of his 1919 diary, quoting from 1 John 4:7. He went on to note that that biblical passage affirms that whoever loves is born of God and Alex Youngson added: 'Whosoever loveth the meanest of His creatures may bring us nearer to Him and may be a proof that we are the Sons of God.' This 1919 footnote is the most theological comment to survive, penned by Alex Youngson: it embodies a simple Christian humanism.

Living in a society where everything local was known and where controversy could lead to invective, Alex Youngson was not appreciated by all. He was not one of the more doctrinally severe of Scottish ministers and some may have criticised his theology as insufficiently rigorous. There were those who tried to burn down his church just before it reopened in October 1911: workmen sleeping in the building 'were awakened by a noise and a smell of burning and found a large pile of sticks and shavings which had evidently just been lighted.'[5] There was the faction that considered that those ministers who supported the social events of early 1919 did not deserve the name of minister. The bulk of the church-going population chose to attend congregations other than his, perhaps for historical reasons and family loyalties, perhaps also because his preaching may have been uninspired. There was some truth in the assessment recorded in the diary for 1911: 'We have worked here for the past years. It is but little we have done.'

There were limitations to Alex Youngson's ministry, some of them geographical. It has been noted that the visiting lists in the diaries for 1911, 1912 and 1915 cover in full Strathy East and West, Strathy Point, Brawl and Baligill, but list only a few selected names for Melvich and Portskerra, and cover Halladale not at all. Headings for Armadale, Lednagullen and Fleuchary were left blank. From this and from his daily notes of where he spent his time, it can be seen that his ministry was mainly conducted within a mile or so of his manse. Indeed, he was welcomed as a 'stranger' at an Armadale entertainment[6] just as folk from Strath Halladale were welcomed as 'strangers' in Strathy. The term did not mean, of course, that he was unknown: it meant, simply and yet importantly, that he came from another settlement. Armadale, however, with its immediate neighbours, was an integral part of the Church of Scotland parish of Strathy to which Alex Youngson was called. Armadale was further from Strathy manse than other settlements of the parish, true, but the doctor travelled from Armadale throughout the whole of Farr. When some rejected Alex Youngson's lead in the 1919 planning for a War Memorial, perhaps he had sown some of that rejection himself.

Alex Youngson was a minister of the 'Auld Kirk'; he had chosen the part of the Established Church, back in the 1860s and 1870s when the Free Church of Scotland had made good its claim to be an alternative national denomination and when those of a decidedly evangelical theology, if presbyterian, were either United Presbyterian or Free Church. Though its theology might be broad-based, the 'Auld Kirk' had an inherited status in Scotland: its ministers, even those of the north coast, lived in large manses and enjoyed the produce of large glebes. Indeed, some historians and critics of the Sutherland Clearances accused the Established Church's ministers of profiting from their co-operation with the landlords. Mr Youngson employed men and women to work his glebe, and to some extent expected that they would make themselves available when he asked. The Church of Scotland had, a century earlier, managed Scotland's national systems of poor relief and parish schools; his ambition was to offer these services through the contemporary vehicles of the Parish Council and the School Board. He was familiar with the administrative agencies of his period and, though through them he sought such economic developments as were or might have been practical, he had no profound vision for a more socially just or mobile society – such as was, perhaps, held by Rev. Hector Macaulay of Strathy Free Church. Further, he was also a graduate of Aberdeen University and possessed a Master of Arts degree in a community where the schools rarely taught anyone above the age of fourteen. He was on social terms with the proprietor; and (certainly only after election) he came to head the Parish Council. When looking for financial support for projects, whether for his own Sabbath School treat or the pier projects for Port Grant and Portskerra, or for the War Memorial, his instinct and expertise were to tap the generosity of landed wealth and the merchant classes of the south. Towards the end of his ministry he was given a commission as a Justice of the Peace. Alex Youngson was an establishment figure, both by status and by orientation. There is little evidence that people in trouble called uninvited at his door, though he diligently went to their homes.

With such establishment backing, Mr Youngson offered a single-minister ministry: he, by himself, represented his congregation and made its decisions. He alone controlled contacts with those offering financial support and to the Presbytery; he led the worship and ran the Sabbath School. Friday men's meetings at the annual communion were not a feature of the parish church at Strathy, and there is no suggestion in Alex Youngson's diaries of the prayer meetings that the UF Synod, for example, saw as a sign of the spiritual health of its congregations. Certainly he made one effort to create a Kirk Session with a proper quorum, but the men chosen seem to have depended more on his selection than on popular recognition and had few if any active spiritual duties. By contrast the UF Church had effective elders in both Strathy and Halladale, and diligent networks of area collectors soliciting donations towards the denomination's central funds, its foreign and its home missions.[7] For Alex Youngson, the sphere for his ministerial work was the parish and not the congregation: he visited all homes, attended all funerals, offered the ordinances of religion to all and placed his administrative talents at the service of local government. With such a vision, a minister could direct mission in the parish entirely alone, and (apart from the assistance of his daughter), Alex Youngson did just that. With a minister with such a very restricted vision for (and perhaps suspicious of) local church leadership besides himself, the Established Church congregation was less of a fellowship and more of an audience, albeit within a society strongly imbued with a presbyterian Christian ethos. If the sample of Strathy was in any way typical, an unselfconsciously arrogant minister-oriented culture constricted his 'Auld Kirk' congregation's life as a Christian community. On his retirement in 1930, Alex Youngson retained in his own hands the post of Session Clerk and Alice Youngson was appointed Clerk to the Vacancy Committee – were there really no others of the congregation able to take on these duties?[8]

How far, then, did Alex Youngson's ministry at Strathy typify that of the Established Church, the 'Auld Kirk', of his day – that of the last decades before the Union? Clearly, ministries of his type were at one end of a scale that stretched all the way to the elite of well-connected ministers of large city congregations, conveners of powerful central committees, Moderators and past-Moderators of the General Assembly. But how many of the Church of Scotland's ministers might identify with Alex Youngson? Because attitudes to church membership differed very considerably from north to south, there is little point attempting to discover how many other parishes had a communicant roll similar to Strathy. What can be attempted, however, is to ask how many ministers were – like Alex Youngson – able to run their congregations without any real need to obtain the permission of a Kirk Session. A survey of the 1929 *Year Book* of the Church[9] has therefore been made, to identify all congregations with only one or two elders (or none). (A Session with fewer than two elders was technically inquorate and, in order to meet at all, would need to be supplemented with an external assessor appointed via the Presbytery.) This statistical approach has its limitations: a well-respected former Moderator with a powerful personality might be able to sway his Session with little debate, no matter how many elders there were. If there were virtually no elders at all, however, then the minister must have had as free a hand as Alex Youngson clearly had. The 1929 *Year Book* printed statistics gathered in 1927 and reported to the 1928 General Assembly. It showed a total of 1,375 ministers in parishes. Of these, 132 served in parishes with zero, one or two elders: say, 10 per cent of the total. The pattern is particularly frequent in the north and west: six out of ten of the ministers in the Presbytery of Tain come into this category; six out of nine in the Presbytery of Dornoch, ten out of thirteen in Lochcarron, eight out of ten in Skye. All six charges in Strathy's Presbytery of Tongue had two or less elders in 1929: indeed, only Tongue and Strathy itself reported having any elders at all, one each. The pattern was repeated in the Western Isles: in Uist, four of the seven charges had two or fewer elders; in Lewis the figure was four out of six; in Islay and Jura, four out of eight. Elsewhere the pattern, though widespread, was not so dominant, being confined entirely to rural Presbyteries. Such parishes as Coulter, Dolphinton and Skirling in the Presbytery of Biggar had either two or one elders – and in those parishes, communicant membership was three or four times larger than that of Strathy. The 'Auld Kirk' ministers of the rural Borders clearly considered that one or two elders were quite sufficient for parishes with a membership of around 200: for example, Eckford (Presbytery of Jedburgh) had one elder and a membership of 229. Parishes with a minimum number of elders can also be found in the Presbyteries of Peebles, Haddington, Dunbar, Duns, Chirnside, Kelso, Earlston, Selkirk, Lochmaden and Langholm. Occasional examples were found in rural Angus, Fife, Perthshire and Argyll; the pattern also occurred in one of the three Orkney Presbyteries, that of the North Isles. Only in and around the cities, in central Scotland and along the Clyde coast, and (interestingly) in Aberdeenshire, Moray and Gordon were Kirk Sessions routinely larger than a minimum number of elders and the minister.

In all, ministries of this pattern could be found in forty-five of the eight-four Scottish Presbyteries of the Church of Scotland, some 53 per cent. It is clear that Alex Youngson's pattern of church government was not at all untypical of the rural ministry of the 'Auld Kirk', even if Strathy's small, scattered, north Highland population placed him at one end of the scale.

Essentially the 'Auld Kirk' rural minister offered by himself whatever pastoral care might be required; he made such policy decisions as might be needed; the session only met to assist with the communion. Congregational leadership came entirely from the minister and the manse. Whatever the personal qualities of the minister, such a pattern may described as institutionally arrogant, being based on the well-meaning assumption that the minister's judgement was better than anyone else's. Such institutional arrogance is part of the legacy of the 'Auld Kirk' to the current Church of Scotland: at the General Assembly of 2000, the Church's Board of Ministry reported 'We must all repent of the wrong belief that ministry is primarily the work of ministers. This prevalent view in the Kirk distorts the New Testament teaching . . .'[10]

Alex Youngson's ability to offer leadership (both spiritual and secular) in his parish, which he clearly saw as part of his calling, also owed something to his non-denominational approach and something to his genuine kindliness; further, he benefited from a culture of deference that was passing away. As the permanent residents living in the largest houses in the parish, we have seen how the teachers, doctors, ministers and the hotel keepers came to take the chair at social gatherings. Ministers also routinely stood for election to public posts, a field of leadership where teachers and doctors, as public employees, had less scope. The crofting communities, however, also generated their own local leadership: those who were spokesmen and representatives like John Mackay, Chilsey; or administrators like Hugh Gunn. John Chilsey, Hugh Mackay (Trantlemore), Thomas Munro (Newlands) and John Munro (Strathy West) were all crofters who successfully competed for votes against the Sutherland Estates' factor from Tongue and against the ministers; the respect in which they were held came not so much from deference to education, status or vocation, but from lifelong personal knowledge. The various settlements looked to their representatives (who were independent in the sense of not standing on the platform of a political party) to see that they were not neglected in the allocation of whatever resources, contracts and grants were available. This was a participatory democracy (albeit largely male orientated).

Although distant from British centres of power, the crofters of the north coast were by no means ignorant of the world: indeed, their horizons were broad. Parents placed a high emphasis on education. Both men and women left for employment elsewhere in Scotland; families maintained contacts across the world to the emigrant communities of the Empire and to the United States. Men returning from wartime service added to the parish's collective experience of the world. Clerks to the Parish Council and individual crofters negotiated, sometimes shrewdly, sometimes naively, with Edinburgh and London's civil servants and politicians. Working in the public eye of their neighbours and local settlements, crofters and their families were always conscious of living in community, but they also valued personal dignity and respect. Asked by the 1901 Census whether their heads of household were employers, workers or 'on own account', their standard reply was 'On own account – at home'. They might be poor, but controlling their own land gave (at least to the men) a quality of life and a frame of mind far removed from that of the industrial worker of the cities, typically living at that time in a one- or two-room flat without sanitation and without security of employment. North coast crofters, therefore, were not 'Bolsheviks'; they did not look to overthrow the state or to engage in class warfare: they were quite willing, as free citizens, to shake the Marquis of Stafford's hand when he visited his estates before 1914.

The people of these communities, even after a hundred years, were nevertheless conscious that they were excluded from lands their forebears had ancestrally occupied; and that it was the landowning classes that had perpetrated this. Writing to the CDB in January 1900, John Mackay of Diamond Cottage, Melvich, criticised plans to offer lands at Syre in Strathnaver to a few selected smallholders: he believed that only the better-off could afford to take on the stock and that therefore the mass of small crofters would be excluded. Nevertheless, he wrote, 'I have always hoped to see this Strath repeopled and I think that even yet it could be accomplished'.[11] The crofters were practical people, making choices in line with what was possible. Challenging the entrenched power of such members of the imperial British Establishment as the Duke of Sutherland was, most of the time, impractical – yet the hopes remained. British culture, the British Empire and the English language offered opportunities for improvement and for a better life for the children; most adults were bilingual – yet the old Gaelic music was best loved during winter socials, even while the new songs of the music hall of the south were also sung. 'Auld Kirk' ministers like Alex Youngson might be, as he seems to have been, individually respected and trusted, yet popular loyalty was mainly given elsewhere, to the free congregations in the tradition of the 1843 Disruption.

In Mr Youngson's time, the people of the east ward of Farr supported seven places of Christian worship: the four churches of Strathy, the UF hall in Melvich, the Free and the UF mission churches of Strath Halladale. Children born in the parish came to Christian baptism as a matter of course; the Christian ministers officiated at funerals. This was a society whose rites of passage took Christian form, and where the passing of time – the arrival of New Year and of Harvest – was a cause for Christian worship. The fast and preparation days associated with the annual communion retained their prior claim to time and attention. No unnecessary work was done on the Sabbath: spinning and knitting were cleared up on Saturday evening, water brought in from the well, the Sunday meal prepared in advance and clothes prepared for church. Within the public schools, children learnt by heart the stories of the Bible, the praise of the psalms and the Christian doctrine of the catechism. People were not well off, yet they contributed with generosity to the appeals for good causes and to benefit events for the distressed, as social custom and their churches' teaching asked them to do. Our earlier judgement that the Established Church's congregation was more of an audience and less of a fellowship needs now to be qualified. This was a society where Christian teaching had been internalised to a significant extent, and families sought to put their faith into practice in the daily and weekly routines of life. Those attending Mr Youngson's congregation may not have enjoyed the devout fellowship of the prayer meetings and Bible studies of the three Free Church traditions, but we should not doubt that they knew themselves to be part of a fundamentally Christian people.

Culture, of course, does not stand still. We have seen the way that, after the Great War, the ex-servicemen and their dancing generation were fully prepared to challenge the strictures of the older puritanism. Having experienced the harsh, humanitarian fellowship of the trenches or of the lower decks, they returned more assertive and more prepared to challenge authority. Those who had been engaged across the world in total war on land or sea could hardly have returned with unchanged attitudes to the small routines of, say, Sabbath observance. Yet even as the war ceased to be a crusade and became a bloodbath to be endured, it nurtured a non-doctrinal piety, suspicious of denominational distinctions but ready to pray.[12] Alex Youngson's personal faith and Christian humanism may not have been too far away, in fact, from the religion of the army. He had been found to be a 'real friend in time of need' and in 1919 he rejoiced in community celebration. His successors would face different challenges.

The population of the Registration District of Strathy continued to decline. The overall total of 1,532 at 1901 had shrunk to 1,197 by 1921: a drop of almost 22 per cent, reflecting the loss of the young emigrants before 1914, of the dead of the First World War and of others who sought employment in the cities of the south. The falling population took some of the pressure off those landholding issues remaining after the purchase of Strathy and Armadale by the Board of Agriculture. Indeed as the twentieth century progressed, depopulation replaced land hunger as the issue of the Highlands.[13] The higher living standards increasingly expected in the twentieth century were not easily provided by a north Highland economy starved of capital, for long without good communications to the south, and whose croft-based agriculture was unable to benefit from economies of scale. Ownership by a public board produced little new investment in the Strathy Estate, but the free market created no more lasting employment at Forsinard, which moved from being a deer forest to a 'commercial' forest of close-planted pine on drained land; and then to a RSPB Reserve that seeks to restore the peat bogs. Land-use decisions, whether of public boards or private companies, were no more responsive to local opinion: the 'valuable salmon fisheries and shooting rights' in Strathy purchased by the Board of Agriculture became no more of a local resource than the River Halladale, which remained a preserve of the non-resident wealthy. In retrospect, the lively local politics of the era of the parish councils and the school boards marked a high point in the self-government of the far north's communities. T. M. Devine correctly states that 'The influence of the presbyterian churches on civil affairs was indeed further curtailed in 1929 when the parish councils and the elected education authorities . . . were abolished'[14] and certainly these changes reduced the viability of a vision for ministry, Alex Youngson-style. As the twentieth century progressed, with the growing power of centralising government and of the autonomous professions (teaching, medicine, local government, social work), something vital and truly local, transparent and accountable was also lost.

Having retired in 1930 in the interests of union, Alex Youngson was entitled to remain in his manse for life; the UF manse became that of the new, united, congregation. Worship was held every third Sunday in the West Church, together with occasional evening services, but the decision to use the former UF Church for two out of every three Sunday services no doubt reflected the relative size of the UF congregation compared with that of the parish church. The post-1930 Church of Scotland parish of Strathy and Halladale was, in effect, the UF congregation under a new name. Rev. Alex Youngson MA JP died in July 1933, as his gravestone records, 'in the 92nd year of his life and the 56th year of his ministry. A beloved minister and father'. The notice in the press said: 'The community learnt with regret of the death of Rev. Alex Youngson, The Manse, Strathy, whose name in the district and far beyond was a household word.'[15] Presbytery then agreed that, from 1933, the West Church would be used for only one evening service a month; after the Second World War it was declared redundant and sold – as, indeed, the church at Newmill in time was also sold. The island of Stroma is now uninhabited. Miss Alice Youngson was permitted to remain in and to rent her father's manse at the discretion of the General Trustees of the Church of Scotland, and she did so until her death in 1961, when it too was sold. The fields allowed after 1828 as a glebe by the successive proprietors of Strathy to the ministers of the Established Church had never been formally conveyed to the church, but were in law occupied from year to year on an unwritten tenancy. They and the lands used as glebe by the Free/UF ministers passed into other hands. Mackay, however, is still the predominant name in the district of Strathy.

As with any ministry, the value of Alex Youngson's ministry was found not in any legacy left in buildings, institutions or even diaries but (his limitations notwithstanding) in faithfulness to Christ in his own day and time. Other, better known, ministers despaired of the divisive nature of Highland presbyterianism. The Very Rev. Norman Maclean found his first parish, Waternish on Skye, 'joyless, song-less, mirth-less and music-less', and left for a career in the south that brought him in time to the Moderator's

chair.[16] Alex Youngson remained in the north, cultivated neigh-
bourly relations with the other denominations active in the
parish, promoted what was good in local culture, worked for
a caring and prosperous society and offered the consolation of
the Christian faith to the distressed. On his family's gravestone in
the Strathy burial ground a verse is inscribed:

I have glorified Thee on the earth,
I have finished the work which Thou gavest me to do
St. John xvii, 4

Notes

1 Introduction

1. James Hunter, *The Making of the Crofting Community*, Edinburgh, 1976, p. 122.

2 The Youngson Diaries

1. Figures given apply to 1911.
2. Frank Bardgett, *North Coast Parish: Strathy and Halladale*, Thurso, 1990.
3. NAS: GD 84.
4. Captain John Henderson, 'A general view of the agriculture of the County of Sutherland', London 1812; microfilm available at NLS.
5. NLS (Map Room) Deposit 313 and Accession 10853.
6. NLS Dep. 313/3622/3.
7. R.J. Adam, 'Papers on Sutherland Estate Management, 1802–1816', Scottish History Society, Edinburgh 1972, vol i, p. 156; cited in Hunter, *Making of the Crofting Community*, p. 27.
8. NLS Dep. 313/3622/2.
9. NLS Dep. 313/3606/1 & 2.
10. NAS: AF42/1754. Rev. Angus Macpherson, minister of Strathy, forwarding correspondence requesting assistance from the Congested Districts Board towards building a landing slip for Strathy Point: 13 January 1902.
11. NLS Dep. 313/3606/1–3. See also NAS: GD 87/4/35, Mackay of Bighouse Muniments.
12. NAS: CH2/508/3, Minutes of the Presbytery of Tongue, 17 July 1833 p. 82; 26 November 1834, pp. 115–16.
13. NAS: CH3/1438/1–5.
14. NAS: CH 2/508/8, p. 297, 22 October 1930. The minute

records the agreement of the Presbytery of Caithness to the boundaries of the new Church of Scotland parish of Strathy and Halladale, 'in view of the fact that the two congregations now united had for many years been responsible for the supply of religious ordinances and for the pastoral oversight of the people of Forsinard and Strathhalladale, the Presbytery of Caithness would offer no objection to the inclusion of these districts in the area proposed to be allocated to the united congregations of Strathy under the scheme of delineation of areas by the Presbytery of Tongue. Rev. Mr Carmichael, minister of Reay, entered his dissent from this finding.' The Presbytery of Tongue thus concluded: 'The boundaries of the said new parish of Strathy now are: On the East the County boundary between Sutherland and Caithness, and on the other sides the old parish boundaries contained in Records of Presbytery of Tongue vol iii pp. 115–116.' The decision was confirmed 18 January 1933 [p. 340]: 'No change from former quoad sacra parish except on the east where now the county boundary and on the south, where the boundary is the old Kildonan parish boundary.'

15. Douglas Willis, *The Story of Crofting in Scotland*, Edinburgh, 1991, pp. 70–94. The report of the Royal Commission under Lord Napier is published as 'Report of Commissioners of Inquiry into the Conditions of Crofters and Cottars in the Highlands and Islands of Scotland', 5 vols, Edinburgh, 1884.

16. Willis, *Crofting in Scotland*, p. 93.

17. Willie Orr, *Deer Forests, Landlords and Crofters*, Edinburgh, 1982, pp. 37–51.

18. NT, 26 December 1912, 'Concert & Dance at Strathy' and NT, 2 January 1919.

19. NAS: AF 42/5124. The Congested Districts Board (31 July 1908) agreed to subsidise any deficit the Parish Council of Farr might incur from their guarantee to repay to the GPO any annual shortfall if receipts for the Strathy Post Office were below £35.

20. *Scotsman*, 28 June 1930.

21. NAS: AF 67/65, 2063/628.

22. JG, 29 September 1912.

23. NAS: IRS 85/37–43. I have also assumed that those homes

controlled by the Parish Council and unlisted for valuation purposes were thatched.

24. Fasti VII, p. 109 and GROS: Register of Marriages for the Parish of Pitsligo, County of Aberdeen, no. 20/1870.
25. GROS: Register of Marriages for the Parish of Pitsligo, County of Aberdeen, no. 20/1870.
26. Fasti VII, p. 109. One daughter, Helen Murray Youngson, died as an infant – GROS: Register of Deaths for the Parish of Skene, County of Aberdeen, no. 22/1874.
27. John J. Graham, *'A vehement thirst after knowledge' Four centuries of education in Shetland*, Lerwick, 1998, pp. 136–64 describes the local impact of the arrival of school boards in the crofting settlements of Shetland.
28. Rev. Stewart Mechie, 'Education for the ministry in Scotland since the Reformation', *Records of the Scottish Church History Society* vol. xiv, 1963, pp. 115–35 and 161–79.
29. NAS: CH2/342/14, Minutes of the Presbytery of Strathbogie, pp. 289, 291, 292. The account of Mr Youngson's career as given in Fasti VI, p. 328 does not accord with the record of the minutes of the Presbytery.
30. Frank D. Bardgett, *Devoted Service Rendered – the Lay Missionaries of the Church of Scotland*, Edinburgh, 2002, pp. 43–86 discusses Home Mission in nineteenth-century Scotland.
31. NAS: CS 318 /41/ 435.
32. NAS: CH2/342/15, Minutes of the Presbytery of Strathbogie, pp. 253, 255–6, 259, 261, 266–9, 281.
33. NAS: AF 56/211, Construction, extension and maintenance of Stroma Pier, 1890–1910. Also, AF 42/844, 29 January 1901, the petition from the inhabitants of Stroma to the Congested Districts Board, with support of Canisbay Parish Council, for an extension to the Pier of Stroma.
34. NE, 3 August 1909.
35. NAS: CH 2/508/8, Minutes of the Presbytery of Tongue, from p. 56.
36. NE, 3 August 1909.
37. NAS: CH 2/476/4. This single volume, created and maintained by Mr Youngson, contains the formal Communion Roll, Registers of Proclamations and of Baptisms, and the Kirk Session Minutes of Strathy for the period of his ministry.

38. GROS: Register of Marriages in the District of St Machar in the Burgh of Aberdeen, no. 111/1898.
39. NAS: IRS 85/40, Valuer's Field Book, Parish of Farr, book 4 ref. 384.

3 *The People of the Parish*

1. GROS: full, searchable, details of the 1901 Census are available on www.scotlandspeople.gov.uk the official website (2005). I have used images of the pro forma completed by the enumerators, downloaded from the site.
2. 'Gaelic speaking in Scotland, demographic history' in Derick S. Thomson (ed.), *The Companion to Gaelic Scotland*, Oxford, 1983, pp. 109–14.
3. NAS: CH 2/508/8 Minutes of the Presbytery of Tongue, pp. 55, 77.
4. HCA: CSVR, *passim.*
5. GROS: Register of Marriages in the District of Strathy in the County of Sutherland, no 6/1910.
6. GROS: Register of Marriages in the District of Strathy in the County of Sutherland, no 3/1894.
7. GROS: Register of Deaths in the District of Strathy in the County of Sutherland, no. 6/1911. Angus Murray Macpherson Mackay died at Strathy Point, 11 February 1911, aged 15 years; son of parents Angus Mackay (fisherman) and Barbara (ms Morrison); meningitis (10 days) certified by Dr J. G. McGregor.
8. NAS: CH2/476/4.
9. NAS: IRS 85/42, Valuer's Field Book, Parish of Farr no. 6 ref. 577.
10. NT, 31 August 1911.
11. GROS: Register of Marriages in the District of Blythswood in the Burgh of Glasgow, no. 525/1915; Register of Deaths for the Burgh of Inverness no. 136/1922; Register of Deaths in the District of Strathy in the County of Sutherland: no. 8/1915, no. 18/1918; no. 24/1919; no. 4/1924. For Daniel Shearer as a communicant and elder, and also for the baptism of his grandson, NAS: CH2/476/4.
12. JG, 12 April 1912.
13. NT, 31 August 1911.
14. HCA: CS 5/3/12/4 and -/5, Farr School Board, 10/9/1914 to

15/8/1918. In February 1916 Mary Gunn was nominated by her father for a post as monitoress at Strathy, being one of his two senior pupils. The School Board had her in mind for a vacant post in the side-school of Bowside in May 1917 and she was appointed in June. In August 1918, however, her resignation from Bowside was accepted.

15. NAS: IRS 85/41, Valuer's Field Book, Parish of Farr no. 5 ref. 406.
16. NT, 9 January 1913: 'Medical Service in the Highlands'.
17. HCA: CS 6/13/11, Farr Parish Council 1903–1905, pp. 12 and 13.
18. NT, 19 August 1915, 'Medical Service in the Highlands'.
19. NAS: CH2/476/4.
20. GROS: Register of Deaths in the District of Strathy in the County of Sutherland nos. 24 and 25/1911.
21. NT, 6 March 1919.
22. Christopher J. Uncles, *Memories of North and West Sutherland*, Catrine, Ayrshire, 2003, pp. 72–5.
23. GROS: Register of Deaths in the District of Strathy in the County of Sutherland nos. 7 and 9/1915.
24. NAS: CH2/476/4.

4 Congregations and Community

1. Report of the Panel on Doctrine in *Reports to the General Assembly 2004*, published for the Church of Scotland 2004.
2. NT, 31 August 1911, 'Mod at Tongue'.
3. NE, 7 February 1911.
4. JG, 7 June 1912. An evening service was also held in the Melvich Hall.
5. NAS: CH3/1438/1, Minutes of the Deacons' Court of the UF congregation of Halladale, 30 July 1906.
6. 'Gaelic-speaking in Scotland, sociology' in Thomson, *Companion to Gaelic Scotland*, pp. 114–15; Douglas Ansdell, *The People of the Great Faith*, Stornoway, 1998, p. 107.
7. Duncan Forrester and Douglas Murray (eds), *Studies in the History of Worship in Scotland*, Edinburgh, 1984, p. 90. See also, A. C. Cheyne, *The Transforming of the Kirk*, Edinburgh, 1983, pp. 88–107.
8. *The Highland News*, Inverness, 31 July 1909 (microfiche in Inverness Public Library).

9. A small risk of error may be admitted as this identification is made. Mr Youngson's diaries never explicitly say who the Precentor was. It is clear from numerous references, however, that he was being visited in Strathy West, and that he was married. The best evidence for the identification is that, in the first week of September 1911 the Precentor and John were noted cutting grass for the manse, and that the Farm Account for the same year shows payments on 4 September to 'John Cooper' and Johnnie Post'. John Mackay Cooper was the father of the Strathy postman.

10. Willie Orr, *Deer Forests, Landlords and Crofters*, Edinburgh, 1982, p. 126 shows hostility between keepers and crofters, though from evidence relating to the West Highlands.

11. Figures courtesy of the General Register Office for Scotland, 2004.

12. NAS: CH 2 /476/2.

13. Rev. Walter Calder, *Strathy*, privately 1897.

14. NAS: IRS 85/40, Valuer's Field Book no. 4 ref. 382. The Valuer's notes also mentioned 'old seatings' and that the whole building was in poor repair.

15. NT, 5 September 1912.

16. Rev. John A Lamb (ed.), *The Fasti of the United Free Church of Scotland 1900–1929*, Edinburgh, 1956, p. 482; GROS: Register of Marriages in the District of Inverness in the County of Inverness, no 19/1908. The Rev. E. Fraser moved from Strathy and Halladale to Tarbat (22 October 1912) and thence to Urray (14 May 1925). At the union of the UF Church with the Church of Scotland, he joined the united church and his congregation was renamed Urray East within the Church of Scotland. He moved from there to Ullapool in 1936 and died in 1938.

17. NAS: IRS 85/39, Valuer's Field Book, Parish of Farr no. 3 refs. 231 and 276.

18. NT, 13 October 1912: 'Departure of Rev. Ewen Fraser'.

19. NT, 7 March 1912.

20. NT, 19 December 1912.

21. Lamb, *Fasti of the United Free Church*, p. 503.

22. NT, 26 June 1919.

23. NAS: CH3 /1438/1, Deacons' Court meeting 29 July 1905.

24. NT, 18 March 1915, Strathy and Halladale UF Church.

25. NT, 4 May 1911, Farr School Board. The motion to re-appoint Ewen Fraser Chair of the Board failed; on a split 3–2 vote, he was replaced by the Factor to the Tongue Estate.
26. NT, 16 May 1912.
27. NT, 20 May 1920.
28. NT, 22 July 1915.
29. JG, 24 February 1911, 'Death of a promising lad'.
30. NT, 11 May 1911 and GROS: Register of Deaths in the District of Strathy in the County of Sutherland, no. 12/1911.
31. NT, 25 September 1919. A tribute to James Macdonald is included in Calder, *Strathy*, p. 18.

5 The Regularities of Life

1. NLS Dep. 313/3590/19.
2. NAS: IRS 85/40, Valuer's Field Book, Parish of Farr no. 3, ref. 309.
3. NT, 17 August 1911.
4. Mairi Robinson (ed.), *The Concise Scots Dictionary*, Aberdeen, 1985, p. 592 under 'scroo etc'.
5. HCA: Minutes of Sutherland County Council, volume 3, p. 239: Finance Committee, 14 February 1908.
6. Mr Youngson entered the communion Sundays of the neighbouring congregations in his diary, but not invariably. While the FP sacrament was recorded in all four diaries, the UF congregation's communion was mentioned only in 1911 and 1919, and that of the Free congregation in 1911, 1912 and 1915.
7. John Kennedy, *The Days of the Fathers in Ross-shire*, Inverness, 1927, pp. 113–15 offers an idealised description of a Highland communion season in an eighteenth-century evangelical parish.
8. Sandra Train, *A memory of Strath Halladale*, Thurso, 1995, pp. 27–33 discusses the social and community customs surrounding the sacrament of communion.
9. NT, 27 June 1912.
10. Train, *Memory of Strath Halladale*, p. 29.
11. NAS, CH 2/476/4.
12. A. L. Drummond and J. Bulloch, *The Church in Late Victorian Scotland 1874–1900*, Edinburgh, 1979, p. 168.
13. JG, 26 January 1912.

14. The family occurs under this surname both in the 1901 Census and in Mr Youngson's diaries. It sounds suspiciously like a byname, however.
15. NAS: CH 2/508/8, p. 87.
16. Ibid., p. 158.
17. *Year Book*, 1912, p. 62.
18. NAS: CH 2/508/8, pp. 129, 132, 133, 145, 147, 153, 162.
19. T. M. Devine, *The Scottish Nation 1700–2000*, London, 2000, p. 530.
20. NT, 4 May 1911.
21. JG, 19 April 1912.
22. NAS, CH 2/ 345/4, pp. 131–206.
23. NT, 9 January 1913, 'Strathhalladale Entertainments'.
24. NT, 2 February 1911 and 16 March 1911; also, GROS: Register of Deaths in the District of Strathy in the County of Sutherland no. 4/1911.
25. NT, 30 March 1911.
26. JG, 31 March 1911.
27. C. Maclean, *Island on the edge of the world – the story of St Kilda*, Edinburgh, 1972, pp. 73, 116–19.
28. NE, 16 May 1911.
29. NT, 2 January 1919.
30. NT, 18 January 1912.
31. JG, 20 January 1911.
32. NT, 3 July 1919.
33. JG, 24 May 1912.
34. See the 2005 company website: www.delmege.com.
35. NAS: IRS 85/40, Valuer's Field Book, Parish of Farr no. 4 ref. 331.
36. NAS: IRS 85/39, Valuer's Field Book, Parish of Farr no. 3 ref. 272.

6 Service on the Public Bodies of the Civil Parish of Farr

1. NAS: CS 2/476/2.
2. NT, 17 June 1915, reporting a meeting of the Parish Council that had received comments on its budget from the Local Government Board. Of Hugh Gunn, the letter mentioned and the paper reported: 'As inspector he receives £55; as Clerk £15; and as infant protection visitor £3/10s. Also £2/10s for travelling . . .'

3. NAS: IRS 85/39, Valuer's Field Book, Parish of Farr no. 3 ref. 218 and 225.
4. NAS: GD 325/4/249, Correspondence and papers of the Scottish Landowners Federation.
5. HCA: CS 6/13/14, Minutes of Farr Parish Council 1909–1910, pp. 14–29. Thanks are due to the Archivist of the Highland Council for access to these and other volumes of the minutes of the Parish Council of Farr for years after 1903 on condition that (a) the research would not be used to support measures or decisions in respect of particular individuals; (b) would not cause or be likely to cause substantial damage or substantial distress to any person who is the subject of the data while he or she is alive or likely to be alive when assuming a life span of 100 years; (c) generally in compliance with the Data Protection Act 1998.
6. These homes were not listed in the Valuation Rolls, nor do they appear in the Inland Revenue's 1912 survey of properties, NAS: IRS 37–43, which took the Rolls as its starting point. Mr Youngson's lists of households, however, clearly show a number of mainly single women (and the occasional single older man) resident in the communities. These homes were referred to by the Parish Council, HCA CS 6 /13 /14, p. 94 (meeting 21 February 1911): 'In order not to disqualify paupers for old age pensions it was resolved to charge £1 rent a year for houses belonging to the Parish Council held by old age pensioners. Asked Inspector to determine which houses the Parish Council could lay claim to.'
7. HCA: CS 6 /13/18, p. 65.
8. HCA: CS 6 /13/17, p. 32.
9. HCA: CS 6 /13/16, p. 96.
10. HCA: CS 6 /13/17, p. 3.
11. HCA: CS 6 /13/14, p. 83.
12. Ibid., p. 5
13. Ibid., p. 8
14. Ibid., p. 19.
15. NT, 29 February 1912 and HCA: CS 6 /13/15, p. 47.
16. HCA: CS 6 /13/14, pp. 12, 34.
17. Ibid., pp. 59, 64.
18. HCA: CS 6 /13/15, pp. 25, 32.

19. NT, 4 December 1919.
20. Ibid.
21. HCA: CS 5/3/12/4, unpaged Minutes of Farr School Board 1908–1914; meetings 22 April 1909, 25 April 1911 and 24 April 1914.
22. JG, 12 April 1912.
23. NT, 9 and 16 January 1919.
24. HCA: CS 5/3/12/4, Farr School Board, vol. 4; meetings held on 30.7.14, 10.9.14, 12.11.14, 24.1.14; CS 5/3/12/5, School Board of Farr: vol. 5; meetings held on 11.2.15, 11.11.15 and 16.12.15.
25. HCA: CS 5/3/12/5, School Board of Farr: vol. 5; meetings held on 21.1.16 and 4.1.17.
26. NT, 27 March 1919, 10 April and 17 April 1919.
27. NE, 22 January 1919, 'From a Halladale correspondent'.
28. NT, 12 June 1919.
29. James Hunter, *The Making of the Crofting Community*, Edinburgh, 1976, p. 185.
30. NT, 1 February 1912.
31. NT, 25 May 1911.
32. NAS: AF 42/927; AF 42/7678; AF 42/4758.
33. NAS: AF 42 /1034.
34. HCA: CS 6/13/15, meeting 1.8.11, p. 9.
35. NAS: AF 42/1754.
36. NAS: AF 42/3743.
37. HCA: CS 6/13/14, p. 45.
38. HCA: CS 3/1/3, Minutes of Sutherland County Council vol.3, pp. 508–9 and 554–6.
39. NT, 28 March 1912 reported his death.
40. JG, 7 June 1912.
41. NE, 12 November 1912.
42. HCA: CS 3/1/4, Minutes of Sutherland County Council vol.4, pp. 144, 165, 182, 220–221, 270, 330, 549–550.
43. NT, 18 September 1919; the meeting in Strathy School was part of a constituency tour by Sir Leicester.
44. NE, 1 October 1919.
45. NE, 20 June 1911: a correspondent reporting opinions held in Portskerra.
46. NT, 29 August 1918.

7 The Tale of Years

1. JG, 10 January 1919.
2. NT, 11 July 1912, 'Portskerra Presentation'.
3. JG, 20 June 1911.
4. NT, 26 September and 10 October 1912. His gravestone still stands in the burial ground.
5. JG, 13 December 1918.
6. JG, 24 May 1912.
7. JG, 21 April 1911.
8. NE, 16 May 1911.
9. NAS: CH 2/508/8, Minutes of the Presbytery of Tongue, p. 86: 30 November 1910.
10. JG, 27 October 1911.
11. JG, 20 October 1911.
12. James Hunter, *The Making of the Crofting Community*, Edinburgh, 1976, pp. 186–92.
13. NT, 25 May 1911.
14. 'Dunrobin Castle, Golspie, Sutherland' – booklet guide, 1988, p. 17.
15. NT, 30 March and 25 May 1911.
16. NT, 25 May 1911
17. JG, 12 January 1912.
18. NT, 22 February 1912; JG, 19 April 1912; NT, 18 April and 9 May 1912.
19. NAS: AF 67/65, 2063/628.
20. NE, 11 February 1911.
21. NE, 23 May 1911.
22. NT, 28 March 1912.
23. JG, 12 April 1912.
24. JG, 22 September 1911.
25. NT, 7 March 1912; JG, 12 March 1912.
26. NT, 29 February 1912.
27. E. King, *Scotland Sober and Free: the Temperance Movement 1829–1979*, Glasgow, 1979, p. 16.
28. NT, 23 March 1911.
29. NE, 21 February and 9 April 1911.
30. NT, 26 Dec 1912; JG, 29 Nov. 1912.
31. NT, 26 December 1912.
32. NT, 14 November 1912.

33. NAS: CH1/40/5, Minutes of Committee on Highlands and Islands (1911 to 1929) pp. 8, 33.
34. Richard Holmes, *Tommy. The British Soldier on the Western Front 1914–1918*, London, 2004, p. xvii, citing Barbara Tuchmann.
35. Colonel John Sym (ed.), *Seaforth Highlanders*, Aldershot, 1962, p. 221.
36. Mr Youngson's diary entry for 21 January 1919 reads: 'Tho Traill – 183699 – 129 Coy A S C Sect 2 – Mesopotamia Expeditionary Force' and his service number and medals are confirmed by the medals' index held by the National Archives, London: catalogue number WO/373/20 image 11659.
37. JG, 29 January 1915.
38. NT, 7 January 1915.
39. Pte Thomas R. Ross is listed among the Men of Melvich on the local War Memorial and further details can be found on the database of the Commonwealth War Graves Commission. He was five at the time of the 1901 Census.
40. JG, 21 February 1919.
41. Major F. W. Bewsher, *The History of the 51st (Highland) Division 1914–1918*, Edinburgh and London, 1921, p. 4.
42. JG, 29 January 1915.
43. HCA: CS 5/3/12/5, School Board of Farr: vol. 5: meetings 22/9/1915, 10/8/1916 and 18/7/1918.
44. NE, 24 August 1915: public notice 'Increased Separation Allowances'.
45. NT, 4 March 1915.
46. HCA: CS 6/13/17, Parish Council of Farr 1915–17, p. 8.
47. NT, 7 January 1915.
48. NT, 17 June 1915, 'Recruiting Appeal'.
49. JG, 7 May 1915.
50. Sym, *Seaforth Highlanders*, p. 152; Bewsher, *History of the 51st (Highland) Division*, p. 20.
51. NT, 17 June 1915.
52. NT, 15 July 1915.
53. NT, 8 July 1915.
54. NT, 1 July 1915.
55. NT, 22 July 1915 and HCA: CS 3 /1/4, Minutes of Sutherland County Council, pp. 267–8.
56. HCA: CS 6/13/17, Parish Council of Farr 1915–17, p. 18.

57. JG, 9 July 1915.
58. NT, 7 January 1915.
59. NT, 7 January 1915.
60. JG, 6 August 1915.
61. JG, 20 August and 8 October 1915. Further details can found in the database of the Commonwealth War Graves Commission, with reference to the Becourt Military Cemetery.
62. NT, 30 September 1915. Thomas Mackay's death was not registered at Strathy, but his funeral was recorded in Alex Youngson's diary.
63. NT, 24 June 1915.
64. NT, 23 September and 15 October 1915.
65. JG, 2 July 1915.
66. NT, 2 September 1915; also, Dugald MacEchern, *The Sword of the North: Highland Memories of the Great War*, Inverness, 1923, p. 51.
67. NT, 20 May and 2 September 1915.
68. NT, 15 July 1915.
69. GROS: Register of Marriages in the District of Gourock, 24/ 1915. Alexander W. Youngson died in 1938, aged 61; and his wife died in 1946, aged 80: GROS, Registers of Deaths in the District of Cathcart, 494/1938 and the District of Eaglesham, 11/1946.
70. J. Hunter, *Last the Free: a Millennial History of the Highlands and Islands of Scotland*, Edinburgh and London, 1999, p. 327.
71. JG, 29 January, 11 and 18 June 1915; NT, 15 July 1915; also NAS: GD 325/4/249, Scottish Landowners' Association, papers relating to Kirkton Farm.
72. JG, 10 January 1919.
73. NT, 9 January 1919.
74. NT, 2 January 1919.
75. JG, 10 January 1919. Further details can be found in the database of the Commonwealth War Graves Commission in relation to the Preseau Communal Cemetery Extension. Donald A. Mackay's brother, who had emigrated to Australia, served in the Australian army and survived the war.
76. NT, 2 January 1919.
77. Further details can be found on the database of the Commonwealth War Graves Commission.

78. JG, 7 March 1919.
79. JG, 28 March 1919.
80. JG, 4 and 11 April 1919.
81. The extant minutes of the Parish Council of Farr for 1919 contain no reference to war memorials.
82. NT, 1 May 1919.
83. NT, 13 February 1919.
84. NT, 8 May 1919.
85. NAS: CH 2/508/8, Minutes of the Presbytery of Tongue, 26 March 1919, p. 182
86. JG, 3 October 1919.
87. NE, 12 March 1919.
88. GROS: Register of Deaths in the District of Strathy in the County of Sutherland no. 4/1919; further details can be found on the database of the Commonwealth War Graves Commission.
89. NE, 16 April 1919.
90. JG, 25 July 1919.
91. Details regarding the purchase of Strathy by the Board of Agriculture were supplied on behalf of the Scottish Executive by letter dated 16 July 2004.
92. JG, 25 July 1919.
93. NT, 4 March 1919.
94. NT, 3 July 1919.
95. NT, 24 July, 16 October and 18 December 1919.
96. NAS: CH3/1438/5, book 5.
97. NT, 2 January 1919.
98. NT, 30 January 1919.
99. NT, 5 June 1919.
100. Hunter, *The Making of the Crofting Community*, pp. 195–201.
101. NT, 13, 20 and 27 March and 24 April 1919 covers the public meetings, protests and development plans, with the report of the exchange in the House of Commons; NLS acc.10225/153 provides a map of the new Bighouse holdings.
102. NAS: GD 325/4/ 249, 'Memo with reference to forcible possession of Kirkton' set out Mr Macandrew's case for the information of the Scottish Landowners Federation.
103. NAS: AF 67/65 and 2063/628 contain files on this incident retained by the Scottish Office.
104. NAS: AF 2063/628 includes a report from the board's local agent, Thomas Noble, that contains these details.

105. NT, 17 June 1920.

106. NAS: AF 67/65 no. 2063/603, letter dated 7 November 1919 relating to Forsinain Farm.

107. NT, 15 July, 5 & 19 August, 7 & 14 October 1920; NAS: AF 67/65 and 2063/628; *The Scotsman*, 23 May 1922, article 'A Sutherland Land Scheme'. A letter on behalf of the Scottish Executive's Environment and Rural Affairs Department dated 16 July 2004 states that Kirkton farm 'was set up as small holdings by the Board of Agriculture' but not acquired by the Board.

108. Holmes, *Tommy*, p. 613.

109. JG, 21 March 1919.

110. JG, 5 September 1919.

111. NAS: CH2/508/8 p. 188.

112. Douglas Murray, *Freedom to Reform,*, Edinburgh, 1993, pp. 1–25; James L. Weatherhead, *The Constitution and Laws of the Church of Scotland*, Edinburgh, 1997, pp. 16–24.

8 Retrospect – Minister and Community

1. NAS: CH 2/508/8, p. 294.

2. In the notes in the diary for 1912.

3. NT, 2 January 1919.

4. NT, 4 December 1919.

5. JG, 20 October 1911.

6. JG, 17 January 1911.

7. NAS: CH3 /1438/1, Minutes of the Deacons' Court, 24 September 1902 lists all these office-bearers and collectors; CH3/1438/5 is a set of collectors' books for the central funds, showing a standard donation of 2/6d. per person.

8. NAS: CH 2/476/4, Kirk Session Minutes 3 November 1930.

9. *The Church of Scotland Year-Book, 1929*, published for the Christian Life and Work Committee of the General Assembly, Edinburgh, 1929.

10. Report of the Board of Ministry, *Reports to the General Assembly 2000*, published for the Church of Scotland, 2000, 2.3.2.2, page 17/2.

11. NAS: AF 42/527.

12. Holmes, *Tommy*, pp. 503–27, discusses the religion of the British Army in France.

13. Hunter, *The Making of the Crofting Community*, p. 207.
14. Devine, *The Scottish Nation*, p. 387.
15. JG, 21 July 1933.
16. Norman Maclean, *Set Free*, London, 1949, pp. 178, 182, 211 and see also the unpaged Dedication.

Index of People

Index of Places

Index of Subjects